This book must be returned immed-
iately it is asked for by the Librarian,
and in any case by the last date
stamped below.

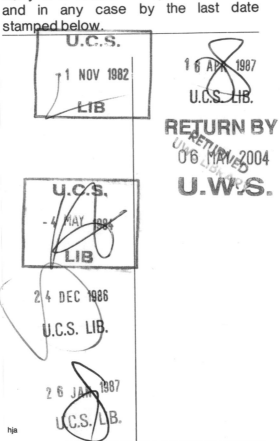
SWANSEA UNIVERSITY COLLEGE LIBRARY

INTER-AMERICAN DEVELOPMENT BANK

# Population and Urban Trends
# in Central America and Panama

Robert W. Fox

Jerrold W. Huguet

Washington, D.C.
1977

297805

The views and opinions expressed in this publication
do not necessarily reflect the official positions
of the Inter-American Development Bank.

Robert W. Fox, a sociologist, is a member of the
Economic and Social Development Department
of the Inter-American Development Bank.

Jerrold W. Huguet, a demographer now with the U.N.
Economic and Social Commission for Asia and
Pacific (ESCAP), participated in the surveys as a
consultant to the Bank.

# CONTENTS

## Appendices

# Introduction

This publication collects in one volume a series of surveys undertaken by the Inter-American Development Bank in 1975 and 1976 on population growth trends in the five countries of Central America—Costa Rica, El Salvador, Guatemala, Honduras and Nicaragua—as well as in Panama.

The surveys focus on two main areas of demographic analysis: the rates of population increase in each of the six countries, and changes in their spatial distribution patterns. Population growth trends during the past 50 years are examined at the national, departmental and city levels, both in terms of rates of increase and of absolute magnitudes. Based on past trends and other demographic characteristics, projections of future population growth have been made to the year 2000.

Shifts in urban-rural distribution patterns are evaluated and discussed in the context of the growth of the cities of the region. Such attendant demographic factors as age and sex structures, urban and rural fertility differentials and changing occupational patterns are also reviewed for each country.

Preceding the individual country surveys is a regional analysis of population trends and projections to the year 2000 based on the interaction of the three population growth variables—the number of births, the number of deaths, and migration. This regional overview facilitates the identification of demographic similarities and differences among these six contiguous countries which, as a region, are experiencing one of the world's fastest rates of population growth.

In publishing this study, the Bank seeks to contribute to a greater understanding of the dimensions, patterns and characteristics of Central America's population expansion, with the hope that it will stimulate greater and more detailed demographic research in the region, and its more intensive application in the development planning process. The Bank will continue to examine, in coordination with other organizations, population growth and related issues that are relevant to its financing activities in such areas as rural and urban development, water supply and sewerage service, health and education.

In this particular study the U.S. Agency for International Development (AID), through its Office of Urban Development, contributed a small grant toward the financing of initial travel and research in Central America.

Washington, D.C.
November 1977

# I. Regional Demographic and Urbanization Trends

## The magnitude of population growth

In the brief span of 25 years, the combined populations of Panama and the five Central American republics—Costa Rica, El Salvador, Guatemala, Honduras, and Nicaragua—more than doubled, increasing from 8.9 million in 1950 to 18.5 million inhabitants in 1975. On an average annual basis, this represents a very high growth rate of 3.1 per cent. Furthermore, current patterns of births and deaths are expected to yield population growth rates over the remainder of the century that are quite similar to those in the quarter just preceding. Accordingly, a high annual rate of increase averaging 2.9 per cent is projected to continue, and by year 2000 the population will again double, producing a regional total of 39 million inhabitants at the close of the century.

This study provides a retrospective analysis of the forces behind the huge population increase in the region, together with a prospective view of the factors that are likely to persist in the decades ahead because of demographic inertia. The purpose is to supply those concerned with change and development in the region with a basic set of facts affecting population growth and spatial distribution that can be useful in assessing the ramifications of the "population explosion" on regional economic and social development.

The effective absorption of very large numbers of people into national life is perhaps the most basic question facing the Central American countries in the coming years. The problem is considerable, since it involves coping not only with future needs of increasing numbers of people, but also relieving existing shortcomings as well, reflected in such deficit areas as employment, housing, health and education. Additionally, fresh demands will be made on the societies as products of social change.

---

[1] In the interest of style and brevity, reference is made throughout the study to the six-country region simply as Central America rather than Central America and Panama, which is the more conventional form.

1

Larger proportions of women than in the past, for example, should seek employment in already crowded and male-dominated labor markets.

Population experts continue to be concerned over the high rate of population growth in developing countries, and the great number of problems on the horizon that demand a demographic focus. Hence these projections and a limited amount of analysis, particularly that dealing with the possibilities for slowing the rate of growth.

Among the longer range problems facing Central America are difficult agrarian issues and choices including the need to provide land to a growing number of landless farmers or otherwise absorb them into the labor force in a productive manner, to develop adequate mechanisms for consolidating fragmented farm units that now are barely able to permit a subsistence living, and to continually face up to economic land use alternatives, opting to satisfy the internal market or the export market in order to generate needed foreign exchange for imports.

Also emerging as a major concern is the quickening pace of urbanization brought on by the high rate of population increase in both the countryside and the cities, but augmented by the constant flow of migrants from rural to urban areas. While the urban growth issue in Central America is not as dramatic as in South America or in neighboring Mexico where some of the world's largest urban agglomerations are found—Mexico City's population is now approximately 13 million, and that of Sao Paulo, Brazil 11 million—it is commanding increasing attention as the undesirable effects of rapid urbanization accumulate.

Another long-range concern arising from rapid population growth is the question of how societies can sustain rising levels of living to keep pace with apparently faster-rising expectations. The ubiquitous transistor radio, rural-to-urban bus service, the newspaper, and the television receiver are among a host of modern conveniences which are rapidly becoming commonplace in all Latin America, bringing with them radically changing values, attitudes and aspirations not dreamed of in the past by traditional rural folk. Yet, how are rising expectations for a better life to be met in the face of population numbers that are increasing at an exponential rate?

### The pace of population growth

Population totals by country and in successive decades since 1920 are shown in Table 1. Also shown are population projections to year 2000. There are marked inter-country differences in population densities. The sharpest contrast is between El Salvador, on the one hand, and Honduras, Nicaragua and Panama—the least crowded countries—on the other. Population densities in the latter countries in 1970 ranged between 14-26 persons per square kilometer. The density level of El Salvador was 170, triple that of Guatemala and comparable to that in Haiti

2

(152) and Jamaica (171). El Salvador's population density should increase to about 230 in 1980. By 2000, the density range for the least-crowded countries will rise to between 43 and 61 people per square kilometer, but in El Salvador it will have reached 420 inhabitants. Bangladesh and Java, which are two of the world's most densely populated countries, at present have 515 and 540 people per square kilometer, respectively.

El Salvador's rising population density has been a matter of some concern in recent years, particularly in view of the fact that it has little idle land. Soil exhaustion and erosion are growing problems, and a very high proportion of its labor force is engaged in agricultural activities with little opportunity for further expansion in this sector, other than higher productivity. Yet population continues to grow at an average annual rate of 3.4 per cent.

The relative advantage in territorial size enjoyed by the other Central American countries could prove in fact to be slight when the severe natural conditions common to the humid tropics have been tested. Vast unpopulated expanses still exist in these countries, but their suitability for absorbing large numbers of people is questionable. Along the Caribbean coast and in the hinterland from Panama to Guatemala, where most of the virgin lands are located, there exist formidable obstacles to agricultural production including oppressive heat, mosquito breeding grounds, extensive swamps and mangroves, and steep mountainous terrain. Heavy rainfall regularly sweeps on to the plains along the Caribbean Sea, and equally large amounts of rainfall produced by orographic wind currents drop on the inland mountain ranges. Soils that are apparently fertile while in their natural state turn rock-hard after vegetation has been cleared, and only a few crops can be produced due to the unaccustomed penetration of sunlight and the absence of organic replenishment that the natural jungle canopy provides. This deterioration process is aggravated by downpours in the rainy season that wash away organic nutrients from the soil, and turn the earth to laterite. In Guatemala's Peten region, on the Caribbean side of the isthmus, farmers scratch a thin limestone-based soil which yields precious little, and through which rainfall quickly percolates and is lost to aquifers far below the surface.

For these reasons the Caribbean side of the Central American continental divide has remained sparsely populated. Roughly 85 per cent of the regional population lives on the Pacific side of the isthmus, compared with a scant 15 per cent on the Caribbean plains. The latter proportion drops to 10 per cent when the population of the San Pedro Sula area in Honduras is subtracted. This is the one heavily populated area along the Caribbean side of the isthmus in which soil conditions for agriculture are good to excellent.

In the 80-year span covered in Table 1, the region's inhabitants are

3

**Table 1**

**Population totals for Central America, enumerated and projected, 1920-2000**
(In thousands)

| Country | 1920 | 1930 | 1940 | 1950 | 1960[a] | 1970[a] | 1980 | 1990 | 2000 |
|---|---|---|---|---|---|---|---|---|---|
| Costa Rica | 421 | 499 | 619 | 801 | 1,336 | 1,872 | 2,286 | 2,954 | 3,695 |
| El Salvador | 1,168 | 1,443 | 1,633 | 1,856 | 2,511 | 3,549 | 4,813 | 6,595 | 8,803 |
| Guatemala | 1,450 | 1,771 | 2,300 | 3,006 | 4,445 | 5,679 | 6,940 | 9,108 | 11,582 |
| Honduras | 783 | 948 | 1,119 | 1,369 | 1,885 | 2,897 | 3,595 | 4,997 | 6,881 |
| Nicaragua | 639 | 742 | 893 | 1,050 | 1,536 | 1,878 | 2,669 | 3,672 | 4,812 |
| Panamá | 429 | 502 | 595 | 805 | 1,075 | 1,428 | 1,931 | 2,532 | 3,230 |
| **Total** | **4,890** | **5,905** | **7,159** | **8,887** | **12,788** | **17,303** | **22,234** | **29,859** | **39,003** |

[a] The statistics for 1960 and 1970 are according to the actual census years, listed on page 57.
Source: 1920-1940, CELADE (Centro Latinoamericano de Demografía).

expected to increase eightfold. What is remarkable is the consistency of this pattern in country after country. El Salvador, Nicaragua and Panama will each contain roughly 7.5 times the number of inhabitants in 2000 as in 1920. Guatemala's numbers will increase by 8 times, and in Costa Rica and Honduras the factors are 8.7 and 8.8 times, respectively.

An analysis of the proportional distribution patterns of each country's population in the Central American context shows that only insignificant shifts have taken place and are projected. El Salvador, for example, accounted for 24 per cent of Central America's population in 1920 and 21 per cent in 1970, and will hold a projected 23 per cent by 2000. In all the countries without exception, their proportional share of the regional total expected by year 2000 will be within 2 percentage points of what it was 80 years earlier.

Urban and rural population distribution patterns in the census years around 1970 are shown in Table 2. The data in the first column refer to the urban sector as defined by the census institution, which encompasses a larger share of the total population than the urban definition employed in this report[1]: cities and towns with 10,000 and more inhabitants. By census definition, numerous villages throughout Central America are considered "urban" if they have such infrastructure as potable water, school and electricity, or serve as administrative centers for small political subdivisions.

The brunt of Central America's population growth in this century is still to be faced. To envision this growing pressure, imagine a man in his middle years contemplating the population changes he has experienced in Central America in his lifetime and the changes facing his immediate descendants. By mid-century, he would already have lived through a period of rapid population growth, a time in which the region's numbers

---

[1] Except for Panama, as explained on page 192.

**Table 2**

**Urban and rural population totals, and percentage distribution patterns, 1970**[a]

| Country | "Urban" segment by census definition | | | | "Urban" segment according to population in cities of 10,000 and more inhabitants | | | |
|---|---|---|---|---|---|---|---|---|
| | Population (thousands) | | Per cent | | Population (thousands) | | Per cent | |
| | Urban | Rural | Urban | Rural | Urban | Rural | Urban | Rural |
| Costa Rica | 760 | 1,112 | 41 | 59 | 575 | 1,297 | 31 | 69 |
| El Salvador | 1,405 | 2,144 | 40 | 60 | 909 | 2,640 | 26 | 74 |
| Guatemala | 1,878[b] | 3,334[b] | 36 | 64 | 1,430 | 4,248 | 25 | 75 |
| Honduras | 825[b] | 1,829[b] | 31 | 69 | 686 | 2,212 | 24 | 76 |
| Nicaragua | 883 | 995 | 47 | 53 | 662 | 1,216 | 35 | 65 |
| Panamá | 679 | 749 | 48 | 52 | 724 | 704 | 51 | 49 |

[a] Data are for the actual census year for each country around 1970.
[b] Not adjusted for census underenumeration.

increased by 80 per cent from their level just 30 years earlier. But it probably would not have occurred to him that this increase was just a minuscule portion of what could be expected, for after all, just 12 per cent of the region's net population increase for the 1920-2000 period had, by that time, taken place. This is a consistent pattern throughout the region. In Costa Rica, just 12 per cent of the increase from 421,000 (1920) to 3,695,000 inhabitants (2000) had occurred by 1950, 9 per cent in El Salvador, 15 per cent in Guatemala, 10 per cent in Honduras and Nicaragua, and 13 per cent in Panama.

During his productive years in the third quarter of the 20th century the term "population explosion" entered into his vocabulary. Starting with a 1950 population of nine million, those in the region numbered 19 million by 1975. Rural migrants came in waves to the capital city and stayed in squatter settlements that soon surrounded the traditional urban settlement. Primary and secondary level school enrollments doubled and redoubled, as did evening vocational training programs. The service sector swelled with new entrants into the labor force, while many stayed unemployed and underemployed. But, escaping his notice, no doubt, was the notion that this extraordinarily large increase that is straining the social, economic and political order throughout the region is just a minor portion of the total population expansion to be expected during the second half of the 20th Century. The increase from nine to 19 million inhabitants in fact represents just 34 per cent of the net gain projected for 1950–2000. Another 66 per cent of the increase—from 19 to 39 million inhabitants—is still to come before the year 2000.

Among the region's countries are some variations in this regard. By 1975 Costa Rica had experienced 40 per cent of the total population increase expected in the second half of the century. The other 60 per cent will come between 1975-2000. Panama experienced 36 and Guatemala 35 per cent between 1950-1975, leaving two thirds of the total increase for the quarter century ahead. But in El Salvador, Nicaragua and Honduras only 32, 31, and 30 per cent of the net population gain for the 1950-2000 period had taken place by 1975, and thus these countries face the remaining and much larger proportions of 68, 69 and 70 per cent, respectively, in the last quarter of the century.

Net population gains in the census intervals and as projected are found in Table 3. The data reflect the expectation that the countries will increase in population by roughly 25-35 per cent during each intercensal period throughout the 1950-2000 period.

The corresponding rates of population increase are shown in Table 4. They are very high, almost without exception. The apparent inconsistency for Nicaragua in the 1960-70 and 1970-80 intervals derives from census data which, as shown, are not adjusted for underenumerations. The necessary adjustments provide a 2.82 average annual rate of increase for 1960-70 and also 2.82 per cent for 1970-80.

**Table 3**

**Total population increases by country, expressed in absolute and percentage terms, 1950-2000 as enumerated[a] and projected**
(In thousands)

| Country | Absolute increases | | | | | Percentage increase | | | | |
|---|---|---|---|---|---|---|---|---|---|---|
| | 1950–60 | 1960–70 | 1970–80 | 1980–90 | 1990–2000 | 1950–60 | 1960–70 | 1970–80 | 1980–90 | 1990–2000 |
| Costa Rica | 384.4 | 498.4 | 602.0 | 668.7 | 740.8 | 48.0 | 42.0 | 35.8 | 29.3 | 25.1 |
| El Salvador | 593.9 | 940.0 | 1,422.9 | 1,782.0 | 2,208.0 | 32.0 | 38.4 | 42.0 | 37.0 | 33.5 |
| Guatemala | 961.8 | 1,233.0 | 1,739.3 | 2,168.1 | 2,474.5 | 32.0 | 31.1 | 33.4 | 31.2 | 27.2 |
| Honduras | 465.3 | 691.7 | 1,069.1 | 1,401.9 | 1,884.9 | 34.0 | 37.7 | 42.3 | 39.0 | 37.7 |
| Nicaragua | 346.4 | 431.4 | 842.1 | 1,002.1 | 1,140.3 | 33.0 | 30.9 | 46.1 | 37.5 | 31.1 |
| Panamá | 262.5 | 383.1 | 489.6 | 602.0 | 697.4 | 33.0 | 36.2 | 34.0 | 31.2 | 27.5 |

[a] Data for each country are adjusted to mid-year 1960 and 1970.

**Table 4**

**Average annual rate of population increase, enumerated and projected, 1950-2000**
(Per cent)

| Country | 1950–1960 | 1960–1970 | 1970–1980 | 1980–1990 | 1990–2000 |
|---|---|---|---|---|---|
| Costa Rica | 3.98 | 3.33 | 2.80 | 2.57 | 2.24 |
| El Salvador | 2.78 | 3.41 | 3.38 | 3.15 | 2.89 |
| Guatemala | 2.79 | 2.74 | 2.76 | 2.72 | 2.40 |
| Honduras | 2.95 | 3.34 | 3.40 | 3.29 | 3.20 |
| Nicaragua | 2.93 | 2.53 | 3.82 | 3.19 | 2.70 |
| Panamá | 2.89 | 3.01 | 2.97 | 2.72 | 2.43 |

Our observer is no doubt well aware of the expansion of his capital city. Each of the six capitals grew rapidly in population size during the 1950's. San Jose, San Salvador, Guatemala City and Panama City all expanded by at least 50 per cent, while Managua and Tegucigalpa increased by roughly 75 per cent. In the 1960's this pattern was repeated. Each city again increased by at least 50 per cent in the decade, while Managua and Tegucigalpa grew by over 80 per cent. The same pattern of growth is foreseen for the 1970's.

The fact of rapidly expanding capital cities, which has persisted for such a long time, would thus seem to be a normal part of the course of events to any observer. But this disguises a very massive impact that is best seen in terms of absolute numbers. This impact is shown in Table 5, which contrasts city population totals in 1950 with net population gains in the 1960's and, separately, the increases projected for the 1970's. The data show that with few exceptions net increases for each decade *alone* in the 1960's and the 1970's exceed city population totals in 1950.

City planners are acutely aware of this urban population growth in the region, which relentlessly outstrips the city's ability to expand its economic base and urban services. The gap is likely to widen in the major cities of Central America, for the projections of net increases in the major cities per decade suggest that by the end of the century population shall have risen even more substantially than at present. The projections for 1990–2000 for Guatemala City, for example, show that the city will add in excess of 850,000 inhabitants and San Salvador and Managua more than one half million inhabitants each. Thus, a massive stimulus of economic and social activity promoting job creation must clearly be a major target of national authorities. The alternative is a continuing swelling of the services sector with youths and adults who are only marginally employed, side by side with rising unemployment levels.

Net population increases per decade over the 1950–70 interval for both the urban and rural sectors are included in Table 6, together with

**Table 5**

Population of Central American capital cities in 1950 and 1980 (projected) and net increases in the 1960–70 and 1970–80 intervals

| City and country | Population | | Absolute increase[a] | |
|---|---|---|---|---|
| | In 1950 | In 1980 | 1960–70 | 1970–80 |
| San José-Costa Rica | 146,000 | 508,000 | 122,000 | 161,000 |
| San Salvador-El Salvador | 213,000 | 858,000 | 202,000 | 327,000 |
| Guatemala-Guatemala | 337,000 | 1,430,000 | 367,000 | 535,000 |
| Tegucigalpa-Honduras | 72,000 | 406,000 | 102,000 | 178,000 |
| Managua-Nicaragua | 109,000 | 662,000 | 163,000 | 305,000 |
| Panamá-Panamá | 217,000 | 794,000 | 188,000 | 274,000 |

[a] Statistics are adjusted to mid-year 1960, 1970 and 1980.

## Table 6

### Regional population increases: total, urban and rural, expressed in absolute and percentage terms, 1950-2000, as enumerated and projected[a]

| Regional | Absolute increase (in thousands) | | | | | Percentage increase | | | | |
|---|---|---|---|---|---|---|---|---|---|---|
| | 1950–60 | 1960–70 | 1970–80 | 1980–90 | 1990–2000 | 1950–60 | 1960–70 | 1970–80 | 1980–90 | 1990–2000 |
| Total | 3,014.3 | 4,177.6 | 6,165.0 | 7,624.8 | 9,146.0 | 34.0 | 35.1 | 38.4 | 34.3 | 30.6 |
| Urban[b] | 931.5 | 1,685.4 | 2,543.5 | 3,313.5 | 4,261.7 | 50.2 | 60.5 | 56.9 | 47.2 | 41.3 |
| Rural | 2,082.8 | 2,492.2 | 3,621.5 | 4,311.3 | 4,884.3 | 29.7 | 27.4 | 31.2 | 28.3 | 25.0 |

[a] Data for 1950, 1980, 1990 and 2000 are from national enumerations and as projected. Because of irregular census years in most of the countries during the 1960's and 1970's, the statistics used in Tables 6-8 are interpolated to 1960 and 1970, based on original census data. Panama census data for December, 1950 are also interpolated to mid-1950.
[b] "Urban" is considered as the population of all cities and towns with 10,000 and more inhabitants in 1970. The population of these localities was tracked back to 1950 and forward in the projections to 2000. "Rural" is considered as all remaining population.


## Table 7

### Net urban population increases by country, expressed in absolute and percentage terms, 1950-2000, as enumerated and projected[a]
(In thousands)

| Country | Absolute increase | | | | | Percentage increase | | | | |
|---|---|---|---|---|---|---|---|---|---|---|
| | 50–60 | 60–70 | 70–80 | 80–90 | 90–2000 | 50–60 | 60–70 | 70–80 | 80–90 | 90–2000 |
| Costa Rica | 106.7 | 171.6 | 219.3 | 251.6 | 291.9 | 60.8 | 52.8 | 44.2 | 35.1 | 30.2 |
| El Salvador | 174.9 | 297.3 | 471.9 | 639.0 | 851.5 | 52.5 | 52.6 | 48.1 | 48.0 | 43.2 |
| Guatemala | 252.9 | 466.2 | 683.7 | 896.0 | 1,114.3 | 50.5 | 61.5 | 56.5 | 47.1 | 39.8 |
| Honduras | 118.9 | 234.7 | 401.0 | 532.1 | 782.3 | 65.7 | 78.3 | 75.0 | 56.9 | 53.3 |
| Nicaragua | 136.0 | 241.1 | 436.9 | 566.2 | 696.9 | 55.0 | 62.7 | 70.2 | 53.4 | 42.8 |
| Panamá | 142.1 | 274.5 | 330.7 | 428.6 | 524.8 | 44.1 | 59.1 | 44.8 | 40.1 | 35.0 |

[a] Footnotes a and b, Table 6 apply.


## Table 8

### Net rural population increases by country, expressed in absolute and percentage terms, 1950-2000, as enumerated and projected[a]
(In thousands)

| Country | Absolute increase | | | | | Percentage increase | | | | |
|---|---|---|---|---|---|---|---|---|---|---|
| | 50–60 | 60–70 | 70–80 | 80–90 | 90–2000 | 50–60 | 60–70 | 70–80 | 80–90 | 90–2000 |
| Costa Rica | 277.2 | 326.8 | 382.7 | 417.1 | 449.0 | 47.7 | 38.0 | 32.2 | 26.7 | 22.6 |
| El Salvador | 419.0 | 642.7 | 951.0 | 1,143.0 | 1,356.5 | 26.6 | 33.9 | 39.8 | 32.8 | 29.3 |
| Guatemala | 708.9 | 767.0 | 1,055.4 | 1,272.1 | 1,360.2 | 28.3 | 24.0 | 26.4 | 25.3 | 21.6 |
| Honduras | 346.4 | 457.0 | 668.1 | 869.8 | 1,102.6 | 29.2 | 29.8 | 33.6 | 32.7 | 31.2 |
| Nicaragua | 210.4 | 190.3 | 405.2 | 435.9 | 443.4 | 26.2 | 18.9 | 33.6 | 27.1 | 21.7 |
| Panamá | 120.4 | 108.6 | 158.9 | 173.4 | 172.6 | 25.4 | 18.3 | 22.6 | 20.1 | 16.7 |

[a] Footnotes a and b, Table 6 apply.

projections for 1970-2000. The data indicate that the urban sector has and will continue to expand at a pace roughly double that of the rural sector. But in absolute terms, rural increases will be far larger. While city population totals increased by about 60 per cent in the 1960-70 interval, for example, and those in the countryside by about 30 per cent, the rural gains in absolute terms were 2.4 million as compared to 1.7 million for the cities.

The data in Table 6 are disaggregated by country and by sector and shown in Tables 7 and 8. Rural increases after 1970 are somewhat exaggerated, while urban sector increases are understated because towns expected to pass the population size threshold of 10,000 and more inhabitants are not taken into account after that date.

In percentage terms, each country follows the regional pattern shown in Table 6, namely, the urban category in all cases should increase at a faster pace than the rural population. However, in absolute terms and excepting Nicaragua and Panama in some intervals, net rural population gains have been and will continue to be larger than those in the urban sector.

Growth trends in rural areas have a very important bearing on future city expansion because of internal migration, which traditionally has played a major role in urban growth. This is increasingly significant in Central America because the rural population reservoir is large and becoming much larger, while even now many rural districts are considered overpopulated relative to a deteriorating resource base, precariously low levels of living, and prevailing social and economic systems. These factors, combined with agriculture's limited prospects for accelerated expansion, can only strengthen the probability that the pace of rural-to-urban migration will quicken beyond the level implicit in the city projections in this study.

Rural population totals throughout the 1950-2000 period are shown in Table 9. In percentage terms, the regional rural component diminishes from a very high 79 per cent in 1950 to 63 per cent by 2000. In comparison to Latin America in general, Central America supports a very large rural population.

Table 10 shows the net population gains each country's rural sector can expect during the 1970-2000 period. In El Salvador, Honduras and Nicaragua the net rural population increases are projected to be so high as to equal or exceed the total population currently found in the countryside.

Rural population totals for each country are shown in Table 11. In all cases, large absolute increases are expected in each 10-year period while the proportion of the total population this sector represents is expected to decline by either a modest amount (Costa Rica) or sharply (Honduras, Nicaragua and Panama).

**Table 9**

**Central American rural population, enumerated and projected, and as percentage of total population, 1950-2000[a]**
(In thousands)

|  | 1950 | 1960[b] | 1970[b] | 1980 | 1990 | 2000 |
|---|---|---|---|---|---|---|
| Rural population | 7,026 | 9,692 | 12,318 | 15,219 | 19,530 | 24,413 |
| As percentage of total population | 79 | 76 | 71 | 68 | 65 | 63 |

[a] "Rural" is defined as all population outside towns and cities with 10,000 inhabitants in 1970. These same cities and towns, regardless of population size, are considered the urban segment of the national total during the entire 1950-2000 period.
[b] Data are shown according to actual census years.


**Table 10**

**Rural population in 1970 (census year), and net rural population increases projected by year 2000**
(In thousands)

| Country | Rural population 1970[a] | Net rural population increase 1970-2000 |
|---|---|---|
| Costa Rica | 1,297 | 1,139 |
| El Salvador | 2,640 | 3,342 |
| Guatemala | 4,249 | 3,421 |
| Honduras | 2,211 | 2,421 |
| Nicaragua | 1,216 | 1,272 |
| Panamá | 704 | 503 |

[a] Outside of existing towns of +10,000 inhabitants in 1970.


**Table 11**

**Rural Population by country, enumerated and projected, and as percentage of total population, 1950-2000[a]**
(In thousands)

| Country | Rural population | | | | | | As % of total population | | | | | |
|---|---|---|---|---|---|---|---|---|---|---|---|---|
|  | 1950 | 1960 | 1970 | 1980 | 1990 | 2000 | 1950 | 1960 | 1970 | 1980 | 1990 | 2000 |
| Costa Rica | 583 | 968 | 1,297 | 1,570 | 1,987 | 2,436 | 73 | 72 | 69 | 69 | 67 | 66 |
| El Salvador | 1,470 | 1,927 | 2,640 | 3,483 | 4,626 | 5,983 | 79 | 77 | 74 | 72 | 70 | 68 |
| Guatemala | 2,506 | 3,543 | 4,249 | 5,037 | 6,309 | 7,669 | 83 | 80 | 75 | 73 | 69 | 66 |
| Honduras | 1,188 | 1,566 | 2,211 | 2,659 | 3,529 | 4,631 | 87 | 83 | 76 | 74 | 71 | 67 |
| Nicaragua | 803 | 1,089 | 1,216 | 1,608 | 2,045 | 2,488 | 76 | 71 | 65 | 60 | 56 | 52 |
| Panamá | 476 | 598 | 704 | 862 | 1,035 | 1,207 | 59 | 56 | 49 | 45 | 41 | 37 |

[a] "Rural" defined accoring to footnote a, Table 9.


## Population growth and the labor force

The present size of the labor force and its projection for year 2000 provides a framework for examining the prospects of accelerating rural to urban migratory flows. The regional economically active population is shown in Figure 1. Information for each country is shown in Figures 2-7.

Rates of participation in the labor force partially determine its size. Since current rates are known, the greatest change in the size of the labor force will result from changes in the total working-age population. This population can be projected quite accurately, because those aged 25 and over in 2000 are already alive. Projecting the under-25 population is more problematical, although the current trend of fertility is a guide to future fertility. Besides, about half the women giving birth in 2000 are already born, so their number is known.

According to CELADE's information, the Central American labor force will increase from 6,184,000 to 13,973,00 persons by 2000, as follows: in Costa Rica the totals are 646,000 in 1975 and 1,364,000 in 2000; in El Salvador, 1,538,000 and 3,545,000; Guatemala, 1,895,000 and 4,127,000; Honduras, 938,000 and 2,265,000; Nicaragua, 641,000 and 1,566,000; and in Panama the labor force now numbering approximately 525,000 individuals will increase to 1,105,000 by 2000.

This means for Costa Rica in the 1995–2000 interval that 33,000 new jobs should be created annually, compared to 23,000 in the 1970–75 period. In like manner, some 106,000 new jobs will be needed annually in El Salvador during 1995–2000 compared to 50,000 in the 1970–75 period. For Guatemala the requirement is 117,000 new jobs annually compared with 56,000 between 1970–75; Honduras, 72,000 jobs compared with 28,000; Nicaragua, 51,000 jobs compared with 20,000; and Panama, 29,000 compared with the 15,000 new jobs that were needed yearly between 1970 and 1975.

When the urban and rural sectors (by census definition) are separated and studied for each country, slightly different labor force participation patterns from the national norms emerge. Female participation rates are much lower in the countryside than in the cities, while rural rates among males are slightly higher than those for their city counterparts. Larger proportions of rural males also join the labor force at an earlier age.

Only a limited number of occupational *roles* have developed in Central America for rural females, and the diversity of these roles is not extensive. This clearly places severe limits on the choices available to rural women. Outside of rural employment, the two most common are early marriage or some other consensual arrangement, or migration to the city. In Costa Rica, just 12 per cent of all rural women (ages 15–64) are economically active, 14 per cent in Panama, and 5 per cent in Guatemala. Seven occupational categories in Costa Rica account for a full 65 per cent of those economically active. These categories are agricultural workers, seamstresses, sales girls, restaurant workers, primary school teachers, household domestics, and concierges.

The dearth of remunerative employment possibilities and the narrow range of occupational skills developed by these rural societies partially explain why large numbers of girls flock to the cities and at a higher

**Figure 1**
**Central America: population, total and economically active;**
**by sex and age group; 1975 and 2000.**

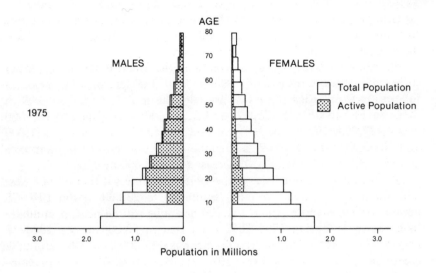

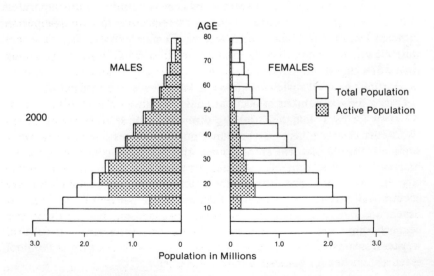

Source:
Centro Latinoamericano de Demografía (CELADE), *Boletín Demográfico*, 7:13 (January 1974) and 8:16 (July 1975).

12

rate than their male counterparts. The city, with its attractions, real, or imagined, seems a far better place than poor country dwellings where economic stagnation is the standard and the likelihood is high that the cycle of an early marriage and large families will be repeated. As rural populations increase, and the gap between the urban and rural levels of living continues to widen, the potential grows for further increases in the number of young females who migrate to the cities of Central America.

The labor force projections in this study assume that female participation rates will stay at around 18 per cent. Should this ratio increase, which would be in keeping with recent social trends, larger numbers of females would have to be added to the above estimates of those who will be seeking work.

The principal employment among the rural male population in Central America is farming and related agricultural activities including livestock-raising. Throughout the region, there is strong evidence that fewer and fewer males are being absorbed by this sector, as available land becomes increasingly scarce or consolidated into larger and less labor-intensive farm units, and as more remunerative employment is found elsewhere. The "saturation" of the agricultural sector appears to be the single most important of the factors that foster higher rates of migration to the cities. Unfortunately, the information available on this subject is limited, but the situation can be reviewed for Costa Rica, Nicaragua, Panama and Honduras.

In Costa Rica in 1963, about 75 per cent of the economically active rural male population was engaged in agriculture. This proportion dropped sharply in 1973 to 64 per cent. In other words, the rural male labor force increased by 30 per cent in the period, but in agriculture just 12 per cent.

According to Nicaraguan census information, the total economically active population increased from 474,960 (1963) to 505,445 in 1971, an increase of 6 per cent. This is a surprisingly small gain, considering that the population in the 15–64 group increased by roughly 40 per cent in the period, and suggests that some major unspecified change in the definition of "economically active" was made in the 1971 census. Nevertheless, those in agriculture in the rural sector are reported to have declined *in absolute terms* from 252,000 (1963) to 209,676 in 1971. The decline is found to be distributed about evenly throughout the country's departments. The amount of the decline strongly suggests that it is real regardless of census definition problems.

In Panama, the agricultural labor force, including males and females, increased by 17 per cent between 1950 and 1960, and by just 10 per cent in the 1960-70 interval. In the meanwhile the entire economically active

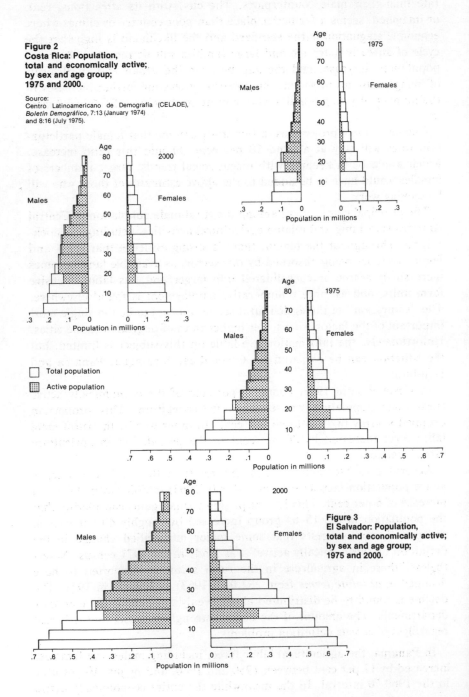

**Figure 2
Costa Rica: Population,
total and economically active;
by sex and age group;
1975 and 2000.**

Source:
Centro Latinoamericano de Demografía (CELADE),
*Boletín Demográfico*, 7:13 (January 1974)
and 8:16 (July 1975).

☐ Total population

▨ Active population

**Figure 3
El Salvador: Population,
total and economically active;
by sex and age group;
1975 and 2000.**

14

population increased by 25 and 36 per cent, respectively, during the two decades.

Between the two most recent census years in Honduras (1961 and 1974), the population increased by 42 per cent, while the economically active population 10 and older increased by 31 per cent. Labor force gains did not keep pace with the overall population rise because of the very high birth rate and resulting differential increases among those under vs. those over 10 years of age—68 and 28 per cent, respectively. The trend in agriculture during the period follows the general pattern found in Central America. Those employed in agricultural activities increased by just 20 per cent, while those in all other occupational categories experienced a much higher gain of 54 per cent.

The trend in employment substitutions to farming in rural Central America is a subject that requires further research. Many are leaving or not entering this occupation in the first place, but are staying in the rural areas. How significant this factor will be in the future in determining the increasing rural-to-urban migratory flow is unknown.

Rural factors that "push" the population from the land into the cities include inequities in the size of agricultural holdings and land tenure systems that result in great numbers of landless farmers. Central American landholdings are highly concentrated, favoring large agricultural units, a characteristic which constrains the ability of rural areas to continue absorbing increasingly larger populations.

Information in Table 12 by size category lists the distribution of land holdings in the region.[1] At one end of the scale are 476,000 landless rural families who find periodic work as farm laborers. In the next two categories are another 837,000 families who subsist on small holdings of 4 hectares or less (under 10 acres). These categories together represent more than 76 per cent of all rural families, but the property they hold accounts for a meager 6.6 per cent of all agricultural land.

The examination of any number of socio-economic indicators would relate the finding that urban Central America is easily better off than its rural counterpart with regard to the welfare of the population. Public services—electrification, communications networks, education, health, sanitation and other social services—are basically limited to the cities in Central America. These advantages, together with the many diversifications a city provides seem to offer to an increasing number a more fulfilling life, and it is just these elements combined with land tenure, size of agricultural holdings and other serious social and economic structure problems in the rural areas that may quite well push the magnitude of urban population growth in the region to a level higher than the projections presently show.

---

[1] Excludes Panama.

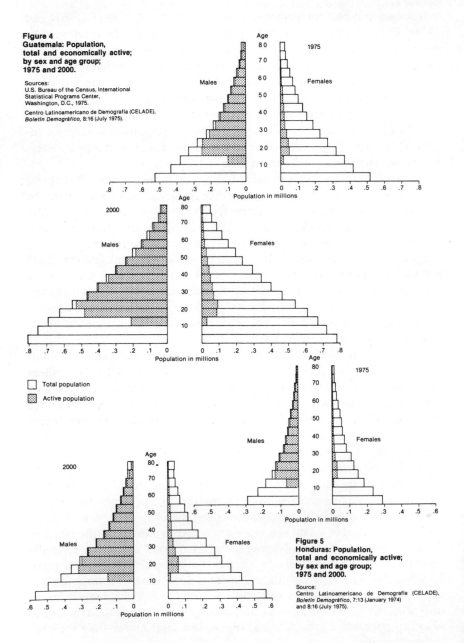

**Figure 4
Guatemala: Population,
total and economically active;
by sex and age group;
1975 and 2000.**

Sources:
U.S. Bureau of the Census, International
Statistical Programs Center,
Washington, D.C., 1975.

Centro Latinoamericano de Demografía (CELADE),
*Boletín Demográfico*, 8:16 (July 1975).

☐ Total population

▨ Active population

**Figure 5
Honduras: Population,
total and economically active;
by sex and age group;
1975 and 2000.**

Source:
Centro Latinoamericano de Demografía (CELADE),
*Boletín Demográfico*, 7:13 (January 1974)
and 8:16 (July 1975).

16

**Table 12**

**Central America: Distribution of agricultural holdings according to size and relative participation, 1970**[a]

| Category | Area | | Number of units or families | |
|---|---|---|---|---|
| | Thousand of hectares | Participation per cent | Thousand of units | Participation per cent |
| Landless Farmers | | | 476.3 | 27.7 |
| "Microfincas" (less than 0.7 ha.) | 85 | 0.6 | 285.1 | 16.6 |
| Subsistence Family Size Holdings (0.7 to 4 ha.) | 868 | 6.0 | 552.3 | 32.2 |
| Medium Subsistence Family Holdings (4 to 7 ha.) | 583 | 4.0 | 126.5 | 7.4 |
| Family Size Farms (7 to 35 ha.) | 2,350 | 16.2 | 180.7 | 10.5 |
| Medium Multifamily holdings (35 to 350 ha.) | 5,121 | 35.2 | 68.8 | 4.0 |
| Large Multifamily Holdings (more than 350 ha.) | 5,535 | 38.0 | 7.0 | 0.4 |
| Administrators | | | 20.5 | 1.2 |
| Total | 14,542 | 100.0 | 1,717.2 | 100.0 |

[a] Excludes Panamá.

Source: *Secretaría Permanente del Tratado General de Integración Económica Centroaméricana* (SIECA) and United Nations Food and Agriculture Organization (FAO), *Perspectivas para el Desarrollo y la Integración de la Agricultura en Centro América.* Guatemala, May 1974, Table G-2, p. 109.

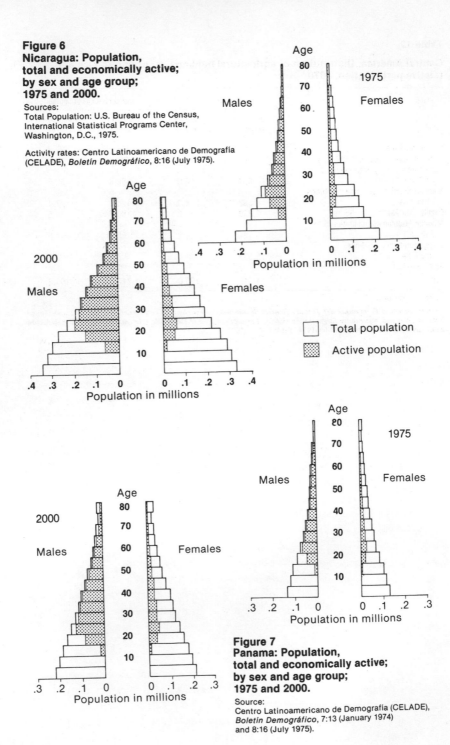

**Figure 6**
**Nicaragua: Population,**
**total and economically active;**
**by sex and age group;**
**1975 and 2000.**

Sources:
Total Population: U.S. Bureau of the Census,
International Statistical Programs Center,
Washington, D.C., 1975.

Activity rates: Centro Latinoamericano de Demografía
(CELADE), *Boletín Demográfico*, 8:16 (July 1975).

☐ Total population
▨ Active population

**Figure 7**
**Panama: Population,**
**total and economically active;**
**by sex and age group;**
**1975 and 2000.**

Source:
Centro Latinoamericano de Demografía (CELADE),
*Boletín Demográfico*, 7:13 (January 1974)
and 8:16 (July 1975).

# The structure and changes in urban systems

This chapter focuses on the growth of the cities of Central America, including the shifts in the urban systems that can be expected to result from population increases. Five categories are examined: cities with 10-20,000 inhabitants; 20-50,000; 50-100,000; 100-250,000; and 250,000 and more inhabitants that encompass the six capitals for 1970 and 1980.

The cities are examined here in two perspectives; First, cities are transferred from one size category to another as their population increases. This permits an examination of urbanization levels for one group of cities relative to another as shifts occur over time, and when viewed in percentage or proportional terms, accounts for changes in urban structures. Feeding into this system at the bottom rung are towns that move from fewer to more than 10,000 inhabitants during intercensal periods.

Second, since urbanization levels do not show the *pace* of growth of cities relative to one another, it is necessary to classify cities by population size in a given year and trace these particular groupings and their rates of increase forward and backward over time. Under this approach, by *cohort* groupings, cities and metropolitan areas are classified relative to size in the base year 1970, and the projected population is totaled for 1980 and traced back to 1960. The resulting aggregates permit comparisons on the velocity of growth among the various components in the Central American urban system.

Throughout South America and in Mexico mushrooming cities are now surrounded by even faster-growing suburbs and shantytowns that fall outside the city's administrative boundaries. In some instances the corridors between large cities have completely filled, forming massive urban agglomerations, and in other cases the core city has simply expanded to enmesh the towns surrounding it.

19

This pattern is beginning to develop in the principal cities of Central America, but on a lesser scale. San Salvador is now a well-defined metropolitan area comprising ten contiguous municipalities. Guatemala City is surrounded by numerous adjacent communities, including Mixco and Villa Nueva. Urban population growth in Panama City led to the development of the San Miguelito residential community in the last 15 years, and to the rapid expansion of the prestigious La Chorrera suburb in the low-lying hills north of the city. Following the Managua earthquake in December 1972, a large portion of that city's population moved to temporary shelter in the suburbs and into nearby towns. The results of this migration can still be seen in the hundreds of commuting automobiles that pour into the capital city each working day from as far away as Masaya, Granada, and Diriamba, some 30–50 kilometers away, and also in the form of now semi-permanent earthquake relief communities found around the periphery of the deserted city center. The suburban portions of all major Central American cities are listed in the individual country chapters in Part II.

The outstanding Central American example of urban sprawl is found in San Jose, Costa Rica where most of the entire Central Valley may be said to comprise a single "urbanizing" unit with the city of San Jose at its core. While the metropolitan area had 401,000 inhabitants in 1973, the metropolitan *region* under a broader definition contained 507,000 inhabitants classified as urban and 260,000 classified as rural by the census. Together, this represents 43 per cent of the country's entire population. The region's urban numbers include those in the provincial capitals of Alajuela, Cartago and Heredia, all located within a short drive of San Jose. The "rural" population of the region is unquestionably caught up in the urbanization transition. It is apparent even to the most casual observer that a very high proportion of those in the countryside earn their livelihood from city-oriented activities. Census data verify this. Only 22 per cent of the economically active in the rural portion of the Central Valley region are principally engaged in agricultural activities, compared to a full 75 per cent outside the region. This feature of Costa Rica's urban development process is more fully explained in the country chapter in Part II.

**Urbanization levels**

The regional pattern of changing urbanization levels is shown in Table 13. By 1980, the number of cities and towns will have tripled in the brief 30-year span since 1950. The pace of urbanization is about double that of the overall population growth average. This is to say that city populations will have jumped by almost five times by 1980, while the six countries collectively will have increased in total population by about 2.5 times during the same period.

**Table 13**

Distribution of the urban population by city size category 1950, 1960, 1970, and projected to 1980[a]

| City size category (thousands) | Number of cities | | | | Number of inhabitants[b] (thousands) | | | |
|---|---|---|---|---|---|---|---|---|
| | 1950 | 1960 | 1970 | 1980 | 1950 | 1960 | 1970 | 1980 |
| 10-20 | 21 | 29 | 41 | 60[c] | 268.0 | 412.9 | 579.3 | 801.9 |
| 20-50 | 5 | 11 | 22 | 35 | 126.2 | 316.2 | 644.1 | 1,054.6 |
| 50-100 | 3 | 3 | 4 | 6 | 191.1 | 210.9 | 265.2 | 401.9 |
| 100-250 | 4 | 2 | 2 | 3 | 685.5 | 368.7 | 264.7 | 500.8 |
| 250 and More | 1 | 4 | 6 | 6 | 336.6 | 1,577.6 | 3,233.1 | 4,657.4 |
| **Total** | **34** | **49** | **75** | **110** | **1,607.4** | **2,886.3** | **4,986.4** | **7,416.6** |

[a] The percentage distribution of the urban population is shown in Table 15.
[b] Data from Tables 16-21.
[c] Includes the population of 34 towns projected to increase from fewer to more than 10,000 inhabitants in the 1970-80 interval.

The number of small urban centers—under 50,000 inhabitants—has increased greatly, jumping from 26 in 1950 to a projected 95 by 1980. This is a significant indication of the continuing strength of small towns within the regional urban system, particularly in Costa Rica, El Salvador and Guatemala.

There has been a very small gain among cities with 50-250,000 inhabitants. Of the seven existing in 1950, five were capitals which have since passed to the open-ended 250,000 + category, and only seven other cities have replaced them. This underscores the very weak position of secondary cities throughout most of the region, and throughout Latin America for that matter. Very few cities can compete outside the capitals in growth and prosperity. The nine urban centers at the present time in this size category encompass virtually all the region's secondary cities, and in most instances they are increasing at a slower or much slower pace than the capitals. Such is the case of San Miguel and Santa Ana in El Salvador; Quetzaltenango, the indigenous population stronghold in Guatemala; La Ceiba in Honduras; Leon in Nicaragua; and the port city of Colon in Panama. Of the group only Escuintla in Guatemala, David in Panama, and San Pedro Sula in Honduras show rates of growth which significantly excede those of their respective national capitals. Escuintla and David, however, are hardly contenders for national urban dominance as they are just 4 and 8 per cent the size of their national capitals, respectively. San Pedro Sula, as the only major secondary city in Central America, is in an altogether different position. It is roughly half the size of Tegucigalpa, quite dynamic, and growing more rapidly than any other major city in the region. By 2000, it is projected to be two-thirds the size of Tegucigalpa.

With the exception of Honduras, in each of the other countries the capital cities thoroughly dominate their national urban systems, holding from 60-75 per cent of the total urban population. But, as seen in Table

21

14, the proportions claimed by the capitals are either just holding their own or are on the decline.

From the Isthmus of Tehuantepec and the Chiapas Highlands in the north to the Darien Gap in Panama at the southern extreme, Central America is easily viewed as one geographic unit divided politically into six republics. In one regard, the existence of six countries serves in the region's interest, since this has promoted the growth of numerous capital cities. Were it one nation, surely the population flow would be to the one central seat of the government. The domination of one city—usually the capital—over all others is a common occurrence throughout Latin America, and goes hand-in-hand with a centralized form of government that concentrates political, economic, social, and cultural functions in one locality. The issue of concentrated functions is no small matter in Latin America today as capital cities in large countries throughout the region are swamped with enormous population gains that cannot be absorbed through existing social and economic systems. School systems cannot meet the demand, nor can meaningful remunerative employment be found for increasing tens of thousands.

In a very real sense, the urban explosion *is* the population explosion in Latin America. Mexico City's population, for example, increased from 5.6 million in 1960 to 8.6 million in 1970, and conservative projections place the population of this one city at 13.6 million by 1980. Witness the large populations and phenomenal growth of Santiago, Chile; Lima, Peru; or Buenos Aires, Argentina which around 1970 contained 54, 57, and 54 per cent respectively of each country's urban population. In each of these three instances the percentage of the total urban population claimed by these capital cities is holding firm according to projections, but underscoring this are enormous population gains in absolute terms. Projections for 1970–80 for the Santiago metropolitan area, for example, show a net population increase of 1.1 million, which compares with a projected gain of just 0.6 million for the remainder of

Table 14

Population of Central American capital cities, and as per cent of total urban population, 1950–70, projected to 1980

| City | Population (thousands) | | | | Per cent of urban total[a] | | | |
|---|---|---|---|---|---|---|---|---|
| | 1950 | 1960 | 1970 | 1980 | 1950 | 1960 | 1970 | 1980 |
| Guatemala City | 337 | 644 | 1,067 | 1,430 | 82 | 78 | 75 | 71 |
| Managua | 109 | 235 | 385 | 662 | 54 | 58 | 58 | 59 |
| Panamá City | 217 | 332 | 520 | 794 | 70 | 72 | 72 | 72 |
| San José | 146 | 257 | 401 | 508 | 70 | 73 | 70 | 65 |
| San Salvador | 213 | 345 | 565 | 858 | 62 | 60 | 62 | 61 |
| Tegucigalpa | 72 | 134 | 295 | 406 | 53 | 49 | 43 | 42 |

[a] Data from Tables 16-21.

22

Chile's urban sector. For Peru, 1.4 million of a total 2.3 million urban increase is projected to accrue to Lima during the same period; and Buenos Aires will gain 1.9 million of a net 3.6 million population increase for the Argentine urban sector between 1970-80.

In Central America in contrast, none of the six capital cities can claim a very large portion of the *region's* total urban population. There is no one primate city in the region, although in a national context each capital does dominate over its own urban system. This is clearly a major strength. Many countries—Mexico, Peru, Venezuela, Brazil and Colombia among them—are urgently attempting to divert increasing populations to secondary cities through such measures as economic incentives for industrial plant relocations, or relocating entire ministries away from the capital to alternative "development poles." These efforts clearly are due to enormous population growth pressures on the capitals, whether in terms of employment, housing, education, water and sewerage, land use or other directly perceived issues. But in spite of these embryonic measures the demographic outlook to year 2000 shows continuously mounting populations for these countries and unrelenting pressures on weakly developed urban systems that focus on one primate city.

Seen as one region, the absorption of increasing urban populations in Central America can more readily be handled, owing to the existence of six moderately populated capital cities instead of one large urban agglomeration. Together, the six hold a majority of the region's total urban numbers, but separately these cities contain far smaller proportions. San Jose holds but 8 per cent of the region's urban population total, San Salvador 11 percent, Guatemala City 21 per cent, Tegucigalpa 6 per cent, Managua 8 per cent, and Panama City 10 per cent.

Shifts in the urban system expressed in proportional terms are found in Table 15. Here, the consistent strength of small towns (under 50,000 inhabitants) can be fully appreciated. This category contained 25 per cent of the total in 1950, and will contain a like share in 1980.

Table 15

**Percentage distribution of the urban population, 1950-70, and projected to 1980**

| City size category | Per cent of urban total[a] | | | |
|---|---|---|---|---|
| | 1950 | 1960 | 1970 | 1980 |
| 10–20 | 16.7 | 14.3 | 12.0 | 10.8 |
| 20–50 | 7.9 | 10.9 | 12.5 | 14.2 |
| 50–100 | 11.9 | 7.3 | 5.3 | 5.4 |
| 100–250 | 42.6 | 12.8 | 5.3 | 6.8 |
| 250 and more | 20.9 | 54.7 | 64.9 | 62.8 |
| Total | 100.0 | 100.0 | 100.0 | 100.0 |

[a] Data from Tables 16–21.

Cities with populations between 50–250,000 have declined in their share of the total, dropping from 20 per cent in 1960 to 12 per cent by 1980, while the capitals are beginning to decline just slightly from a high of 65 per cent in 1970. In interpreting these numbers it should be noted that only one capital city had moved out of this category to the 250,000 category in 1950, four by 1960 and all six by 1970 (see Table 13). Thus it can be seen that all cities of 100,000 and more inhabitants accounted for 63.5 per cent of the region's total urban population in 1950, 67.5 per cent in 1960, a maximum of 70.2 per cent in 1970, and will account for 69.6 per cent in 1980.

Information on each country's urban system is presented in Tables 16–21. Included are examinations of proportional shifts in the structure according to population size in the 1950–70 period and as projected to 1980.

While urban levels have risen considerably throughout Central America, they began in 1950 almost without exception from a very low base. At mid-century the region was overwhelmingly rural, and only Panama had as many as two in five persons in the cities. This was due to the existence of two port cities, Panama City and Colon, located at either end of the inter-oceanic canal. The urban proportion was lowest in Honduras where only one in ten lived in cities of 10,000 and more inhabitants, followed by Guatemala (14 per cent), El Salvador (18 per cent), and Nicaragua (19 per cent).

Three cities of over 100,000 inhabitants existed in the latter four country group—San Salvador, Guatemala City, and Managua—while Tegucigalpa contained just 72,000 inhabitants. In Costa Rica (1950) the urban system encompassed 26 per cent of the total population—a proportion second only to Panama—and was comprised of San Jose and a very consistent group (in population size) of five provincial capitals, three of which can be observed in the distance from downtown San Jose.

Table 16

Costa Rica: Urban population distribution by city size category, 1950–1973 and projected to 1980

| City size category | Number of cities | | | | Population (thousands) | | | | Percentage of total urban | | | |
|---|---|---|---|---|---|---|---|---|---|---|---|---|
| | 1950 | 1963 | 1973 | 1980 | 1950 | 1963 | 1973 | 1980 | 1950 | 1963 | 1973 | 1980 |
| 10–20 | 5 | 5 | 2 | 8[a] | 63.4 | 95.9 | 23.0 | 99.7 | 30 | 27 | 4 | 13 |
| 20–50 | — | — | 5 | 5 | — | — | 150.9 | 179.9 | — | — | 26 | 23 |
| 50–100 | — | — | — | — | — | — | — | — | — | — | — | — |
| 100–250 | 1 | — | — | — | 146.1 | — | — | — | 70 | — | — | — |
| 250 and more | — | 1 | 1 | 1 | — | 257.2 | 401.0 | 507.8 | — | 73 | 70 | 64 |
| Total | 6 | 6 | 8 | 14 | 209.5 | 353.1 | 574.9 | 787.4 | 100 | 100 | 100 | 100 |

[a] Includes the towns of San Ramón, Grecia, Ciudad Quesada, Paraíso, Nicoya, and San Isidro projected to increase from fewer to more than 10,000 inhabitants in the 1973–1980 interval.

## Table 17

### El Salvador: Urban population distribution by city size category, 1950-1971, and projected to 1980

| City size category | Number of cities | | | | Population (thousands) | | | | Percentage of urban total | | | |
|---|---|---|---|---|---|---|---|---|---|---|---|---|
| | 1950 | 1961 | 1971 | 1980 | 1950 | 1961 | 1971 | 1980 | 1950 | 1961 | 1971 | 1980 |
| 10-20 | 4 | 7 | 8 | 10[a] | 49.2 | 89.5 | 130.4 | 123.8 | 14 | 16 | 14 | 9 |
| 20-50 | 1 | 2 | 2 | 8 | 26.7 | 63.6 | 53.3 | 216.5 | 8 | 11 | 6 | 15 |
| 50-100 | 1 | 1 | 2 | 1 | 51.7 | 72.8 | 160.3 | 89.9 | 15 | 13 | 18 | 6 |
| 100-250 | 1 | — | — | 1 | 213.4 | — | — | 131.1 | 63 | — | — | 9 |
| 250 and more | — | 1 | 1 | 1 | — | 344.6 | 565.0 | 857.8 | — | 60 | 62 | 61 |
| Total | 7 | 11 | 13 | 21 | 341.0 | 570.5 | 909.0 | 1,419.1 | 100 | 100 | 100 | 100 |

[a] Includes the towns of Atiquizaya, Metapan, Izalco, Armenia, Arcatag, La Libertad, Sensuntepeque, and Santiago de Mario projected to increase from fewer to more than 10,000 inhabitants in the 1971-1980 interval.

## Table 18

### Guatemala: Urban population distribution by city size category, 1950-1973, and projected to 1980

| City size category | Number of cities | | | | Population (thousands) | | | | Percentage of total urban | | | |
|---|---|---|---|---|---|---|---|---|---|---|---|---|
| | 1950 | 1964 | 1973 | 1980 | 1950 | 1964 | 1973 | 1980 | 1950 | 1964 | 1973 | 1980 |
| 10-20 | 4 | 7 | 14 | 19[a] | 46.7 | 96.1 | 202.9 | 251.3 | 11 | 12 | 14 | 13 |
| 20-50 | 1 | 3 | 4 | 8 | 26.9 | 85.5 | 110.3 | 209.9 | 7 | 10 | 8 | 10 |
| 50-100 | — | — | 1 | 2 | — | — | 50.1 | 120.8 | — | — | 3 | 6 |
| 100-250 | — | — | — | — | — | — | — | — | — | — | — | — |
| 250 and more | 1 | 1 | 1 | 1 | 336.6 | 664.0 | 1,067.1 | 1,430.0 | 82 | 78 | 75 | 71 |
| Total | 6 | 11 | 20 | 30 | 410.2 | 825.6 | 1,430.4 | 2,012.0 | 100 | 100 | 100 | 100 |

[a] Includes the towns of Santa Cruz del Quiché, Comalapa, San Andrés Iztapa, Esquipulas, Palín, Asunción Mita, Sumpango, Santa María de Jesús, Ciudad Vieja, and Totonicapán projected to increase from fewer to more than 10,000 inhabitants in the 1973-1980 interval.

## Table 19

### Honduras: Urban population distribution by city size category, 1950-1974, and projected to 1980

| City size category | Number of cities | | | | Population (thousands) | | | | Percentage of urban total | | | |
|---|---|---|---|---|---|---|---|---|---|---|---|---|
| | 1950 | 1961 | 1974 | 1980 | 1950 | 1961 | 1974 | 1980 | 1950 | 1961 | 1974 | 1980 |
| 10-20 | 3 | 4 | 6 | 9[a] | 41.4 | 55.9 | 79.9 | 139.5 | 31 | 21 | 12 | 14 |
| 20-50 | 1 | 1 | 5 | 4 | 21.1 | 24.9 | 149.1 | 133.9 | 15 | 9 | 22 | 14 |
| 50-100 | 1 | 1 | — | 1 | 72.4 | 58.6 | — | 54.1 | 54 | 21 | — | 5 |
| 100-250 | — | 1 | 1 | 1 | — | 134.1 | 161.7 | 238.9 | — | 49 | 23 | 25 |
| 250 and more | — | — | 1 | 1 | — | — | 295.5 | 405.6 | — | — | 43 | 42 |
| Total | 5 | 7 | 13 | 16 | 134.9 | 273.5 | 686.2 | 972.0 | 100 | 100 | 100 | 100 |

[a] Includes the towns of Choloma, Catacamas, and San Lorenzo projected to increase from fewer to more than 10,000 inhabitants in the 1974-1980 interval.

Table 20

Nicaragua: Urban population distribution by city size category, 1950–1971, and projected to 1980

| City size category | Number of cities | | | | Population (thousands) | | | | Percentage of urban total | | | |
|---|---|---|---|---|---|---|---|---|---|---|---|---|
| | 1950 | 1963 | 1971 | 1980 | 1950 | 1963 | 1971 | 1980 | 1950 | 1963 | 1971 | 1980 |
| 10–20 | 3 | 4 | 8 | 10$^a$ | 40.1 | 49.4 | 105.1 | 127.6 | 20 | 12 | 16 | 11 |
| 20–50 | 2 | 4 | 4 | 8 | 51.1 | 119.3 | 116.8 | 263.2 | 26 | 30 | 18 | 23 |
| 50–100 | — | — | 1 | 1 | — | — | 54.8 | 75.3 | — | — | 8 | 7 |
| 100–250 | 1 | 1 | — | — | 109.4 | 234.6 | — | — | 54 | 58 | — | — |
| 250 and more | — | — | 1 | 1 | — | — | 384.9 | 661.9 | — | — | 58 | 59 |
| Total | 6 | 9 | 14 | 20 | 200.6 | 403.3 | 661.6 | 1,128.0 | 100 | 100 | 100 | 100 |

$^a$ Includes the towns of El Viejo, Juigalpa, Nagarote, Masatepe, Ocotal, and Prinzapolka projected to increase from fewer to more than 10,000 inhabitants in the 1971–1980 interval.


Table 21

Panama: Urban population distribution by city size category, 1950–1970, and projected to 1980

| City size category | Number of cities | | | | Population | | | | Percentage of urban total | | | |
|---|---|---|---|---|---|---|---|---|---|---|---|---|
| | 1950 | 1960 | 1970 | 1980 | 1950 | 1960 | 1970 | 1980 | 1950 | 1960 | 1970 | 1980 |
| 10–20 | 2 | 2 | 3 | 4$^a$ | 27.2 | 26.1 | 38.0 | 60.0 | 9 | 6 | 5 | 5 |
| 20–50 | — | 1 | 2 | 2 | — | 22.9 | 63.7 | 51.2 | — | 5 | 9 | 5 |
| 50–100 | 1 | 1 | — | 1 | 67.0 | 79.5 | — | 61.8 | 21 | 17 | — | 6 |
| 100–250 | 1 | — | 1 | 1 | 216.6 | — | 103.0 | 130.8 | 70 | — | 14 | 12 |
| 250 and more | — | 1 | 1 | 1 | — | 331.8 | 519.6 | 794.3 | — | 72 | 72 | 72 |
| Total | 4 | 5 | 7 | 9 | 310.8 | 460.3 | 724.3 | 1,098.1 | 100 | 100 | 100 | 100 |

$^a$ Includes the town of La Concepción projected to increase from fewer to more than 10,000 inhabitants in the 1970–1980 interval.


By 1980, nine cities in the region will contain more than 100,000 inhabitants: the six capitals and Santa Ana, San Pedro Sula, and Colon. The urban sector's share of the total population will continue on the upswing in all countries. This trend, which became more pronounced after 1950 can be seen in Table 22. The urban share of the Nicaraguan population will have risen from 19 to 42 per cent—a gain of 23 percentage points and the largest increase of the six countries. This is followed by Panama (18 points), Honduras (17), Guatemala (15), El Salvador (11), and Costa Rica (8).

The relatively low gains in the share of the total population held by the urban sector in Costa Rica and El Salvador over the 30-year span appear to be due to two reasons. First, rural population growth has been very high in these countries. Rural increases amount to 117 per cent on average for the region, but in Costa Rica rural gains will amount to a level of 169 per cent, and in El Salvador 137 per cent. Thus, the existence of very rapid rural population growth tends to restrict relative urban gains in these two countries. The other countries, incidentally,

Table 22

Central America: Urban sector as percentage of total population, 1950–1970, and projected to 1980[a]

| Country | Per cent urban[b] | | | |
| --- | --- | --- | --- | --- |
| | 1950 | 1960 | 1970 | 1980 |
| Costa Rica | 26 | 26 | 31 | 34 |
| El Salvador | 18 | 23 | 26 | 29 |
| Guatemala | 14 | 19 | 25 | 29 |
| Honduras | 10 | 15 | 24 | 27 |
| Nicaragua | 19 | 26 | 35 | 42 |
| Panamá | 39 | 43 | 51 | 57 |

[a] Years given are those nearest the actual census date for each country.
[b] Data from Tables 16–21.

should register rural increases amounting roughly to 124 per cent (Honduras), 100 per cent (Nicaragua), 101 per cent (Guatemala), and 81 per cent (Panama) over the 30 year period.

Secondly, the emergence and consequent influence of "new cities" (e.g. those increasing from fewer to more than 10,000 inhabitants in any of the three 1950–80 intercensal periods) on the overall urban system in both cases will be modest. Without this component, a limit is placed on the urban sector's ability to surge ahead in urban vs. rural population distribution patterns. Just 13 per cent of Costa Rica's total 1950–80 urban population growth will be attributed to the entrance of "new cities" into the urban system, and for El Salvador only 16 per cent will be so attributed. In other words, 87 and 84 per cent, respectively, of urban population growth in the two countries is due to population increases in those cities existing in 1950. A similar pattern is found in Nicaragua and Panama; just 15 and 10 per cent, respectively, of their total urban population growth for 1950–80 will be attributed to "new cities" passing the population size threshold of 10,000 and more inhabitants. For Guatemala and Honduras the "new city" contribution to total urban population growth is higher; 20 and 31 per cent, respectively.

Compared to six other countries of Latin America, and applying an "urban" definition of 20,000 and more inhabitants instead of 10,000 and more, Central America was regionally the least urbanized of the group in 1950 (Table 23). This situation will persist in 1980, at which time Central America will be in a situation comparable to that of the other countries some 20 and 30 years earlier. Only Panama's urban level presently compares favorably with several of the Latin American countries.

Information in Table 24 relates the extent to which the urban sector (1950–80) absorbs total national population gains. The further projection of this trend (1980–2000) is seen in Table 25. Clearly, there is an

27

**Table 23**

**Urban sector as percentage of total population, for 12 Latin American countries, by census year 1950-1970, and projected to 1980**

| Country | Per cent urban[a] | | | |
|---|---|---|---|---|
| | 1950 | 1960 | 1970 | 1980 |
| Costa Rica | 18 | 19 | 29 | 30 |
| El Salvador | 16 | 19 | 22 | 27 |
| Guatemala | 12 | 16 | 22 | 25 |
| Honduras | 7 | 11 | 21 | 23 |
| Nicaragua | 15 | 23 | 30 | 37 |
| Panamá | 35 | 40 | 48 | 54 |
| **Central America Regional Average** | **15** | **19** | **25** | **30** |
| Argentina | 50 | 59 | 66 | 73 |
| Brazil | 22 | 29 | 40 | 50 |
| Chile | 43 | 50 | 60 | 67 |
| Mexico[b] | 28 | 36 | 44 | 51 |
| Peru | 23 | 30 | 43 | 49 |
| Venezuela | 36 | 50 | 61 | 71 |

[a] "Urban" for all countries is defined as cities of 20,000 and more inhabitants. Central American data from Tables 27-33.
[b] An alternative set of urban percentages for Mexico is based on the study of Juan Fernández de la Vega, *Ensayo sobre las aglomeraciones urbanas en los Estados Unidos Mexicanos*, Secretaría de Hacienda y Crédito Público, Fondo de Operación y Descuento Bancario a la Vivienda, México, D.F. 1969, 163 pp.. For 1950 the urban percentage is 43 per cent; 50 per cent in 1960; 57 per cent in 1970, and 62 per cent in 1980.

**Table 24**

**National population increases, and increases absorbed by the urban sector, 1950-60, 1960-1970, and 1970-80 as projected (by census year)**
(In thousands)

| Country | (a) National Population | | | (b) Population Increase | | | Urban absorption ratio | | |
|---|---|---|---|---|---|---|---|---|---|
| | Increase in interval | | | Urban sector[a] | | | (b as % of a) | | |
| | 1950-60 | 1960-70 | 1970-80 | 1950-60 | 1960-70 | 1970-80 | 1950-60 | 1960-70 | 1970-80 |
| Costa Rica | 535 | 536 | 414 | 144 | 222 | 212 | 27 | 41 | 51 |
| El Salvador | 655 | 1,038 | 1,263 | 230 | 339 | 510 | 35 | 33 | 40 |
| Guatemala | 1,439 | 1,234 | 1,261 | 415 | 605 | 582 | 29 | 49 | 46 |
| Honduras | 516 | 1,013 | 697 | 139 | 413 | 286 | 27 | 41 | 41 |
| Nicaragua | 486 | 342 | 791 | 202 | 258 | 466 | 42 | 75 | 59 |
| Panamá | 270 | 353 | 503 | 150 | 264 | 374 | 56 | 75 | 74 |

[a] Data from Tables 16-21.

expected strong relationship between these absorption ratios and the degree to which a country is urbanized in the first place. A highly urban country is more apt to absorb a larger proportion than one with a small urban sector. This occurs through natural increases in the cities and through the constant process of rural to urban migration. Thus, it follows that in Central America the urban absorption ratios for Panama are quite high and this is followed by Nicaragua, the next most highly urbanized country.

**Table 25**

**National population increases, and increases absorbed by the urban sector, 1980-90, and 1990-2000 as projected**
(In thousands)

| Country | (a) National Population increase in interval | | (b) Population Increase urban sector[a] | | Urban absorption ratio (b as % of a) | |
|---|---|---|---|---|---|---|
| | 1980-90 | 1990-2000 | 1980-90 | 1990-2000 | 1980-90 | 1990-2000 |
| Costa Rica | 669 | 741 | 435 | 651 | 65 | 88 |
| El Salvador | 1,782 | 2,208 | 855 | 1,249 | 48 | 57 |
| Guatemala | 2,168 | 2,475 | 1,169 | 1,634 | 54 | 66 |
| Honduras | 1,402 | 1,885 | 624 | 961 | 45 | 51 |
| Nicaragua | 1,002 | 1,140 | 730 | 1,002 | 73 | 88 |
| Panamá | 602 | 697 | 463 | 586 | 77 | 81 |

[a] In this context, urban centers include cities with 10,000 and more inhabitants in the base year 1970 and the population of those same cities projected to 1980, 1990, and 2000 as shown in the respective country tables. At each interval past 1970 the population of "new" cities is added— those that are estimated to increase from under to over 10,000 inhabitants in size during the preceding period.

**Table 26**

**Growth rates in the 1950-60, 1960-70 and 1970-80 (projected) intervals for all cities over 50,000 inhabitants**

| Country and city | Rate of population growth (per cent) | | |
|---|---|---|---|
| | 1950-60 | 1960-70 | 1970-80 |
| **Costa Rica** | | | |
| San José | 4.4 | 4.4 | 3.3 |
| **El Salvador** | | | |
| San Miguel | 3.7 | 4.3 | 4.1 |
| San Salvador | 4.4 | 4.9 | 4.6 |
| Santa Ana | 3.1 | 3.0 | 3.2 |
| **Guatemala** | | | |
| Esquintla | 6.4 | 6.2 | 5.2 |
| Guatemala City | 4.6 | 5.6 | 4.0 |
| Quetzaltenango | 3.1 | 2.1 | 2.8 |
| **Honduras** | | | |
| La Ceiba | 3.7 | 4.1 | 3.9 |
| San Pedro Sula | 9.4 | 7.9 | 6.2 |
| Tegucigalpa | 5.7 | 6.1 | 5.0 |
| **Nicaragua** | | | |
| León | 3.0 | 2.5 | 3.4 |
| Managua | 5.9 | 6.2 | 5.9 |
| **Panamá** | | | |
| Colón | 1.7 | 2.7 | 2.3 |
| David | 4.3 | 6.1 | 4.0 |
| Panama City | 4.3 | 4.8 | 4.2 |

The urban absorption ratio is shown to accelerate for all countries almost without exception in the 1950-2000 period. While just half the net population gain in Costa Rica in the 1970's will accrue to the cities, this is projected to rise to 88 per cent in the 1990-2000 decade. Similar ratios are seen for Panama and Nicaragua by year 2000. This finding compares quite favorably with information from other Latin American countries. Central America, as noted earlier, is approximately 20-30 years behind the much higher urban levels in these nations. For the five South American countries considered plus Mexico the current urban absorption percentages are roughly equal to where Costa Rica, Nicaragua, and Panama will be by year 2000.

Costa Rica, El Salvador, Guatemala and Honduras currently maintain urban absorption levels in the 40-51 per cent range. The pace as shown in Table 25 should accelerate in the coming decades in each of these countries, rising to more than 50 per cent in all cases. The impact on individual cities will unquestionably be severe, viewed either in absolute or growth rate terms. Guatemala City, for example, is projecting a population increase from 1,067,000 (1971) to 3,021,000 inhabitants by year 2000. However, it is evident that in the remaining years of this decade and well into the 1980's, rural areas (and activities) will have to absorb roughly half of the net population gains in Central America with the exception of Panama.

### Growth by cohort groupings

Table 27 and the accompanying graph show the pace of urban growth by various cohort groupings for the six countries. The basic regional trend relates a persistent decline in the proportion of the urban population held by cities of fewer than 100,000 inhabitants, and in like manner a proportional increase among those in the eight major cities over 100,000 inhabitants. The former group held 36 per cent of the total in 1950, 30 per cent in 1970, and is projecting 25 per cent by 2000, while the six capitals plus San Pedro Sula, and Colon comprised 64 (1950), 70 (1970), and a projected 75 per cent by 2000.

The breakdowns by country are shown in Tables 28-33 and in the accompanying graphs. Excepting the rapid decline of Colon's proportion of Panama's urban total, each country follows precisely in the regional pattern. Colon's slow rate of growth is related in Table 26 which presents growth rates for all Central American cities over 50,000 inhabitants.

**Central America and Panama**

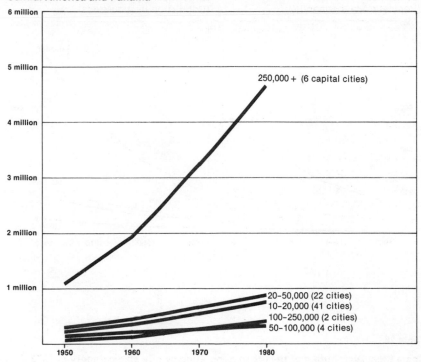

250,000 + (6 capital cities)

20-50,000 (22 cities)
10-20,000 (41 cities)
100-250,000 (2 cities)
50-100,000 (4 cities)

1950    1960    1970    1980

**Table 27**

**Central America and Panamá: Distribution of the urban population by city size category in census years around 1970**
(In thousands)

| City size category (thousands) | Number of cities | Population | | | | | | Per cent of total urban | | | | | |
|---|---|---|---|---|---|---|---|---|---|---|---|---|---|
| | | 1950 | 1960 | 1970 | 1980 | 1990 | 2000 | 1950 | 1960 | 1970 | 1980 | 1990 | 2000 |
| 10–20 | 41 | 261.5 | 397.4 | 579.3 | 774.2 | 1,084.6 | 1,465.1 | 14 | 13 | 12 | 11 | 10 | 10 |
| 20–50 | 22 | 281.5 | 415.7 | 644.1 | 856.2 | 1,198.2 | 1,616.3 | 15 | 13 | 13 | 12 | 12 | 11 |
| 50–100 | 4 | 135.8 | 199.0 | 265.2 | 357.8 | 483.9 | 631.4 | 7 | 6 | 5 | 5 | 5 | 4 |
| 100–250 | 2 | 88.1 | 138.1 | 264.7 | 369.7 | 565.0 | 851.6 | 5 | 5 | 5 | 5 | 5 | 6 |
| 250+ | 6 | 1,094.5 | 1,946.3 | 3,233.1 | 4,657.4 | 6,997.6 | 10,026.1 | 59 | 63 | 65 | 67 | 68 | 69 |
| **Total** | **75** | **1,861.4** | **3,096.5** | **4,986.4** | **7,015.3** | **10,329.3** | **14,590.5** | **100** | **100** | **100** | **100** | **100** | **100** |

31

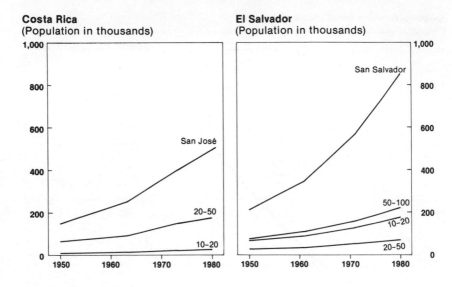

**Costa Rica**
(Population in thousands)

San José

20-50

10-20

**El Salvador**
(Population in thousands)

San Salvador

50-100

10-20

20-50

---

Table 28

**Costa Rica: Distribution of the urban population by city size category in 1973**
(In thousands)

| City size category (thousands) | Number of cities | Population | | | | | | Per cent of total urban | | | | | |
|---|---|---|---|---|---|---|---|---|---|---|---|---|---|
| | | 1950 | 1963 | 1973 | 1980 | 1990 | 2000 | 1950 | 1963 | 1973 | 1980 | 1990 | 2000 |
| 10-20 | 2 | 8.8 | 14.7 | 23.0 | 28.2 | 37.3 | 47.3 | 4 | 4 | 4 | 4 | 4 | 4 |
| 20-50 | 5 | 63.4 | 95.9 | 150.9 | 179.9 | 233.8 | 292.5 | 29 | 26 | 26 | 25 | 24 | 23 |
| 50-100 | — | — | — | — | — | — | — | — | — | — | — | — | — |
| 100-250 | — | — | — | — | — | — | — | — | — | — | — | — | — |
| San José | 1 | 146.1 | 257.2 | 401.0 | 507.8 | 696.4 | 919.6 | 67 | 70 | 70 | 71 | 72 | 73 |
| Total | 8 | 218.3 | 367.8 | 574.9 | 715.9 | 967.5 | 1,259.4 | 100 | 100 | 100 | 100 | 100 | 100 |

---

Table 29

**El Salvador: Distribution of the urban population by city size category in 1971**
(In thousands)

| City size category (thousands) | Number of cities | Population | | | | | | Per cent of total urban | | | | | |
|---|---|---|---|---|---|---|---|---|---|---|---|---|---|
| | | 1950 | 1961 | 1971 | 1980 | 1990 | 2000 | 1950 | 1961 | 1971 | 1980 | 1990 | 2000 |
| 10-20 | 8 | 66.2 | 91.2 | 130.4 | 178.5 | 247.3 | 334.4 | 17 | 16 | 14 | 13 | 12 | 12 |
| 20-50 | 2 | 27.9 | 35.1 | 53.3 | 72.7 | 100.2 | 134.3 | 7 | 6 | 6 | 5 | 5 | 5 |
| 50-100 | 2 | 78.4 | 112.7 | 160.3 | 221.0 | 306.5 | 412.5 | 21 | 19 | 18 | 17 | 16 | 14 |
| 100-250 | — | — | — | — | — | — | — | — | — | — | — | — | — |
| San Salvador | 1 | 213.4 | 344.6 | 565.0 | 857.8 | 1,315.0 | 1,939.3 | 55 | 59 | 62 | 65 | 67 | 69 |
| Total | 13 | 385.9 | 583.6 | 909.0 | 1,330.0 | 1,969.0 | 2,820.5 | 100 | 100 | 100 | 100 | 100 | 100 |

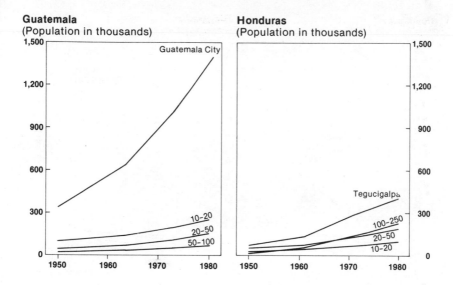

**Guatemala**
(Population in thousands)

**Honduras**
(Population in thousands)

## Table 30

### Guatemala: Distribution of the urban population by city size category in 1973
(In thousands)

| City size category (thousands) | Number of cities | Population | | | | | | Per cent of total urban | | | | | |
|---|---|---|---|---|---|---|---|---|---|---|---|---|---|
| | | 1950 | 1964 | 1973 | 1980 | 1990 | 2000 | 1950 | 1964 | 1973 | 1980 | 1990 | 2000 |
| 10–20 | 14 | 92.6 | 140.1 | 202.9 | 253.1 | 349.3 | 464.5 | 19 | 16 | 14 | 13 | 13 | 12 |
| 20–50 | 4 | 44.2 | 76.3 | 110.3 | 158.5 | 233.2 | 328.5 | 9 | 8 | 8 | 9 | 8 | 8 |
| 50–100 | 1 | 26.9 | 41.3 | 50.1 | 61.5 | 79.4 | 99.1 | 5 | 5 | 3 | 3 | 3 | 3 |
| 100–250 | — | — | — | — | — | — | — | — | — | — | — | — | — |
| Guatemala City | 1 | 336.6 | 664.0 | 1,067.0 | 1,430.0 | 2,137.2 | 3,021.3 | 67 | 71 | 75 | 75 | 76 | 77 |
| Total | 20 | 500.3 | 901.7 | 1,430.4 | 1,903.1 | 2,799.1 | 3,913.4 | 100 | 100 | 100 | 100 | 100 | 100 |

## Table 31

### Honduras: Distributions of the urban population by city size category in 1974
(In thousands)

| City size category (thousands) | Number of cities | Population | | | | | | Per cent of total urban | | | | | |
|---|---|---|---|---|---|---|---|---|---|---|---|---|---|
| | | 1950 | 1961 | 1974 | 1980 | 1990 | 2000 | 1950 | 1961 | 1974 | 1980 | 1990 | 2000 |
| 10–20 | 6 | 29.8 | 45.8 | 79.9 | 103.1 | 148.7 | 211.7 | 16 | 14 | 11 | 11 | 10 | 10 |
| 20–50 | 5 | 57.7 | 80.8 | 149.1 | 188.0 | 279.7 | 406.5 | 32 | 25 | 22 | 20 | 19 | 18 |
| 50–100 | — | — | — | — | — | — | — | — | — | — | — | — | — |
| 100–250 | 1 | 21.1 | 58.6 | 161.7 | 238.9 | 401.9 | 657.6 | 12 | 19 | 24 | 26 | 27 | 29 |
| Tegucigalpa | 1 | 72.4 | 134.1 | 295.5 | 405.6 | 637.4 | 974.2 | 40 | 42 | 43 | 43 | 44 | 43 |
| Total | 13 | 181.0 | 319.3 | 686.2 | 935.6 | 1,467.7 | 2,250.0 | 100 | 100 | 100 | 100 | 100 | 100 |

33

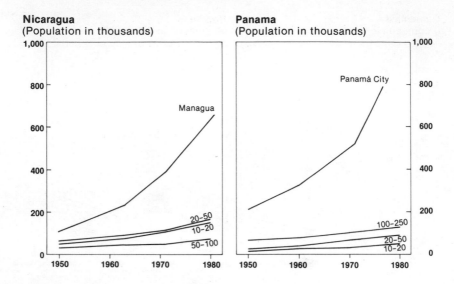

**Nicaragua**
(Population in thousands)

**Panama**
(Population in thousands)

**Table 32**

**Nicaragua: Distribution of the urban population by city size category in 1971**
(In thousands)

| City size category (thousands) | Number of cities | Population | | | | | | Per cent of total urban | | | | | |
|---|---|---|---|---|---|---|---|---|---|---|---|---|---|
| | | 1950 | 1963 | 1971 | 1980 | 1990 | 2000 | 1950 | 1963 | 1971 | 1980 | 1990 | 2000 |
| 10–20 | 8 | 46.2 | 77.8 | 105.1 | 158.2 | 229.3 | 313.1 | 19 | 17 | 16 | 15 | 14 | 14 |
| 20–50 | 4 | 61.6 | 89.3 | 116.8 | 165.8 | 224.9 | 287.3 | 25 | 20 | 18 | 16 | 14 | 12 |
| 50–100 | 1 | 30.5 | 45.0 | 54.8 | 75.3 | 98.0 | 119.8 | 12 | 10 | 8 | 7 | 6 | 5 |
| 100–250 | — | — | — | — | — | — | — | | | | | | |
| Managua | 1 | 109.4 | 234.6 | 384.9 | 661.9 | 1,075.2 | 1,604.1 | 44 | 53 | 58 | 62 | 66 | 69 |
| Total | 14 | 247.7 | 446.7 | 661.6 | 1,061.2 | 1,627.4 | 2,324.3 | 100 | 100 | 100 | 100 | 100 | 100 |

**Table 33**

**Panamá: Distribution of the urban population by city size category in 1970**
(In thousands)

| City size category (thousands) | Number of cities | Population | | | | | | Per cent of total urban | | | | | |
|---|---|---|---|---|---|---|---|---|---|---|---|---|---|
| | | 1950 | 1960 | 1970 | 1980 | 1990 | 2000 | 1950 | 1960 | 1970 | 1980 | 1990 | 2000 |
| 10–20 | 3 | 17.9 | 27.8 | 38.0 | 53.1 | 72.7 | 94.1 | 6 | 6 | 5 | 5 | 5 | 5 |
| 20–50 | 2 | 27.2 | 38.3 | 63.7 | 91.3 | 126.4 | 167.2 | 8 | 8 | 9 | 9 | 8 | 8 |
| 50–100 | — | — | — | — | — | — | — | | | | | | |
| 100–250 | 1 | 67.0 | 79.5 | 103.0 | 130.8 | 163.1 | 194.0 | 20 | 17 | 14 | 12 | 11 | 10 |
| Panamá City | 1 | 216.6 | 331.8 | 519.6 | 794.3 | 1,135.9 | 1,567.6 | 66 | 69 | 72 | 74 | 76 | 77 |
| Total | 7 | 328.7 | 477.4 | 724.3 | 1,069.5 | 1,498.1 | 2,022.9 | 100 | 100 | 100 | 100 | 100 | 100 |

# Population growth

The Central American population doubled between 1950 and 1975, a period when the region exhibited one of the highest growth rates in the world. Individual countries attained very high rates—Costa Rica 4.0 per cent, El Salvador 3.4 per cent, and Honduras 3.3 per cent during various intervals—and in no country did the rate of increase fall below a level of 2.8 per cent. By year 2000 another doubling of the population to 39 million is projected. On what grounds do these projections rest, and how firm are the underpinnings? Can lower population projections be established, and on what basis? And as the year 2000 is no more than a convenient cut-off date, what can be said of demographic tendencies past that point should the projections in this study be realized?

The projected high rates of population increase are supported by three main factors that will be reviewed in turn: a death rate that is still falling rapidly in some of the countries, high birth rates that show only modest signs of declining, particularly among the younger female population, and national populations in which the existence of very high proportions under age 20 serve to almost insure the continuation of high levels of growth.

All changes in population numbers depend on three and only three factors: the number of births, the number of deaths, and changes due to migration. In a national setting, and applicable to the Central American republics, the natural increase—the excess of births over deaths—is normally more important than changes due to emigration or immigration.

Net international migration is generally negative and of small magnitude, with the exception of Salvadoreans returning to their homeland from Honduras during 1969–70. As seen in the country chapters, estimates of national net migration are quite low. Consequently, the major determinants of growth are found in the constant interplay between the number of births and the number of deaths.

## The rate of natural increase, 1950-1970

### The birth rate

From 1950 to 1963 the region's crude birth rate was nearly static, but in the 1965-69 period it entered a stage of incipient decline (Table 34). Throughout this 20-year span the crude death rate declined steadily, continuing a trend begun prior to 1950 with strong efforts to reduce infant mortality, and bring transmissible diseases under control. These rates, by country, are plotted on Figure 8 which shows how they have generally fallen in parallel fashion. The two factors combined—high birth and falling death levels—served to produce rates of natural increase that were higher in 1965-70 than in 1950-55. Thus, what is termed the population "explosion" can be more accurately described as greater numbers surviving than in the past, particularly among infants, and a longer life expectancy for the population in general.

An examination of the crude birth rate (CBR)[1] for the region in Table 34 shows that it declined by only two points from a level of 49.8 in 1950-54 to 47.9 in 1960-64. The rate then dropped by three points to 44.7 for the 1965-69 period. When the countries of the region are considered individually, it is seen that the birth rate in Panama was about the same in 1965-69 and in 1950-54, although it increased then decreased slightly during the intervening period. Panama's CBR, in fact, has been very near to 40 per thousand throughout this century.

## Table 34

### Crude birth rates in the Central America region, 1950-1969
(Per cent)

|  | 1950-54 | 1955-59 | 1960-64 | 1965-69 |
|---|---|---|---|---|
| Region | 49.8 | 49.0 | 47.9 | 44.7 |
| Costa Rica | 47.1 | 48.2 | 45.6 | 38.3 |
| El Salvador | 49.0 | 49.0 | 48.7 | 44.4 |
| Guatemala | 50.9 | 49.0 | 47.6 | 44.0 |
| Honduras | 54.6 | 53.3 | 51.8 | 51.1 |
| Nicaragua | 53.4 | 51.3 | 50.0 | 48.6 |
| Panamá | 37.5 | 39.8 | 40.2 | 39.0 |

Notes and sources: the region: A weighted average of the rates for the countries. Costa Rica, El Salvador, Guatemala, and Panama: from registration data as shown in the country chapters of this report. Honduras and Nicaragua: The rates refer to 1950-55, 1955-60, etc., and are from Centro Latinoamericano de Demografía (CELADE), *Boletín Demográfico* 7:13 (January 1974), p. 31.

---

[1] The crude birth rate is the annual number of births per 1,000 inhabitants.

Costa Rica's historic and unprecedented fertility decline is reflected in its CBR after 1960. The 1960-64 CBR is 2.6 points under the 1955-59 rate, and the 1965-69 rate exhibits a further decrease of over seven points. El Salvador and Guatemala demonstrated incipient decreases in their crude birth rates after 1965, similar to the trend of the regional average. The birth rates of Honduras and Nicaragua are estimated by CELADE to have declined slightly from 1950-54 to 1965-69 but were still at extremely high levels in the latter period, 51.1 and 48.6 per thousand, respectively.

To facilitate comparisons, crude birth rates above 40 per 1,000 may be designated as very high, 30-39 high, 20-29 medium, and below 20 low. On a world-wide comparative basis the Costa Rican and Panamanian rates are high. In more industrialized nations, the rate is commonly below 20. The rates in 1970 and 1973 in Canada were 17.4 and 15.5; 18.3 and 15.0 in the United States; 16.8 and 16.5 in France; and 19.6 and 19.1 in Spain.[1]

Central America has the highest crude birth rate in Latin America. The 1970-75 rate of 42.3 compares with rates of 23.3 in temperate South America, 32.8 in the Caribbean, and 38.3 in tropical South America for the same period.[2] At the end of the century the Central American rate is projected to remain the highest—32.1 compared with 29.3 in tropical South America.

The crude birth rate estimated by the United Nations for all less developed regions is 37.5 in 1970-75 and is projected to decline to 27.8 by 1995-2000. Africa has the greatest CBR, 46.3 in 1970-75. The rate is expected to decrease less rapidly than that in the Central American region and to equal 39.1 in 1995-2000. South Asia's CBR, 41.9, is nearly the same as that in Central America but is projected to decline to 28.4 by the end of the century. The rate in East Asia is just 26.2. In Europe (16.1), North America (16.5), the Soviet Union (17.8), and Australia (21.0) the crude birth rates are less than half that of Central America.

*The death rate*

While the crude birth rate for the region decreased by 10.2 per cent from 1950-54 to 1965-69, the crude death rate (CDR)[3] was lowered by over one-third (34.7 per cent) during a similar period, thus accounting for the rise in the rate of natural increase. In general, the countries

---

[1] United Nations, *Demographic Yearbook* 1974, New York City, 1975, Table 9, pp. 244-254.

[2] United Nations Population Division, *World Population Prospects, 1970-2000, as Assessed in 1973,* ESA/P/WP.53, New York: 10 March 1975, Table 2.1, medium variant.

[3] The crude death rate is the annual number of deaths per 1,000 inhabitants.

with the highest death rates (Table 35) in 1950-55 experienced the greatest absolute declines of their CDR by 1965-70, although the percentage decline was between 30 and 39 per cent for all six countries. Consequently, the range among the crude death rates in the region has narrowed. The CDR's of Guatemala, Honduras, and Nicaragua, however, are still approximately double those of Costa Rica and Panama.

Honduras had the highest death rate in the region both in 1950-55 (28.5) and in 1965-70 (17.5), but also experienced the largest decline in the rate during the period. The death rates in El Salvador, Guatemala, and Nicaragua were all similar in 1950-55 (between 21.3 and 23.4), and all decreased by moderate amounts by 1965-70 to a range between 13.0 and 16.4. The lowest death rates were found in Costa Rica and Panama in 1950-55 (11.8 and 12.5, respectively) and in 1965-70 (7.8 and 8.1).

The interaction between birth and death rates for the region yielded an annual average population growth rate of 2.82 per cent in 1950-55. Declining deaths and stable or slightly falling birth levels underscore the increase in the growth rate of 3.04 per cent in 1955-60, which reached 3.17 per cent in 1960-65. In the subsequent period (1965-70) the population growth rate of 3.06 per cent was nearly the same as that for 10 years earlier.

### The rate of natural increase, 1970-2000

*The birth rate*

A continuing decline in both the crude birth and death rates is anticipated in all countries of the region for the 1970-2000 period (Figure 8). The crude birth rate for the region is projected to decrease by about 10 points between 1970-2000 (Table 36). Most importantly, however, since the projected decline of the crude death rate is approximately six points

**Table 35**

**Crude death rates in the Central American region, 1950-70**
(Per cent)

|  | 1950-55 | 1955-60 | 1960-65 | 1965-70 |
|---|---|---|---|---|
| Region | 21.6 | 18.6 | 16.2 | 14.1 |
| Costa Rica | 11.8 | 9.9 | 8.9 | 7.8 |
| El Salvador | 21.3 | 18.8 | 15.5 | 13.0 |
| Guatemala | 23.4 | 20.0 | 18.0 | 16.4 |
| Honduras | 28.5 | 24.4 | 20.7 | 17.5 |
| Nicaragua | 22.5 | 20.1 | 17.8 | 15.6 |
| Panamá | 12.5 | 10.8 | 9.4 | 8.1 |

Notes and sources: The region: A weighted average of the rates for the countries. Costa Rica and Guatemala: The rates refer to 1950-54, 1955-59, etc., and are estimates as shown in the country chapters of this report. El Salvador, Honduras, Nicaragua, and Panama: Centro Latinoamericano de Demografía (CELADE), *Boletín Demográfico* 7:13 (January 1974), p. 32.

**Figure 8
Estimates of crude birth and death rates for
Central America, 1920-70,
and projected rates for 1970-2000.**[a]

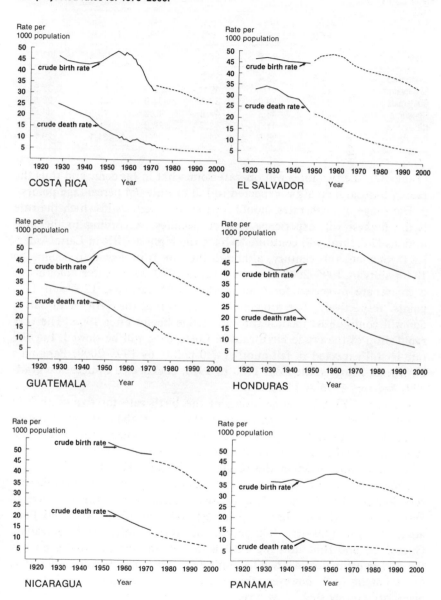

[a] The discontinuities in the crude rates, particularly for Honduras, Guatemala and Nicaragua, result from estimates taken from the different sources available.

39

**Table 36**

**Projected crude birth rates in the Central American region, 1970-2000**
(Per cent)

| | 1970-1975 | 1975-1980 | 1980-1985 | 1985-1990 | 1990-1995 | 1995-2000 |
|---|---|---|---|---|---|---|
| Region | 42.3 | 40.5 | 38.8 | 36.7 | 34.4 | 32.1 |
| Costa Rica | 33.4 | 32.4 | 31.2 | 29.1 | 27.1 | 26.4 |
| El Salvador | 42.2 | 41.1 | 40.0 | 38.3 | 36.1 | 33.5 |
| Guatemala | 42.5 | 39.9 | 37.5 | 34.9 | 32.3 | 29.6 |
| Honduras | 49.3 | 46.3 | 44.0 | 42.2 | 40.5 | 38.5 |
| Nicaragua | 45.2 | 44.3 | 42.7 | 39.9 | 36.3 | 33.0 |
| Panamá | 36.2 | 35.5 | 34.6 | 33.1 | 31.1 | 29.2 |

(Table 37), the two rates will operate somewhat in tandem, and thus the rate of natural increase is expected to fall by only 0.4 percentage points.

The range of birth rates should narrow as countries in which the rate is the highest will experience greater declines. According to the projections Honduras will continue to have the highest CBR in Latin America throughout this century, although the rate is projected to decline by 10.8 points by 1995-2000 from its level in 1970-75. Greater amounts of decrease are projected for Guatemala and Nicaragua, 12.9 and 12.2 points, respectively. The projection indicates that the CBR in El Salvador will continue its modest rate of decline begun after 1965. The very rapid drop of the crude birth rate in Costa Rica will be slowed, but the rate is still expected to fall another 7.0 points by 1995-2000. Panama's birth rate, nearly static from 1950 to 1970, is expected to decrease gradually between 1970 and 2000.

A recent CELADE reevaluation of the birth rate for five of the six countries confirms that in the mid-1970's it is at about the level shown in Table 36. Aside from providing a check on earlier information, the value of the CELADE study is that it is based on data from sources other than those used in the original estimates. This involved careful consideration of new census materials, and recent data from sample surveys and birth registries. The revised information shows a "recent" lower crude birth rate than in prior estimates for Costa Rica and Panama, 31.0 and 33.9 per 1,000 population, respectively. For El Salvador, Guatemala and Honduras the CBR is roughly the same as that shown in the earlier estimates, 43.2, 42.1, and 49.2 per 1,000, respectively.[1] It is to be emphasized, however, that these are new estimates, and do not necessarily imply sharp new directions in birth rate trends.

---

[1] CELADE, *American Latina. Evaluacion de la Situacion en el Quinquenio 1970–1975. Comparación de la Estimaciones Previas con las que Resultan de Datos Recientes*, Santiago, Chile, November, 1976.

**Table 37**

Projected crude death rates in the Central American region, 1970–2000
(Per cent)

|  | 1970–1975 | 1975–1980 | 1980–1985 | 1985–1990 | 1990–1995 | 1995–2000 |
|---|---|---|---|---|---|---|
| Region | 12.0 | 10.2 | 8.9 | 7.9 | 7.1 | 6.3 |
| Costa Rica | 5.9 | 5.1 | 4.6 | 4.4 | 4.4 | 4.4 |
| El Salvador | 11.1 | 9.5 | 8.2 | 7.2 | 6.3 | 5.6 |
| Guatemala | 14.5 | 11.8 | 10.0 | 9.0 | 8.0 | 7.3 |
| Honduras | 14.6 | 12.7 | 11.0 | 9.5 | 8.2 | 6.9 |
| Nicaragua | 12.2 | 11.0 | 9.9 | 8.8 | 7.8 | 6.9 |
| Panamá | 7.2 | 6.6 | 6.2 | 5.8 | 5.5 | 5.2 |

The age-specific fertility rate (ASFR) is the number of live births during one year to women in a given five-year age group per 1,000 women in the same age group.

ASFR's for the six countries by five year age groups are graphed in Figure 9. The graph is based on the information available covering two or three periods, consisting in some cases of "prior" and "recent" estimates made by CELADE, while in other cases the ASFR's are for stated years. El Salvador, Guatemala, Nicaragua, and Panama show tendencies in the direction of slightly declining fertility rates among women of all age groups. In Honduras the opposite trend appears—fertility rates appear to have risen slightly. All of these countries, however, should be examined in comparison to Costa Rica, which through its ASFR trends shows the pattern that ought to develop if birth rates are to begin falling sharply in the region, instead of the modest decline currently found.

Costa Rica since 1960 has experienced the most rapid long-run decline in fertility ever recorded for a Latin American country. Its total fertility rate[1] decreased from a peak of 7.26 in 1960 to 4.37 in 1972, and it is still declining. Recent estimates of the total fertility rates in the other countries are: El Salvador, 6.33; Guatemala, 5.92; Honduras, 7.50; Nicaragua, 6.67; and Panama, 4.72. The decline in fertility since 1960 in Costa Rica affected women 20–24 first of all, and then made an impact on successively older age groups. This is significant for two reasons: since there is the strong possibility that women in the younger age groups will maintain a lower ASFR throughout their reproductive years, they will have more of an impact on total fertility than a similar decline would produce among older groups of women who soon pass out of their reproductive years. This trend among younger women in Costa Rica

---

[1] The total fertility rate is the number of children that a woman would bear in her lifetime if she experienced at each age the average fertility of all women at each age measured for a given year.

**Figure 9**
**Estimates of age-specific fertility rates for Central America.**[a]

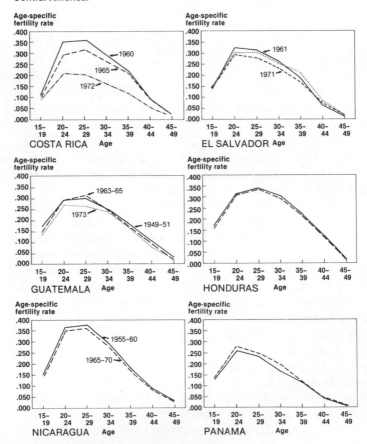

[a] The rates for Honduras and Panama are not identified by year and refer to "prior" and "recent" estimates given by CELADE in "America Latina, Evaluación de la Situación Demográfica en el Quinquenio 1970–1975. Comparación de las Estimaciones Previas con las que Resultan de Datos Recientes", CELADE, San José, Costa Rica, 1976. A "recent" estimate for Guatemala is also shown.

may also be seen as the possible leading edge and reflection of quickly changing values and attitudes among younger people in the country, and a forecast of lower fertility patterns to come. As seen in Figure 9, a similar pattern producing a sizable drop in fertility among younger women has not yet developed in other countries and there is no certainty that it will soon. Freedman, *et. al.* have shown that while fertility declines in Korea in the 1960's were most significant among women under 25, in Taiwan the greater proportional declines occurred for women over age 30.[1] Although marriage rates in Taiwan were falling, marital fertility rose because of earlier marriage of women in the 15–19 age group and because the interval between marriage and the first birth was shortened. If other countries in Central America should follow the Taiwan pattern of fertility reduction rather than the Costa Rican pattern, population growth rates will be slow to fall, first because there are more women in the younger age groups (where fertility rates would be declining less) than the older age groups. Secondly, declining fertility at the older ages has the effect of shortening the length of generation[2] and thus modifying reductions of the growth rate. Consequently, there is no present firm basis for conjecture that birth rates in the region during the next few years will fall much beyond levels now taken into account in the projections.

*The death rate*

The countries which now have the highest crude death rates are expected to show the greatest declines in the rate by the year 2000 (Table 37), as was also true for the birth rates. For this reason, the range in the death rate in the region is projected to decrease from 8.7 points in 1970–75 (Costa Rica vs. Honduras) to a much tighter 2.9 points in 1995–2000 (Costa Rica vs. Guatemala).

Unlike the crude birth rate, the crude death rate has little distance left in which to fall. It is now very low in Costa Rica (5.9), with no possibility that further large reductions will occur. It is expected to decline slightly to 4.4 by 1985–90, then to remain constant at least to year 2000. The decline in Panama's low crude death rate can also only be moderate. Nicaragua's death rate is projected to decline by 5.3 points to a level of 6.9 by 1995–2000. The rate in El Salvador and Guatemala is expected to be nearly halved, while in Honduras it is projected to be more than halved between 1970–75 and 1995–2000.

---

[1] R. Freedman, A. Hermalin, and T. H. Sun, "Fertility Trends in Taiwan, 1961–1970", *Population Index* 38:2 (1972)

[2] The length of generation is defined as the mean age of mothers at the births of their daughters. A population in which women replace themselves in 20 years will grow faster than one in which they replace themselves in 25 years.

**Figure 10.**
**Rates of natural increase for Central América, 1920–1970
and as projected for 1980–2000.**

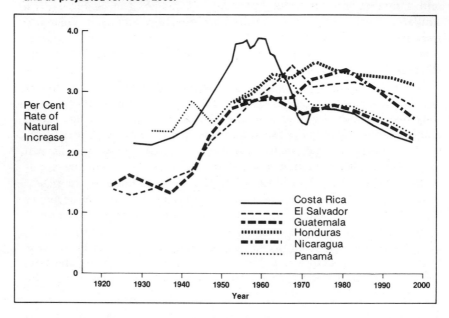

Since projected declines in the crude birth rate of the region are expected to be partially offset by decreases in the death rate, the rate of natural increase will remain quite high at least until the year 2000. The level of natural increases for each of the countries, experienced since 1920 and projected to 2000, is plotted in Figure 10. The rate of natural increase, derived from Tables 34–37, will remain above 3.0 per cent a year until 1980 on the regional level, and should equal 2.99 per cent per annum in 1980-85. Thereafter, it is projected to decrease moderately to 2.88 per cent in 1985-90, to 2.73 per cent in 1990-95, and to 2.58 per cent in 1995-2000. A growth rate such as the region will have at the end of the century would cause a population to again double in under 27 years.

Each of the countries in the region is projected to have a rate of natural increase of 2.2 per cent per year or greater in the 1995-2000 period. Costa Rica and Guatemala are expected to be growing at rates of 2.2 per cent. Panama's projected rate of natural increase is 2.4 per cent, Nicaragua's is 2.6 per cent, El Salvador's is 2.8 per cent, and Honduras' is over three per cent. Thus, even with a substantial decline in fertility between now and the year 2000 which regionally should amount to 25 per cent from present levels, the population in all the countries will continue to grow rapidly.

44

The third major factor underpinning the projections concerns the momentum of growth that derives from "young" age structures. The effect this has on sustaining continuing increases is threaded into the following discussion on possibilities for reducing growth and reaching a zero population growth level.

## Minimum growth projections

Since the populations of urbanized areas are projected in this study by an allocation of the projected national population, the assumptions of the national population projections are critical. As seen in Tables 36 and 37, all the projections employed in this report are based on an assumption of steady declines in both fertility and mortality from 1970 to 2000.

How different would the results be if fertility decreased much more rapidly? One method of investigating this question is to observe population projections for the countries concerned in which the fertility assumption is that the net reproduction rate will be linearly reduced to 1.0 by a specified date. Such projections have been prepared by the U.S. Bureau of the Census and their results are summarized in Table 38.

The net reproduction rate (NRR) is a rather complex demographic measure which reflects both current fertility and mortality conditions. It is the number of daughters per woman who would be born and survive to the age of their mother at the time of their own birth if current fertility and mortality schedules were fixed. Hence, the NRR in a stable population represents the ratio of the size of one generation to the size of its predecessor. A net reproduction rate of 1.0 indicates that one generation exactly replaces itself, or that fertility is at the replacement level. A NRR of 1.0 has been explained by the U.S. Bureau of the Census in these terms:

> In order for a population to cease growing, or to become stationary, its number of births per year must only equal its number of deaths. To hypothetically transform any given population into a stationary population over time, one could utilize a measure of fertility called the Net Reproduction Rate (NRR). The NRR may be defined as the total number of female children that would be born per woman to a cohort of women as they pass through the reproductive ages (15 to 49 years), allowing for mortality of some of the women up to and during this period. Thus, an NRR of 1.0 means that woman would produce an average of one daughter, who may be said to "replace" her mother in the population with the presumed eventual result that no growth of the population would take place. Actually, those women in the fertile years

must average slightly more than one female birth to compensate for the females in the birth cohort who die before they produce a daughter. Although not implicit in the rate, it may, of course, be supposed that each woman would also produce a son, who in turn, "replaces" his father. Thus, it could be considered that about two surviving children per family would eventually result in mere "replacement" of the population.[1]

In 1970, the net population rates in the region ranged from 2.29 in Guatemala to 2.56 in El Salvador, with a regional average of 2.41. Although Costa Rica had the lowest fertility in 1970, its NRR was above that of the high fertility countries of Guatemala, Honduras, and Nicaragua because of its low mortality rates. The smaller number of births in Costa Rica is compensated for by the higher percentage of the births which survive to childbearing age.

The U.S. Bureau of the Census prepared three projection series based on the assumption that the net reproduction rate will decline linearly to 1.0, then remain at that level for the remainder of the projections which extend to the year 2075. The NRR reaches 1.0 in 1980-85, 1990-95, and 2000-2005 in the three projection series. In each of the series it is assumed that mortality decreases gradually until the life expectancy at birth for females equals 75.0 years. For the construction of Table 38, the series which seemed to provide the minimum feasible fertility level for each

**Table 38**

**Population of Central America in the year 2000, and vital rates for 1995-2000, assuming a net reproduction rate of 1.0 is achieved by either 1990 or 2000**[a]

| | NNR in 1970 | Population in 2000 (millions) | Vital rates in 1995-2000[b] | | |
|---|---|---|---|---|---|
| | | | CBR | CDR | RNI (%) |
| Region | 2.41 | 33.7 | 23.1 | 5.8 | 1.73 |
| Costa Rica | 2.48 | 3.3 | 19.0 | 4.7 | 1.43 |
| El Salvador | 2.56 | 7.4 | 23.9 | 5.3 | 1.86 |
| Guatemala | 2.29 | 10.6 | 23.5 | 6.2 | 1.73 |
| Honduras | 2.43 | 5.5 | 24.8 | 6.4 | 1.84 |
| Nicaragua | 2.36 | 4.3 | 24.3 | 6.4 | 1.79 |
| Panamá | 2.41 | 2.6 | 19.4 | 5.1 | 1.43 |

[a] The projections employed assume that an NRR if 1.0 is reached in 1990-1995 in Costa Rica and Panama, and in 2000-2005 in the other four countries.
[b] CBR crude birth rate, CDR crude death rate, RNI rate of natural increase.
Source: U.S. Bureau of the Census, *The Two Child Family and Population Growth: An International View.* U.S. Government Printing Office, Washington, D.C., 1971.

---

[1] U.S. Bureau of the Census, *The Two-Child Family and Population Growth: An International View.* U.S. Government Printing Office, Washington, D.C., 1971.

country was selected. For Costa Rica and Panama the series in which the NRR equals 1.0 in 1990-95 has been chosen. The population projection series in which the NRR reaches 1.0 in 2000-2005 is used for the other four countries.

These projections combined yield a regional crude birth rate of 23.1 in 1995-2000. This is considered the minimum feasible rate for the region in that period and may be compared with the crude birth rate of 32.1 obtained from the projections in this study (see Table 36). The rate of natural increase, however, would still be a substantial 1.73 per cent per year in 1995-2000. This compares with the 2.58 per cent projected in this study.

Thus, even if fertility declines at this maximum feasible rate between now and the end of the century, and a "two child" family average is reached, the resultant population of 33.7 million would be just 13.6 per cent smaller than the 39.0 million currently projected for the region in the year 2000. But to attain this transition to drastically lower birth rates would require profound changes at the family level in the values and attitudes that contribute to human reproduction. From today's vantage point only modest changes appear on the horizon, and these, in the form of slowly declining birth rates, are incorporated into the population projections.

The vital rates by country and in 5 year intervals underlying this hypothetical rapid decline are found in Table 39, along with the rates of natural increase. Fertility levels by year 2000 would be roughly cut in half relative to 1970, ranging from a birth level reduction of 42 per cent in Guatemala to 47 per cent in Panama. The CDR's show declines based on assumed gradual improvements in life expectancy at birth, and hence in age-specific mortality. The fact that the number of births is diminished in these projections helps to lower the CDR temporarily, but the consequent older populations actually cause the CDR to rise again in Costa Rica and Panama (Table 39). Note that in the base period 1970-75 some variations exist between the crude birth rate statistics provided in the U.S. Census Bureau's publication and similar information provided elsewhere in this report, as well as small variations in the CDR throughout the entire 1970-2000 period, but these differences are relatively minor. Finally, net migration is not considered as a factor in these lower fertility projections.

The rapid fertility decline in Costa Rica discussed earlier is frequently cited as a model for reducing growth levels in developing countries, although a point often overlooked is that its current rate of increase still stands at a high 2.7 per cent. Taking this as a model produces some sobering facts. It is clear that a slight or moderate drop in fertility levels is underway throughout the region, and although this force is not projected to be as strong, countries outside Costa Rica should experience

**Table 39**

**Estimates of vital rates and rates of natural increase in Central America for 1970-2000, assuming a net reproduction rate of 1.0 is achieved by either 1990 or 2000**
(Per cent)

| Country | 1970-75 | | | 1975-80 | | | 1980-85 | | |
|---|---|---|---|---|---|---|---|---|---|
| | CBR | CDR | RNI | CBR | CDR | RNI | CBR | CDR | RNI |
| Costa Rica | 34.7 | 5.8 | 2.89 | 32.1 | 4.6 | 2.75 | 28.9 | 4.2 | 2.47 |
| El Salvador | 41.8 | 10.6 | 3.12 | 38.5 | 9.2 | 2.93 | 35.5 | 7.5 | 2.80 |
| Guatemala | 40.3 | 12.3 | 2.80 | 37.6 | 10.9 | 2.67 | 34.9 | 9.4 | 2.55 |
| Honduras | 45.2 | 14.1 | 3.11 | 41.2 | 12.1 | 2.91 | 37.4 | 10.4 | 2.70 |
| Nicaragua | 42.5 | 13.4 | 2.91 | 40.1 | 11.8 | 2.83 | 37.2 | 10.1 | 2.71 |
| Panamá | 36.5 | 7.1 | 2.94 | 32.1 | 6.4 | 2.57 | 28.0 | 5.4 | 2.26 |

| Country | 1985-90 | | | 1990-95 | | | 1995-2000 | | |
|---|---|---|---|---|---|---|---|---|---|
| | CBR | CDR | RNI | CBR | CDR | RNI | CBR | CDR | RNI |
| Costa Rica | 24.3 | 3.9 | 2.04 | 18.8 | 4.2 | 1.46 | 19.0 | 4.7 | 1.43 |
| El Salvador | 32.2 | 6.6 | 2.56 | 28.3 | 5.9 | 2.24 | 23.9 | 5.3 | 1.86 |
| Guatemala | 31.6 | 7.8 | 2.38 | 27.7 | 6.8 | 2.09 | 23.5 | 6.2 | 1.73 |
| Honduras | 33.5 | 8.5 | 2.50 | 29.3 | 7.3 | 2.20 | 24.8 | 6.4 | 1.84 |
| Nicaragua | 33.3 | 8.3 | 2.50 | 28.9 | 7.2 | 2.17 | 24.3 | 6.4 | 1.79 |
| Panamá | 23.8 | 5.1 | 1.87 | 18.9 | 4.8 | 1.41 | 19.4 | 5.1 | 1.43 |

Source: U.S. Bureau of the Census, *The Two-Child Family*.

crude birth rate reductions on the order of 40 to 80 per cent in 1975-2000 of that achieved by Costa Rica in 1950-75. These reductions are incorporated into the regional population projections of 39 million by year 2000. Looking at the lower end of the projection scale, the fact is that even should much stronger fertility reductions occur than contemplated, even to the point of matching the dramatic and earlier Costa Rican experience, the revised population total for Central America would still be well above the 33 million limit achieved by reaching the NRR level of 1.0 as shown in the earlier examples.

### Zero population growth

Attaining a net reproduction rate of 1.0 does not mean that growth will immediately stop. To reach this level in a country's demographic development is simply a step along the way to zero population growth. The reason for this is the enormous momentum for further increases built into the age structure, particularly in countries containing large proportions of children and adolescents. Simply stated, until the age structure of a population *has time* to shift away from one with a high proportion of young people to a so-called older population such as that found in the United States and in Argentina, there will be more younger couples having births than older people dying, and the population will continue to grow.

In each of the Central America countries, age structures follow a similar pattern whereby the majority of all inhabitants are under 20 years of age. In Costa Rica approximately 42 per cent of the inhabitants are under 15 years of age, in El Salvador 46 per cent, Guatemala 44 per cent, Honduras 47 per cent, Nicaragua 48 per cent, and Panama 43 per cent. By comparison, in 1970 just 25 per cent of the population of the United States was in this age bracket, and in 1975, 28 per cent of the population of Argentina.

If net reproduction rates of 1.0 were reached throughout Central America in the time periods described earlier, *and maintained at that level* to a point of zero population growth, each country's population would further increase from 38 to 62 per cent in subsequent decades. Before leveling off, El Salvador's would total 11.7 million in 2055, for example, and Guatemala's 16.4 million by 2060. If each country achieved a NRR of 1.0 in 1990–95 or 2000–05, then maintained it, its population would continue to increase until 2050 or 2060. The region's numbers would stabilize at 52.1 million, just triple the population in 1970.

Using the U.S. Bureau of the Census' thorough description of shifting age structures to zero population growth levels, falling birth rates in Guatemala are taken as a hypothetical example:

> Perhaps even more striking is the fact that from one-half to three-quarters of the population growth between 1970 and the time a zero growth rate is reached would take place after the two-child average has been achieved.
>
> How can this be? If fertility begins to decline immediately, and particularly when it reaches the point that each couple is having only the two children required to replace themselves, how can it be that the population does not immediately cease to grow?
>
> It is clear that the two parents will probably survive for a considerable period of time after the birth of their second child. Thus, if there is to be a zero rate of population growth (equal numbers of births and deaths in the absence of any net international migration), enough other people must die in order to offset the number of births each year. These deaths will occur primarily at the older ages. However, in countries like Guatemala, where large families have been prevalent for a long time, an extremely large proportion of the population is concentrated at the younger ages, as illustrated by the broad base of the 1970 population pyramid for Guatemala (Figure 11).
>
> At the same time these population pyramids (particularly

**Figure 11**
**Guatemala: Estimated and projected population by age and sex, 1970, 1980, 2000 and 2040, assuming a two child family average (Nrr = 1.0) beginning in 1990.**

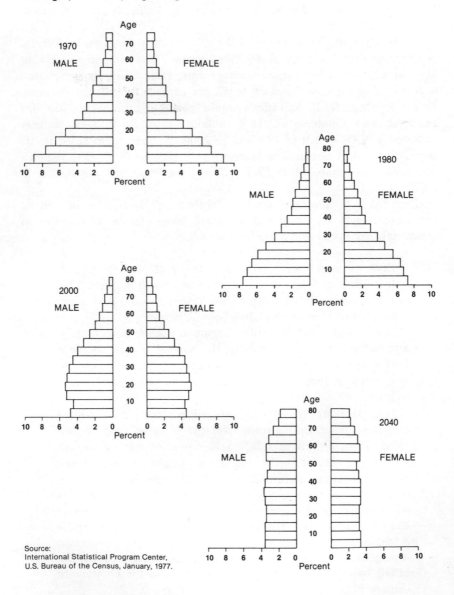

Source:
International Statistical Program Center,
U.S. Bureau of the Census, January, 1977.

those for 1970 and 1980) show relatively few people at the older ages, where most of the deaths occur once improved health conditions have allowed for reductions in mortality among the young. Thus, even after a two-child average family size is reached, there still continue to be more people being born than are dying because of an age structure in which there are a relatively large number of younger people (potential mothers and fathers), and a relatively small number of the aged.

Eventually, as shown in the population pyramid for 2040, the generation will come when the number of parents having their two children will no longer be so large relative to other age groups. Then there will also be larger numbers of older people who are survivors of the period 65 years earlier when two-child families became the average and who are now experiencing higher mortality due to their advanced age. At this point in the population's development, the number of births will finally equal the number of deaths, and the population will stop growing.[1]

The age and sex structure data used in Figure 11 past 1970 are, of course, hypothetical and only serve to illustrate the required relationship between the number of births and the number of deaths to attain zero growth levels.

In actuality the age and sex structures of the six countries projected for the year 2000 follow a far different pattern and point to continued growth. These population pyramids are shown in Figure 12. Age structures will continue to be dominated by large proportions of younger people, although these percentages will be cut back relative to 1970. In a reciprocal manner, those in their productive years will represent a larger share of the total, thus reducing the exceptionally high dependency burdens that now prevail. The shifts in Costa Rica are most pronounced in this regard.

The outstanding feature noted from these population pyramids is that they will still be broadly based, and the continued domination of these youthful age distribution patterns will contribute to further large population increases on an ever-expanding scale. Extrapolating the national rates of increase projected for the 1990–2000 period, for example, would yield a regional population total of around 75 million in the year 2025.

Thus the effects of annual 2 to 3 per cent population growth rates cast long shadows into the future, and the lesson becomes clear that instead

---

[1] Modified from an unpublished ISPC report, issued as a supplement to the report *The Two-Child Family.*

51

**Figure 12
Age-sex population pyramids for
Central America in 1975,
and as projected for 2000.**

Source:
CELADE, *Boletín Demográfico*, Año VII, No. 13, Santiago, Chile,
January, 1974, Table 2.

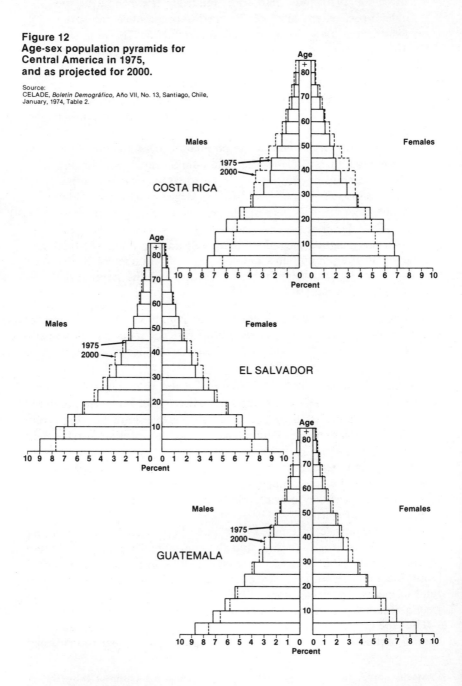

COSTA RICA

EL SALVADOR

GUATEMALA

52

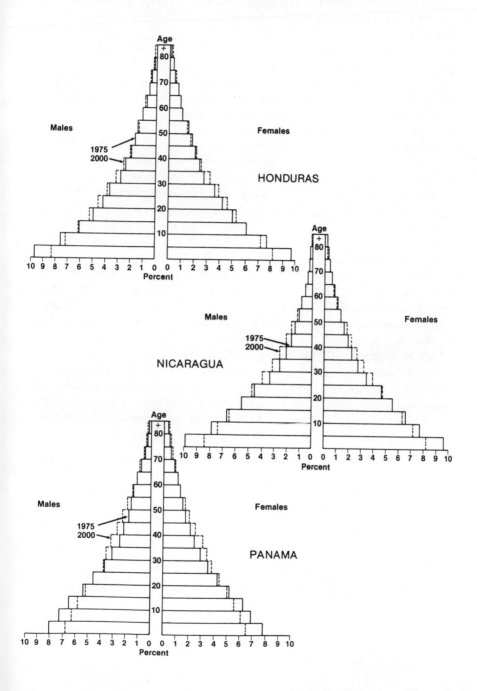

Age
+
80
70
60
Males                    50            Females
1975                                   HONDURAS
2000          40
30
20
10
10 9 8 7 6 5 4 3 2 1 0   0 1 2 3 4 5 6 7 8 9 10
Percent

Age
+
80
70
60
Males            50            Females
1975
2000          40
NICARAGUA              30
20
10
10 9 8 7 6 5 4 3 2 1 0   0 1 2 3 4 5 6 7 8 9 10
Percent

Age
+
80
70
60
Males            50            Females
1975
2000          40
30            PANAMA
20
10
10 9 8 7 6 5 4 3 2 1 0   0 1 2 3 4 5 6 7 8 9 10
Percent

of the short-term life cycle of national administrations, proper attention to population growth is a subject that must be monitored in terms of decades.

In sum, the small likelihood that population growth rates will fall considerably below the projected levels for year 2000 that are shown in this study depends basically on whether the region experiences a very sharp drop in the birth rate, such as one associated with attaining a net reproduction rate of 1.0 in the next two decades. But, under present conditions of values, attitudes, and patterns of behavior, the region's exceptionally high birth rate is expected to drop only moderately, and in the short run in turn the age structure will not shift drastically in its proportional composition, leading once again to continuing population increases. Supporting the expectation of a modest fertility decline is the fact that Central America is still predominantly rural, a condition that is positively associated with high fertility levels and a slow pace of social change.

Barring further national calamities such as the Managua earthquake of 1972 and the earthquake that leveled a part of Guatemala in 1976 taking 24,000 lives, death rates for the region can otherwise be reasonably projected and the range of flexibility within which they operate rather accurately estimated. This population growth variable is less elusive to follow than the future path of fertility trends. Finally, the effect of migration on future regional growth trends has not been examined since there are simply no reasonable statistics to gauge its importance—particularly illegal migration—to destinations outside the area, but on the other hand it would appear that most migration occurs among the Central American countries, and consequently, would have no bearing at the regional level.

# II. Country Summaries on Demographic Trends and Urbanization

## Regional Considerations

This section contains individual country reports for each of the Central American republics. These examine the patterns of population growth since 1950 and the behavior of the three contributing factors to population increases—the level of births and deaths, and net migration. They also include a brief review of changing occupational structures. Data on city population totals are also presented, together with projections for the cities and provinces to year 2000. The reports conclude with a statistical table showing the age and sex composition of the population in the period 1975-2000. Incorporated into each study are method notes describing how technical difficulties were resolved in the course of the research.

In an earlier study special attention was paid to identifying and accounting for the suburbs of large metropolitan areas which have emerged in the past 20 years in practically every major Latin American country.[1] This has been repeated for the Central American countries, but as the populations are considerably smaller, the task is far simpler. Excepting Costa Rica, the suburbs of urbanized areas are identified in a footnote to the principal population projection table. The suburbs of San Jose, Costa Rica are identified in a separate listing on page 82.

Statistical aspects of the study are given a prominent place throughout the report and numerous discussions are included on related topics such as data comparability, variations in statistics according to different sources, and levels of census underenumeration. A complete listing of source materials is included to facilitate the identification of studies

---

[1]Robert W. Fox, *Urban Population Growth Trends in Latin America.* Inter-American Development Bank, Washington, D.C., 1975.

that otherwise are quite isolated, exist only in unpublished form, or in one or two known copies.

It was at first thought that the amount of reliable demographic data available in Central America would be woefully inadequate to meet this study's requirements, but it soon became evident that due to the increasing importance of this topic, several reliable benchmark studies at the national level had already been completed and were available. The considerable amount of information available from the Central American regional office of the Latin American Demographic Center (CELADE), located in San Jose, Costa Rica and the International Statistical Programs Center (ISPC), of the U.S. Bureau of the Census was particularly useful.

Latin America has evolved dramatically in the last three decades from a region where systematic population data were gathered sporadically or not at all, to one where basic information is readily available on total numbers, spatial distribution, and characteristics of the population. Very few serious problems remain related to processing and publishing decennial census returns[1]. Perhaps the most significant matter outstanding that requires attention, aside from improving the quality of responses, is the need to conduct sample surveys immediately following each enumeration to determine the level of census undercount. The purpose of these surveys would be to pinpoint the percentage of the population missed by the census within a narrow range. These surveys would be extremely useful for later scientific investigations aimed at determining the rate of population increase in a particular interval. In the absence of postcensus surveys, an apparent sharp increase or decline in the growth rate may in fact reflect little more than different levels of census completeness. This is a central concern in this report and is addressed in detail in the separate country chapters. To round out the subject, attention is also given to the degree of completeness of vital registries—the other important data source—which contain information on births and deaths.

Population censuses have been conducted regularly in Central America since 1950, while in several of the countries—Honduras and Panama in particular—the tradition extends much longer. In 1950 the "Census of the Americas" was undertaken, a successful hemispheric-wide effort designed to normalize decennial population counts and develop and apply common standards. Each of the six countries participated and since 1950 have followed the original proposal. In subsequent decades several countries have delayed enumerations one or more years past the

---

[1]Major advances in processing census data in the 1970's are discussed in the IDB's annual report for 1975, *Economic and Social Progress in Latin America.* See Chapter V, "Evaluating Social Change in Latin America: The Statistical Foundations."

1960 and 1970 target dates. The actual census years are listed in Table 40.

Finding data at irregular intervals presents the dilemma of having to elect to use it according to each country's census years, or alternatively, to derive a common set of statistics by interpolating the information back to mid-year 1960 and 1970. The data for 1950 did not require adjusting since all countries took their census that same year. The projections to the year 2000 are, of course, to mid-year 1980, 1990, and 2000. For the intervening years the choice was made to follow the actual census year in the presentation of data and the regional analysis. While *rates* of population increase are unaffected, this choice does throw some comparisons out of balance such as the increased level of urbanization attained by Honduras in a 13-year intercensal period (1961–74) as opposed to that same level in Guatemala which conducted two enumerations in a nine year period (1964 and 1973). For the convenience of other investigators, however, and to assist in some comparisons in the report, population statistics for the nation, provinces, cities, and rural areas (labeled "remainder") were also interpolated and are found in Appendix 3 on pages 207–11. It was not necessary to interpolate the data for Panama, since it maintained an enumeration in regular 10-year cycles.

**Table 40**

**Population census enumerations, 1950 to the present**

|  | Census Dates | | |
|---|---|---|---|
| Country | 1950 | 1960 | 1970 |
| Costa Rica | May, 1950 | April, 1963 | May, 1973 |
| El Salvador | June, 1950 | May, 1961 | June, 1971 |
| Guatemala | April, 1950 | April, 1964 | March, 1973 |
| Honduras | June, 1950 | April, 1961 | March, 1974 |
| Nicaragua | May, 1950 | May, 1963 | April, 1971 |
| Panama | Dec., 1950 | Dec., 1960 | May, 1970 |

# COSTA RICA

Costa Rica provides a dramatic case with which to begin this series of country studies. Like all other countries of Central America it is going through an extended period of enormous population growth, but at the same time that rate has fallen sharply in recent years due to the most rapid long-run decline in fertility ever recorded for a Latin American country.

Recently available data indicate that the decline is continuing. In 1960, the crude birth rate (CBR) was 47.5 per thousand population. By 1971, the CBR had fallen to 31.5 per 1,000—a decline of 16 points in just 11 years. Another rapid decrease in fertility in Latin America, by comparison, has also occurred in Trinidad and Tobago where the CBR dropped 16.5 points in 16 years, from 41.9 in 1955 to 25.4 in 1971. Other substantial decreases in fertility on a world-wide basis which match or exceed the speed of decline in Costa Rica have taken place in Taiwan and Singapore. The CBR in Taiwan fell by 16.8 points during the 12-year period from 1955 to 1967, and that in Singapore dropped by 19.9 points in the 14 years between 1957 and 1971.

Taking both the birth and death rates into account, the rate of natural increase in Costa Rica declined from 3.9 per cent in 1960—exceptionally high by any standard—to a level of 2.5 per cent in 1971. But even with this drop, given the still moderately high present rate of natural increase combined with the momentum for future growth built into the age structure of the population, total numbers are projected to double in the span of 27 years from 1,872,000 in 1973 to 3,695,000 inhabitants by the year 2000.

## Growth Rate

The total population of Costa Rica as enumerated by the latest five censuses and the implied growth rates are shown in Table 41. The growth rates based on census totals differ from those estimated by Jimenez (Table 42) due to differing degrees of completeness of enumeration from census to census.[1]

Jimenez estimates that the population in 1927 was 487,410, or 3.4 per cent larger than enumerated. The 1950 population is estimated to be 856,220, or 6.9 per cent greater than the census total. These adjusted totals imply an average annual growth rate of 2.45 per cent between the 1927 and 1950 censuses. The 1963 population total is adjusted by 3.2 per cent to 1,378,705, which produces a 1950-63 annual rate of growth of 3.7 per cent. Net international migration for these intercensal periods was negligible.

The 1973 population census has not yet been evaluated for completeness of coverage. The 1963-1973 rate of growth implied by the unadjusted census totals is 3.3 per cent a year, whereas the average annual rate estimated by Gomez and Bermudez[2] from vital statistics (Table 42) is 3.0 per cent. The actual rate of increase probably lies between these two figures, but its estimation awaits a thorough evaluation of the 1973 census and new estimates of vital rates which take into account the revised total population time series.

The population of Costa Rica has grown at a rapid rate throughout this century—a rate near or above 2.0 per cent a year. A consistently

Table 41

**Enumerated population and intercensal growth rates of Costa Rica, 1892 to 1973**

| Date of census | Enumerated population | Average annual rate of increase (%) during intercensal period |
|---|---|---|
| February 18, 1892 | 243,205 | — |
| May 11, 1927 | 471,524 | 1.88 |
| May 22, 1950 | 800,875 | 2.30 |
| April 1, 1963 | 1,336,274 | 3.98 |
| May 14, 1973 | 1,871,780 | 3.33 |

Sources: 1892 to 1950: Robert E. Nunley, *The Distribution of Population in Costa Rica*. National Academy of Sciences—National Research Council, Publication 743, Washington, D.C., 1960.

1963: Costa Rica, Dirección General de Estadística y Censos, *Censo de Población 1963*, San José.

1973: Costa Rica, Dirección General de Estadística y Censos, *Censos Nacionales de 1973. Población*. Volume 1, San José, December 1974.

---

[1] Ricardo Jimenez, "Proyección de la Población de Costa Rica por Sexo y Grupos de Edad, 1965-1990," in Costa Rica, Dirección General de Estadística y Censos, *Revista de Estudios y Estadísticas*, No. 8, Serie Demográfica No. 5, San José, October 1967, p. 37.

[2] Miguel Gomez B. and Vera V. Bermudez M., "Costa Rica," Country Profiles, The Population Council, New York, April 1974.

**Table 42**

**Vital rates in Costa Rica, 1927 to 1972**

| Years | Crude birth rate | Crude death rate | Rate of natural increase (%) | Total fertility rate[a] |
|---|---|---|---|---|
| 1927–29 | 46.4 | 24.8 | 2.16 | — |
| 1930–34 | 44.4 | 23.1 | 2.13 | — |
| 1935–39 | 43.5 | 20.9 | 2.26 | — |
| 1940–44 | 43.3 | 19.0 | 2.43 | — |
| 1945–49 | 43.9 | 14.5 | 2.94 | — |
| 1950–54 | 47.1 | 11.8 | 3.53 | 6.72 |
| 1955 | 48.9 | 10.7 | 3.82 | |
| 1956 | 48.5 | 9.8 | 3.87 | |
| 1957 | 47.9 | 10.4 | 3.75 | 7.11 |
| 1958 | 47.2 | 9.2 | 3.80 | |
| 1959 | 48.3 | 9.3 | 3.90 | |
| 1960 | 47.5 | 8.9 | 3.86 | 7.26 |
| 1961 | 46.9 | 8.2 | 3.87 | 7.18 |
| 1962 | 45.4 | 8.9 | 3.65 | 6.97 |
| 1963 | 45.3 | 9.0 | 3.63 | 7.01 |
| 1964 | 43.0 | 9.4 | 3.36 | 6.64 |
| 1965 | 42.3 | 8.6 | 3.37 | 6.46 |
| 1966 | 40.5 | 8.1 | 3.24 | 6.19 |
| 1967 | 38.5 | 7.8 | 3.07 | 5.82 |
| 1968 | 35.9 | 7.1 | 2.88 | 5.35 |
| 1969 | 34.4 | 7.2 | 2.72 | 5.04 |
| 1970 | 33.3 | 7.2 | 2.61 | 4.94 |
| 1971 | 31.5 | 6.5 | 2.50 | 4.65 |
| 1972 | 31.5 | 6.6 | 2.49 | 4.37 |

[a] Assuming a sex ratio at birth of 1.05 males per female.

Sources: 1927-1965 (except total fertility rate): Ricardo Jiménez Jiménez, "Proyección de la Población de Costa Rica por Sexo y Grupos de Edad, 1965-1990," in Costa Rica, Dirección General de Estadística y Censos, *Revista de Estudios y Estadísticas*, No. 8, Serie Demográfica No. 5, San José, October 1967, p. 35.

1966-1972 and total fertility rates: Miguel Gómez B. and Vera V. Bermúdez M., "Costa Rica," Country Profiles, The Population Council, New York, April 1974.

high birth rate and a declining death rate caused the rate of increase to grow steadily to a peak of 3.9 per cent per annum in the late 1950's. Since then, the rapid decline in fertility and the very gradual decrease in the death rate have combined to lower the growth rate, which equaled 2.5 per cent in 1971 and 1972. Costa Rica's population has more than doubled since 1950 and is still growing at a rapid rate. The current growth rate of 2.5 per cent implies a doubling of the population in a little less than 28 years. Of course, current trends suggest that the growth rate may continue to decline and that the doubling time may be substantially more than 28 years.

## Birth Rate

The crude birth rates for Costa Rica from 1927 to 1972 are given in Table 42. The rates are calculated using census data corrected for underenumeration and vital statistics corrected for underregistration and delayed registration. Jimenez adjusts the recorded number of births for two per cent underregistration. Gomez and Bermudez make an adjustment for underregistration of an unspecified amount.

During the 1950's the crude birth rate increased quickly from a previous level of 43 to 44 per thousand to a level of 48 or 49. Huyck[1] attributes the observed rise in fertility to increased survivorship and to a decrease in age of marriage. An increase in the survival rates of infants meant that more of their births were registered. The improved registration would raise the observed birth rate separate from an actual increase in fertility. Improved health standards and survivorship among females 15–49 also contributed to a higher birth rate. Huyck explains the greater increase in fertility among all women than in fertility of married women due to a lower age at marriage and a higher proportion of women marrying. The high level was maintained for about eight years, then declined quickly. The decline in the CBR after 1960 did not result from inaccuracies in the vital statistics, a changing age structure, or variations in marriage patterns, but reflects an actual decline in the fertility of Costa Rican women.

The total fertility rate (TFR) is the number of children that a woman would bear in her lifetime if she experienced at each age the average fertility of all women at each age measured for a given year; thus this measure is not affected by the age distribution of females or of the total population. The total fertility rate has decreased from a peak of 7.26 in 1960 to 4.37 in 1972. This is a decline of nearly three children per woman. Although the CBR registered no decline from 1971 to 1972, the TFR decreased significantly, as it has in each year since 1964. The total fertility rate must still be said to be quite high, since its 1972 level implies that women are continuing on average to bear over four children apiece.

The age-specific fertility rate (ASFR) is the average number of children born to the women of a given age during a one-year period. The ASFR's of Costa Rica by five-year age groups are graphed in Figure 13 for 1960, 1965, and 1972. The decline in fertility since 1960 affected women 20–24 first of all, then made an impact at successively older age groups. The percentage decline between 1960 and 1972 has been quite

---

[1] Earl E. Huyck, "Fecundidad y Planificación Familiar: El Caso de Costa Rica, *Quinto Seminario Nacional de Demografía, Informe, San José:* Asociación Demográfica Costarricense; Dirección General de Estadística y Censos; School of Economic and Social Sciences, University of Costa Rica, September 24–25, 1970.

similar for all age groups 20-24 and above—near 40 per cent for each group. Fertility of the 15-19 age group decreased by only 16 percent between 1960 and 1972.

The government of Costa Rica sponsors an active family planning program through the Population Office of the Ministry of Health. Ninety-five government facilities offer family planning services, and two private clinics provide pilot programs. However, the extensive family planning services cannot be credited with much of the decline in fertility since 1960 because they were not implemented until the mid-1960's.

The government program was not put into operation until 1968. Ravenholt and Chao have pointed out that, "In most cases, at least five years must elapse between the initiation of the national family planning program and clear evidence of its impact on fertility."[1]

Several economic and social indicators which may have a bearing on the fertility level are presented in Table 43 for Central America and Panama. The figures are not strictly comparable due to variations in their quality and definition among the countries. If a more standardized definition of urban place is used such as a city of 10,000 and more inhabitants, for example, Honduras is clearly the least urbanized of the six countries. However, on several of the measures Costa Rica and Panama occupy the first two ranks. Costa Rica's crude birth rate is the lowest in the region. It also has the highest expectation of life at birth and the second highest per capita gross domestic product and primary school enrollment ratio. On the other hand, Costa Rica is merely average in terms of the percentage of its labor force in manufacturing or the percentage of its population living in urban areas. Costa Rica appears to have by far the most dynamic agricultural sector in the region, as measured by the increase in per capita food production from the early 1960's to 1970.

Urbanization and industrialization have no doubt been factors in the decline of fertility. Gomez and Bermudez[2] report that the decrease in fertility "started in the urban areas of the Central Valley and gradually extended to other urban areas and then to rural zones." However, it is suggested by Table 43 that the provision of educational and health services and agricultural development may be the key variables in explaining the lower level of fertility in Costa Rica relative to the other Central American nations.

In the survey of fertility and family planning conducted by CELADE and the University of Chicago in San Jose in 1964, education was also

---

[1] R. T. Ravenholt and J. Chao, "Availability of Family Planning Services, the Key to Rapid Fertility Reduction," *Family Planning Perspectives,* 6:4, Planned Parenthood Federation of America, New York, Fall 1974.
[2] Gomez and Bermudez; "Costa Rica," *Country Profiles.*

**Figure 13.**
**Age-specific fertility rates, Costa Rica; 1960, 1965, and 1972.**

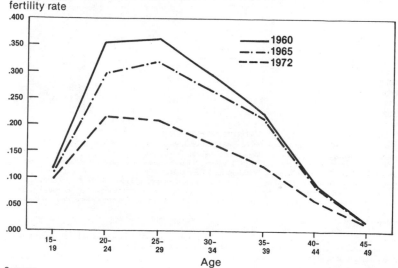

Age-specific
fertility rate

Age

Sources:
1960 and 1965: Miguel Gómez B. and Jack Reynolds, "Numerator Analysis of Fertility Change in Costa Rica: A Methodological Examination." *Studies in Family Planning,* 4:12, The Population Council (December 1973) 317–326.
1972: Miguel Gómez B. and Vera V. Bermúdez M., "Costa Rica," *Country Profiles,* The Population Council (April 1974).

shown to have a strong negative influence on fertility.[1] Greater education for both husband and wife was associated with lower fertility. Women who were employed had significantly lower fertility than those who were not, and higher level occupation of both wife and husband corresponded to lower fertility. The urban or rural origin of the couple was not strongly associated with the fertility of the couple, perhaps because current residence (San Jose) had greater influence on fertility than past residence. This study tends to confirm the conclusion drawn in the preceding paragraph that the provision of social services, particularly education, has been of major importance in the decline of fertility in Costa Rica.

**Death Rate**

Jimenez estimates the crude death rate shown in Table 42 up to 1965 by adjusting the reported number of deaths upward by ten per cent for underregistration. The death rate after 1965 estimated by Gomez and

---

[1]Centro Latinoamericano de Demografia (CELADE) and University of Chicago Community and Family Study Center, *Fertility and Family Planning in Metropolitan Latin American,* University of Chicago, 1972.

## Table 43

### Economic and social measures, Central America

| Country | Crude birth rate[a] | Per capita GDP[b] | % of labor force in mfg | Index of p.c. food produc- tion[c] | Percent urban[d] | % 5–14 in primary school[k] | Life ex- pectancy at birth[l] |
|---|---|---|---|---|---|---|---|
| Costa Rica | 32 | $572 | 11.4 | 138 | 40.6[e] | 68.7 | 69 |
| El Salvador | 42 | 306 | 14.0 | 108 | 39.5[f] | 56.9 | 59 |
| Guatemala | 42 | 415 | 11.4 | 112 | 33.6[g] | 38.3 | 54 |
| Honduras | 49 | 289 | 7.9 | 107 | 38.5[h] | 53.1 | 51 |
| Nicaragua | 47 | 488 | 11.9 | 112 | 48.0[i] | 50.8 | 52 |
| Panama | 36 | 802 | 8.9 | 106 | 47.6[j] | 71.9 | 67 |

[a] Refers to 1972, U.S. Bureau of the Census, International Statistical Programs Center, *World Population: 1973, Recent Demographic Estimates for the Countries and Regions of the World*, Washington, D.C.: 1973.
[b] Per capita gross domestic product for 1972, in 1970 dollars. Inter-American Development Bank, *Statistical Data on the Latin American and Caribbean Countries*, Washington, D.C.: no date.
[c] Refers to 1970 with 1961-65 = 100. Includes all products which contribute energy to the diet, regardless of the extent to which they were used as food. Coffee is not included. U.S. Agency for International Development, Bureau for Latin America, *Summary Economic and Social Indicators, 18 Latin American Countries*: 1960-1971, Washington, D.C.: June 1972.
[d] Percentage of the total population living in urban areas as nationally defined and as reported in census volumes.
[e] 1973. [f] 1971. [g] 1964. [h] 1961. [i] 1971. [j] 1970.
[k] Percentage of the population ages 5-14 enrolled in primary school in 1972. Inter-American Development Bank, *Economic and Social Progress in Latin America, Annual Report 1973*, Washington, D.C., p. 373.
[l] Refers to 1972. U.S. Bureau of the Census, see note a.

## Table 44

### Percentage of population in broad age groups, and dependency ratios for Costa Rica, 1963 and 1973

| Age | 1963 | 1973 Total | 1973 Urban | 1973 Rural |
|---|---|---|---|---|
| All ages | 100.0% | 100.0% | 100.0% | 100.0% |
| 0–14 | 47.7 | 44.0 | 38.1 | 48.1 |
| 15–64 | 49.1 | 52.4 | 57.7 | 48.8 |
| 56+ | 3.2 | 3.5 | 4.3 | 3.0 |
| Dependency ratio[a] | 103.7 | 90.6 | 73.5 | 104.7 |

[a] The dependency ratio is $\left(P(0\text{-}14) + P(65+)\right)/\left(P(15\text{-}64)\right)$ X 100, where P(a) is the population age "a".

Sources: 1963: Ricardo Jiménez Jiménez, "Proyección de la Población de Costa Rica por Sexo y Grupos de Edad, 1965-1900," in Costa Rica, Dirección General de Estadística y Censos, *Revista de Estudios y Estadísticas*, No. 8, Serie Demográfica No. 5, San José, October 1967, p. 46.

1973: Costa Rica, Dirección General de Estadística y Censos, *Censos Nacionales de 1973, Población*, Volume 1, San José, December 1974.

Bermudez takes into account an unspecified degree of underregistration. From 1927 to 1942 the crude death rate in Costa Rica declined very gradually while displaying relatively large annual fluctuations. Between 1943 and the mid-1950's the death rate dropped substantially, to the level of about ten per thousand. The sharp increase in fertility beginning in 1950, together with the lower death rate, yielded the exceptionally high rate of natural increase observed during the 1950's. The death rate has descended slowly since 1955 and currently must be quite near its

**Table 45**

Percentage of population in broad age groups, and dependency ratios for Costa Rica, 1980-2000 as projected by CELADE

| Age group | 1980 | Projected population 1990 | 2000 |
|---|---|---|---|
| Total population | 2,285,721 | 2,954,369 | 3,695,303 |
| 0-14 | 896,305 | 1,089,789 | 1,257,894 |
| 15-64 | 1,308,638 | 1,749,286 | 2,273,464 |
| 65+ | 80,778 | 115,294 | 163,949 |
| Dependency Ratio | 75 | 69 | 63 |

Source: Centro Latinoamericano de Demografía (CELADE) *Boletín Demográfico* 7:13 (January 1974).

anticipated minimum. The somewhat older population resulting from declining fertility can be expected to produce a leveling off of the crude death rate even as general mortality levels continue to improve.

### Age Distribution

The high level of fertility and the declining mortality rates of the 1950's and early 1960's yielded a young age structure, with nearly 48 percent of the population below age 15 (Table 44). During a period of declining mortality, increases in survivorship are proportionately greater for infants and children than for adults. Hence, decreasing mortality has the paradoxical effect of making the population somewhat younger. For every 100 persons ages 15-64 in 1963, there were 104 who were either younger or older than this conventional definition of working age. Decreasing fertility after 1960 reduced the percentage of the population below age 15 in 1973 to 44. The dependency ratio had declined to 91 by 1973.

The projected continued decline in population growth rates has enormous significance for shifts in the age structure of Costa Rica. A basic consequence will be a downward trend in the dependency ratio. From a high dependency ratio of 104 reported in 1963, a decline to 91 is found for 1973, and the decline continues according to CELADE projections (Tables 45) to 75 in 1980, 69 in 1990, and 63 in 2000. This information is given in more detail in Appendix B of this chapter.

### Urban-Rural Fertility Differentials

The Costa Rican General Bureau of Statistics and Censuses does not publish annual birth rates by urban or rural residence of the mother, but other tabulations give an impression of the fertility differentials between these areas. Jimenez has calculated the 1965 total fertility rate of cantons grouped by the proportion of their population residing in urban areas (Table 46). The TFR is lower at each successive greater degree of urbanization. Fertility in the most urban cantons is only 56 percent as great as that in the least urban cantons.

The average number of children ever born alive per woman, by age and residence of mother, may be calculated from the 1973 census report (Table 47). By this measure, rural fertility in Costa Rica is approximately 60 percent higher than urban fertility. Since the table refers to residence in 1973, some amount of the reported fertility occurred in areas different from the current classification, but this fact does not significantly alter the impression of lower urban fertility. The observation that the relative fertility differential between urban and rural places is greater at the younger ages does not necessarily indicate that the differential is increasing with time. The great differentials at younger ages could occur if urban women marry later, but then bear children at a rate to compensate for the delayed fertility.

Child/woman ratios are an imperfect measure of fertility because they are affected by completeness of census enumeration and by the survival rates for infants and children. The child-woman ratios in Table 48 appear to demonstrate that the urban-rural fertility differential has increased gradually since 1950, but most of the change could be accounted for by a more rapid improvement in census coverage and survival rates in rural areas than in urban areas.

A much smaller percentage of the urban than of the rural population is under age 15 (Table 44). The combination of lower urban fertility and the concentration of rural-urban migrants between the ages of 15 and 30 produces an urban population which is older than the rural counterpart. Consequently, the urban dependency ratio (73.5) is considerably lower than the rural (105).

The much greater propensity for females than for males to migrate to urban areas is demonstrated in Figures 14 and 15. Figure 14 shows the urban residence ratios (URR) by sex and 5-year age group, based on the 1973 census of Costa Rica. The URR is the percentage of each sex-age group which lives in an urban area. Males and females below age 10 are about equally urbanized in 1973, but females ages 10 to 25 are increasingly more urban than their male cohorts. Above age 20 the percentage of males living in urban areas is similar for all ages, about 41 or 42 per cent. For females, the URR declines slightly from the 20-24 age group to the 30-34 age group, but then increases steadily for older ages. The fact that Costa Rica's sex ratios above age 20 remain near to 100 is most likely explained by an excess of females over males among emigrants (Figure 15).

**Urban Population Growth**

Costa Rica has eight cities with more than 10,000 inhabitants. San Jose, the capital, is the primate city in the network. It is 11.6 times larger

**Table 46**

**Total fertility rate by degree of urbanization for cantons of Costa Rica, 1965**

| Percent urban[a] | Number of cantons | Total fertility rate |
|---|---|---|
| Costa Rica | 68 | 6.46 |
| 0-9 | 20 | 8.04 |
| 10-19 | 23 | 7.76 |
| 20-29 | 11 | 6.94 |
| 30-49 | 8 | 6.62 |
| 50-74 | 4 | 4.88 |
| 75-100 | 2 | 4.50 |

[a] In the 1963 census.

Source: Ricardo Jiménez Jiménez, "Proyección de la Población de Costa Rica por Sexo y Grupos de Edad, 1965-1990," in Costa Rica, Dirección General de Estadística y Censos, *Revista de Estudios y Estadísticas*, No. 8, Serie Demográfica No. 5, San José, October 1967, p. 67.

**Table 47**

**Average number of children born alive per woman, by age and residence of mother, Costa Rica, 1973**

| Age of mother | Residence in 1973 | | | |
|---|---|---|---|---|
| | Costa Rica | Urban | Rural | Rural ÷ Urban |
| 15-49 | 2.80 | 2.11 | 3.43 | 1.63 |
| 15-19 | 0.16 | 0.10 | 0.21 | 2.10 |
| 20-24 | 1.10 | 0.76 | 1.42 | 1.87 |
| 25-29 | 2.53 | 1.86 | 3.13 | 1.68 |
| 30-34 | 4.12 | 3.12 | 4.98 | 1.60 |
| 35-39 | 5.50 | 4.20 | 6.63 | 1.58 |
| 40-44 | 6.39 | 4.91 | 7.73 | 1.57 |
| 45-49 | 6.66 | 5.12 | 8.14 | 1.59 |

Source: Calculated from Costa Rica, Dirección General de Estadística y Censos, *Censos Nacionales de 1973. Población*, Volume 1, San José, December 1974, Table 25.

**Table 48**

**Number of children aged 0-4 per 1,000 women ages 15-44 by urban and rural areas, Costa Rica; 1950, 1963 and 1973**

| Year | Total | Urban | Rural | Rural ÷ Urban |
|---|---|---|---|---|
| 1950 | 739 | 543 | 866 | 1.59 |
| 1963 | 950 | 681 | 1,134 | 1.67 |
| 1973 | 654 | 461 | 826 | 1.79 |

Sources: 1950 and 1963: Earl E. Huyck, "Fecundidad y Planificación Familiar: El Caso de Costa Rica," *Quinto Seminario Nacional de Demografía. Informe*, San José: Asociación Demográfica Costarricense; Dirección General de Estadística y Censos; Escuela de Ciencias Económicas y Sociales, Universidad de Costa Rica, September 24-25, 1970, p. 485.

1973: Costa Rica, Dirección General de Estadística y Censos, *Censos Nacionales de 1973. Población*, Volume 1, San José, December 1974.

**Figure 14**
**Urban Residence Ratios by Age and Sex, Costa Rica, 1973.**

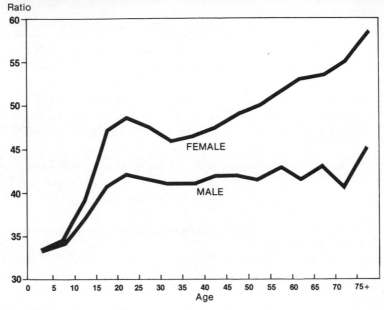

**Figure 15**
**Sex Ratios by Age Group for the Total, Urban, and Rural**
**Populations of Costa Rica, 1973.**

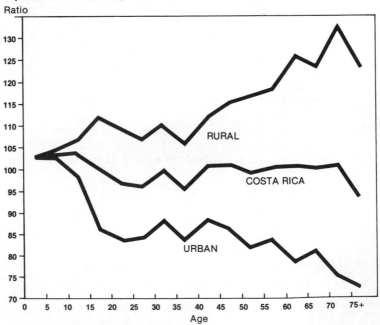

68

than Cartago, and 4.1 times the size of Cartago, Alajuela, and Puerto Limon combined. The population of the seven cities other than San Jose tabulated here includes the urban population of the respective central cantons as presented in census reports.[1] The population of the urbanized area of San Jose includes the urban population (by census definition) of the nine cantons listed in Table 49. For this analysis the same cantons have been considered as comprising the urbanized area for each of the three most recent censuses. However, because the urban area within the cantons has expanded from census to census, the urbanized area have grown partially as a result of the redefinition of their boundaries.

The total population of the eight urbanized areas in 1973 was 574,949, or 30.7 per cent of the national population. After San Jose, containing 401,000 inhabitants in its urbanized area, there is a second tier of five cities of remarkably similar size. These cities all contained between 11,000 and 13,000 inhabitants in 1950, between 18,000 and 20,000 in 1963, and between 26,000 and 35,000 in 1973 (Table 60). The urbanized areas of San Jose, Alajuela, Cartago, Liberia and Puerto Limon grew at rates in excess of four per cent a year between 1963 and 1973 (Table 61). Heredia and Puntarenas increased at rates below that of the national population, although in the latter case the growth rate of the actual urbanized area is quite a bit higher when the population in the suburbs and industrialized area of the adjacent district of Barranca is considered. The city proper of Puntarenas, located on a very narrow peninsula, has simply outgrown the available land area within its boundaries.

The seven largest cities lie on an east-west axis from Puntarenas through the Central Valley, to Puerto Limon. Four of these cities are located within a 40-mile radius of the Central Valley: San Jose, Alajuela, Cartago and Heredia. The latter three cities with their surrounding

## Table 49

Component cantons of the San José urbanized area and urban population in 1973

| Canton | Urban population | Canton | Urban population |
|---|---|---|---|
| **San José** | | | |
| **Urbanized Area** | **401,038** | Alajuelita | 6,673 |
| Central | 215,441 | Tibás | 35,602 |
| Escazú | 13,903 | Moravia | 14,381 |
| Desamparados | 35,469 | Montes de Oca | 27,536 |
| Goicoechea | 43,418 | Curridabat | 8,615 |

Source: Costa Rica, Dirección General de Estadística y Censos, *Censos Nacionales de 1973. Población.* Volume 1, San José, December 1974, Table 1.

[1] Costa Rica, Dirección General de Estadística y Censos, *Censos Nacionales de 1973, Población,* Vol. 1, San José, December 1974, pp. XL and XLVII-LII.

rural populations are all contained within the metropolitan region of San Jose.

An alternative definition of "urban area" is the one employed by the *Dirección de Estadística y Censos* of Costa Rica. In general, the administrative centers of cantons are considered urban. However, urban areas are delimited by physical criteria such as squares, streets, sidewalks, electric lights and other urban services, so that some cantons have no urban area, while in others more than one district may contain areas classified as urban. In all, outside the San Jose metropolitan area and the seven remaining cities, there exist 18 towns with 5-10,000 inhabitants and 36 urban places with populations of fewer than 5,000 persons. Thus, under the census definition, some 760,079 persons, or 40.6 per cent of the population, resided in urban places in 1973. By one criterion—the occupational structure of the population—all areas classified as urban by the *Dirección* regardless of size, appear to warrant the urban label. This point will be examined later on.

At first glance, the process of very rapid urbanization which is so apparent in most of Latin America does not seem to be taking place in Costa Rica. Between 1963 and 1973, the five cities of over 20,000 inhabitants increased their share of the national total only slightly—from 26.4 to 29.5 per cent, and they are projected to reach 30.1 per cent for 1980. A similar pattern emerges when the three towns holding between 10-20,000 inhabitants are included. A gain is seen from 27.5 to 30.7 per cent for 1963-73 and the percentage for 1980 is 31.3. Measured either way, the increase is less than 4 percentage points in the the 17-year span.

A far different pattern emerges for the six other countries of Latin America which have been studied earlier (Table 50). In each of these, the change-over from a rural to an urban-based society has been much more rapid.

Does this apparently slow shift for Costa Rica compared to the other countries mean that it is unique in the region? Not necessarily, when a more extensive urban population is considered.

It is evident that Costa Rica, with a population of fewer than 2 million and a significant rural component, cannot have too many large cities. This is simply a matter of scale. But, as discussed, there are numerous towns classified as urban with fewer than 10,000 inhabitants. These will be taken into account below, and justifiably so as evidenced by occupational structures, disregarding for the moment the population size criterion (20,000) applied to the other countries.

In Costa Rica the occupational structure in small towns is very "urban" oriented; that is, small towns do not serve as large agricultural villages as do many towns in Mexico and elsewhere where much of the labor force travels some distance daily to work in the fields. In Nicaragua, for example, bordering Costa Rica, large proportions of the small-town

70

Table 50

Six countries, urban increases, 1960-80[a]

| Country | Per cent urban | | Urban percentage gain |
| | 1960 | 1980 | in the interval |
|---|---|---|---|
| Argentina | 60 | 71 | 11 |
| Brazil | 31 | 47 | 16 |
| Chile | 50 | 65 | 15 |
| Mexico | 52 | 62 | 10 |
| Peru | 31 | 48 | 17 |
| Venezuela | 53 | 69 | 16 |

[a] "Urban" considered cities of 20,000 and more inhabitants.

Source: Robert W. Fox, *Urban Population Growth Trends in Latin America*: Inter-American Development Bank, Washington, D.C., 1975, Table 3.

Table 51

Costa Rican urban sector: Distribution by occupational category of the economically active population, 1973

| | San Jose province urban population | | 7 Remaining cities with 10,000 & more inhabitants | | Remaining urban population | |
|---|---|---|---|---|---|---|
| Professionals, technicians | 22,199 | 15.8 | 8,118 | 15.4 | 6,168 | 14.0 |
| Managers, administrators | 5,532 | 3.9 | 1,354 | 2.6 | 992 | 2.3 |
| White collar workers | 18,667 | 13.3 | 4,984 | 9.5 | 3,334 | 7.6 |
| Salesmen | 18,286 | 13.0 | 6,270 | 11.9 | 5,422 | 12.3 |
| Farmers, cattlemen | 3,069 | 2.2 | 2,822 | 5.4 | 6,000 | 13.7 |
| Transportation workers | 5,241 | 3.7 | 2,621 | 5.0 | 2,485 | 5.7 |
| Industrial workers | 24,506 | 17.4 | 8,943 | 17.0 | 7,154 | 16.3 |
| Other craftsmen and workers | 6,966 | 4.9 | 2,818 | 5.4 | 2,114 | 4.8 |
| Unskilled workers | 7,304 | 5.2 | 5,084 | 9.7 | 2,854 | 6.5 |
| Service workers | 27,625 | 19.6 | 9,181 | 17.5 | 1,078 | 16.1 |
| Non-specified activities | 1,286 | 0.9 | 405 | 0.8 | 336 | .8 |
| | 140,681 | | 52,600 | | 43,948 | |

Source: Costa Rica, Dirección General de Estadistica y Censos, *Censos Nacionales de 1973. Población*. Volume 2, San José, April 1975.

Table 52

Urban population increases in Costa Rica, 1963-73
(In thousands)

| | 1963 | 1973 |
|---|---|---|
| Population of cities with more than 10,000 inhabitants (8 cities) | 367.8 | 574.9 |
| Remaining urban population | 92.7 | 185.2 |
| Total | 460.5 | 760.1 |
| Percentage of total population | 34.5% | 40.6% |

Source: Calculated from Costa Rica, Dirección General de Estadística y Censos, *Censos Nacionales de 1973. Población*. Volume 1, San José, December 1974, Table 1.

male population are engaged in farm work. A glance at the appropriate census table for Nicaragua will show that roughly 30 to 70 per cent of the male labor force in small towns works in agricultural activities. The norm for Costa Rica is quite different. As seen in Table 51, even in small towns the proportion engaged in agriculture averages just 14 per cent of the total. Quite understandably, an increase in the population size of the urban center shows a decrease in the percentage in agriculture.

Thus, taking into account the entire urban population of the country as defined by the Census Office as shown in Table 52, the urban level in 1973 increases to 40.6 per cent from 34.5 per cent in 1963. The gain of 6.1 percentage points compares favorably with the other countries studied.

It should be pointed out that in 1973 there are few persons newly counted as urban, brought about by an arbitrary reclassification of towns from rural to urban status in the intercensal period. In the San Jose Metropolitan *region* (to be defined in the next paragraph), all urban places listed in the 1973 census report but not listed for 1963, do in fact represent the extension of residential suburbs radiating out from the cities of San Jose, Alajuela, Cartago and Heredia. Outside the metropolitan region, a few newly listed urban places crop up in the 1973 report, but the total population they contain is very insignficant.

A third possible urban definition (Table 53), includes the nationally defined urban population plus the populations of those living in rural areas of the San Jose metropolitan region. This geographic area, the metropolitan region, encompassing San Jose, the cities of Alajuela, Cartago, and Heredia and the rural portions of several cantons, has been established and delineated by the National Institute of Housing and Urbanization (INVU) in the report *Estudio Regional Metropolitano*. The districts and cantons which fall within the region are listed in Appendix A to this chapter.

Table 53

Costa Rica, adjusted urban and rural population totals, 1963-73

| | Population (in thousands) | |
|---|---|---|
| Category | 1963 | 1973 |
| Population classified urban in the metropolitan region | 334 | 547 |
| Population classified rural in the metropolitan region | 210 | 260 |
| Remaining population classified urban in Costa Rica | 126 | 213 |
| Adjusted urban total | 670 | 1,020 |
| Percent of total population | 50% | 54% |
| Remaining rural population of Costa Rica | 666 | 852 |

Source: Costa Rica, Dirección General de Estadistica y Censos, *Censos Nacionales de 1973. Población.* Volume 1, San José, December 1974.

The emerging character of the metropolitan region including its rural environs is quite well-stated in an unpublished document from the Presidential Planning Office prepared by Dr. Fernando Zumbado. The pertinent section is quoted below at length.

According to census data, Costa Rica is a predominately rural country. In 1950 and in 1963, around 35 per cent of the population was classified as urban, while in 1973 this increased to 40.6 per cent. In comparison to other Latin American countries, an urban population of just 40 per cent is relatively low. Only the most rural countries show lower percentages than Costa Rica. Yet when the geographic distribution patterns of the economically active population (by industrial classification) are analyzed, one arrives at the conclusion that Costa Rica is not, after all, a predominately agricultural country. The 1973 population census indicates that 36 per cent of the economically active population is engaged in agricultural activities representing a sharp drop in this category from the census 10 years earlier. Owing to this, one can observe that in 1973 the percentage of the active population in the tertiary sector of the economy is larger than the percentage in the primary sector (40.6 and 38.7 per cent, respectively).

To explain the existence of a relatively high percentage of persons in non-agricultural activities in a country with an apparently low level of urbanization, one must examine population distribution patterns. The observation that Costa Rica has a very high concentration of population in a small portion of its territory is a well known fact. This concentration is not a recent development, but rather results from settlement patterns dating from the Colonial Period. The area situated to the South of the Central Volcanic Cordillera, known as the "Central Valley" or "Intermont Valley" has for four centuries been the most heavily populated zone in the country. In fact, until the last century, an even higher proportion of the total population resided here than at present.

The origins of densely populated rural zones stem from this historically high population concentration in the Central Valley. These areas, located in the outskirts of the cities of San Jose, Alajuela, Cartago and Heredia have little by little lost their rural character as agricultural districts and have changed over to residential areas for a large number of persons dedicated to "urban" oriented activities. A high proportion of traditional agriculturalists have changed their basic activities, and have begun to work in the secondary or tertiary sectors of the economy. At the same time migration movements have brought people from the cities to these areas.

Yet, the majority of these rapidly urbanizing zones are still classified as rural in census reports, thus explaining the apparent low level of urbanization in Costa Rica as shown by official statistics.

Table 54 shows the population totals and growth for the urban and rural components of the San Jose metropolitan region. The rural segment is not insignificant, numbering 260,000 persons in 1973, representing 23 per cent of the entire national rural population.

The occupational structures of the rural population of Costa Rica Rica inside and outside the metropolitan region are very different as can be seen in Table 55. Only 22 per cent of the entire economically active population in the metropolitan region is engaged in agriculture, compared to 75 per cent for the remainder of Costa Rica's rural numbers. The 22 per cent, incidentally decreases to around 18 per cent when the population of just a few marginal districts is dropped from consideration, and similarly the remaining 75 per cent rural population jumps to roughly 79 per cent when just a few districts outside the metropolitan region where industrialization is occurring are deleted. Many common urban types of employment are shown to be quite well represented in the metropolitan region's rural area—such as salesmen (9.0 per cent), industrial workers (19.5 per cent) and service workers (15.6 per cent).

Another finding supporting the urban character of this area is the fact that only 8 per cent of the entire Costa Rican agricultural labor force lives in the San Jose metropolitan region, although it holds 24 per cent of the national rural population. Farmers in the region are generally older than in the rest of the country (Table 56) which suggests that farming is not attracting younger people—a reasonable conclusion given the close proximity of San Jose and possibilities of other types of employment. There is also a "push" factor: since there is no new farmland available in the region, the possibilities for younger people to engage in agricultural pursuits are quite limited. Consequently, with little turnover of properties, the farming population in the metropolitan region will tend to be older than in other parts of the country where the development of new land is possible, and to which younger farmers will migrate.

Finally, in Table 57 the region's rural segment is examined from the point of view of its dominance over the remainder of the national rural population engaged in non-agricultural occupations. A full half of all rural non-agricultural jobs in the country are claimed by the metropolitan region. These data support Zumbado's conclusions on the regions's "urban" character.

It seems, therefore, reasonable in this reassessment to consider the entire metropolitan region as one urban unit, in addition to placing in this category the populations of all other large and small towns. Accord-

**Table 54**

**Population totals and increases for the San Jose metropolitan region, 1963-73**

| Sector | Population 1963 | 1973 | Percentage increase |
|---|---|---|---|
| Urban | 334,469 | 546,938 | 64 |
| Rural | 210,426 | 259,884 | 24 |
| **Total** | **544,895** | **805,822** | **48** |

Source: Costa Rica, Dirección General de Estadistica y Censos, *Censos Nacionales de 1973. Población.* Volume 1, San José, December 1974.

**Table 55**

**Costa Rica: The economically active rural population (1973)**

| Category | San Jose metropolitan region Number | Percentage | Remainder of country Number | Percentage |
|---|---|---|---|---|
| Professionals, technicians | 3,529 | 4.7 | 6,129 | 2.7 |
| Managers, administrators | 886 | 1.2 | 863 | 0.4 |
| White collar workers | 3,481 | 4.7 | 2,607 | 1.1 |
| Salesmen | 6,669 | 9.0 | 7,974 | 3.5 |
| Farmers, cattlemen | 16,545 | 22.3 | 173,284 | 75.1 |
| Transportation workers | 3,457 | 4.7 | 3,214 | 1.4 |
| Industrial workers | 14,462 | 19.5 | 10,711 | 4.6 |
| Other craftsmen and workers | 5,252 | 7.1 | 5,360 | 2.3 |
| Unskilled workers | 7,843 | 10.6 | 8,337 | 3.6 |
| Service workers | 11,575 | 15.6 | 11,445 | 5.0 |
| Non-specified activities | 649 | 0.9 | 851 | 0.4 |
| **Total** | **74,328** | | **230,775** | |

Source: Costa Rica, Dirección General de Estadistica y Censos, *Censos Nacionales de 1973. Población.* Volume 2, San José, April 1975.

**Table 56**

**Age structure of total economically active agricultural population. Metropolitan region rural population vs. remaining Costa Rican rural population, 1973**

| | Percentage distribution by age groups 12-14 | 15-19 | 20-24 | 25-29 | 30-34 | 35-44 | 45-54 | 55-64 | 65+ |
|---|---|---|---|---|---|---|---|---|---|
| Rural population of metropolitan region | 4.4 | 16.4 | 12.1 | 8.6 | 7.8 | 16.2 | 14.6 | 12.2 | 7.7 |
| Remaining rural of Costa Rica | 5.3 | 18.8 | 14.7 | 11.0 | 9.4 | 16.3 | 11.8 | 7.7 | 4.5 |

Source: Costa Rica, Dirección General de Estadistica y Censos, *Censos Nacionales de 1973. Población.* Volume 1, San José, December 1974.

ingly, in Table 53 an aggregated urban total for Costa Rica of 54 per cent is shown. This is a far higher proportion than the 30 per cent of the population discussed earlier and found in cities of 20,000 and more. Yet even on this revised basis the pace of Costa Rican urbanization is quite slow. The urban proportion of the total jumped from just 50 to 54 per cent in the 1963-73 interval.

## Population Projections

In earlier comments, three alternative definitions have been used to quantify and examine the urban sector in Costa Rica. The urban definition used in the projections (Table 60) takes into account the San Jose metropolitan area, and the country's seven other cities with populations in excess of 10,000 inhabitants. Accordingly, the total population of urbanized areas in Costa Rica is projected to the years 1980, 1990, and 2000 by allocating the projected national population first to provinces then to urbanized areas using the ratio-trend methodology elaborated by Jerome P. Pickard.[1] Since this method progresses from a population projection for the country as a whole, to regional projections, to urbanized area projections, it is termed a "step-down" system. The projection methodology is explained on pages 207-11.

### Table 57

Distribution of the rural economically active population in Costa Rica by occupational category, 1973[a]

| Category | Total | Percentage | Metropolitan region | Other rural |
|---|---|---|---|---|
| | | Economically active population in rural Costa Rica | | |
| Professionals, technicians | 9,658 | 8.4 | 3.1 | 5.3 |
| Managers, administrators | 1,729 | 1.5 | .8 | .7 |
| White collar workers | 6,088 | 5.3 | 3.0 | 2.3 |
| Salesmen | 14,643 | 12.7 | 5.8 | 6.9 |
| Transportation workers | 6,671 | 5.8 | 3.0 | 2.8 |
| Industrial workers | 25,173 | 21.8 | 12.5 | 9.3 |
| Other craftsmen and workers | 10,612 | 9.3 | 4.6 | 4.7 |
| Unskilled workers | 16,180 | 14.0 | 6.8 | 7.2 |
| Service workers | 23,020 | 19.9 | 10.0 | 9.9 |
| Non-specified activities | 1,500 | 1.3 | .6 | .7 |
| | 115,274 | 100.0 | 50.2 | 49.8 |

[a] Excluding those in agricultural activities.

Source: Costa Rica, Dirección General de Estadística y Censos, *Censos Nacionales de 1973. Población.* Volume 2, San José, April 1975.

---

[1] Jerome P. Pickard, *Dimensions to Metropolitanism,* Urban Land Institute Research Monograph 14A, Washington, D.C. 1966. pp. 53-56.

## National Projection

Three population projections for Costa Rica were considered for use in this study (see Table 58). All of the projections are based on the 1963 census results. The projections by CELADE and Gomez were able to incorporate more years of observation of the declining birth rate than the earlier Jimenez projection, and yield quite similar results. The CELADE projection is employed for this report. The population as projected to May 14, 1973 is 1,881,000, which is close to the 1,872,000 enumerated by the census of that date.

Table 58

Projected population of Costa Rica, 1965 to 2000.

| | Population in thousands | | |
| Year | CELADE[a] | Jiménez[b] | Gómez[c] |
|---|---|---|---|
| 1965 | 1,494.7 | 1,489.8 | 1,494.7 |
| 1970 | 1,736.8 | 1,766.1 | 1,736.2 |
| 1975 | 1,993.8 | 2,095.9 | 1,991.0 |
| 1980 | 2,285.7 | 2,493.1 | 2,280.9 |
| 1985 | 2,610.9 | 2,961.3 | 2,604.2 |
| 1990 | 2,954.4 | 3,493.3 | 2,945.3 |
| 1995 | 3,311.2 | — | 3,300.7 |
| 2000 | 3,695.3 | — | 3,682.4 |

Sources:

[a] Centro Latinoamericano de Demografía (CELADE), *Boletín Demográfico* 7:13 (January 1974).

[b] Ricardo Jiménez Jiménez, "Proyección de la Población de Costa Rica por Sexo y Grupos de Edad, 1965-1990," in Costa Rica, Dirección General de Estadística y Censos, *Revista de Estudios y Estadísticas,* No. 8, Serie Demográfica No. 5, San José, October 1967.

[c] Miguel Gómez B., "Proyección de la Población de Costa Rica por Sexo y Grupos de Edades", University of Costa Rica, Center for Social and Population Studies, Research Unit, San José, 1971.

Table 59

Projected population, crude birth rate, crude death rate, and rate of increase; Costa Rica; 1965 to 2000

| Period | Population at beginning of period (in thousands) | Crude birth rate | Crude death rate | Average annual rate of increase (%) |
|---|---|---|---|---|
| 1965–70 | 1,495 | 37.3 | 7.3 | 3.00 |
| 1970–75 | 1,737 | 33.4 | 5.9 | 2.76 |
| 1975–80 | 1,994 | 32.4 | 5.1 | 2.73 |
| 1980–85 | 2,286 | 31.2 | 4.6 | 2.66 |
| 1985–90 | 2,611 | 29.1 | 4.4 | 2.47 |
| 1990–95 | 2,954 | 27.1 | 4.4 | 2.28 |
| 1995–2000 | 3,311 | 26.4 | 4.4 | 2.19 |
| 2000 | 3,695 | | | |

Source: Centro Latinoamericano de Demografía (CELADE), *Boletín Demográfico* 7:13 (January 1974).

The population of Costa Rica projected to the year 2000 by CELADE is shown in Table 59 along with the projected rates of the components of population change. Although CELADE assumes a 31 per cent decline in the total fertility rate during the 25 years from 1970-75 (4.65) to 1995-2000 (3,22), comparison with Table 42 suggests that the CELADE projection is higher than the 2.53 per cent rate for 1970-72 based on vital registration. The CELADE projection does not yield a growth rate as low as the 1972 rate of 2.49 per cent until 1985-80. If the growth rate of the Costa Rican population maintains some of the momentum of its recent sharp decline, the population will be somewhat less than that projected by CELADE for any future year. Some revision of the results of this study may be necessary when projections based on the 1973 census returns and on later vital rates are prepared.

The decline in both fertility and mortality projected by CELADE would produce a population in the year 2000 which would be older than the 1973 urban population. At the end of the century, 34.0 per cent of the population would be in the ages 0-14, 61.5 per cent in the ages 15-64, and 4.4 per cent in ages 65 and above (compare with Table 44). The dependency ratio would be reduced to 62.

**Table 60**

**Enumerated and projected population of provinces and urbanized areas in Costa Rica, 1950 to 2000**

| Province and urbanized area | Enumerated population in thousands | | | Projected population in thousands (midyear) | | |
|---|---|---|---|---|---|---|
| | May 22 1950 | April 1 1963 | May 14 1973 | 1980 | 1990 | 2000 |
| **National total** | **800.9** | **1,336.3** | **1,871.8** | **2,285.7** | **2,954.4** | **3,695.3** |
| Alajuela | 148.8 | 240.7 | 326.0 | 390.5 | 489.7 | 593.9 |
| Alajuela | 13.9 | 19.6 | 34.3 | 40.7 | 54.0 | 69.1 |
| Remainder | 134.9 | 221.1 | 291.7 | 349.8 | 435.7 | 524.8 |
| Cartago | 100.7 | 155.4 | 204.7 | 239.3 | 290.6 | 341.2 |
| Cartago | 12.9 | 18.1 | 34.6 | 40.9 | 55.0 | 70.6 |
| Turrialba | 5.4 | 8.6 | 12.2 | 14.6 | 18.4 | 22.4 |
| Remainder | 82.3 | 128.7 | 158.0 | 183.8 | 217.2 | 248.2 |
| Guanacaste | 88.2 | 142.6 | 178.7 | 210.8 | 254.7 | 297.6 |
| Liberia | 3.4 | 6.1 | 10.8 | 13.6 | 18.9 | 24.9 |
| Remainder | 84.8 | 136.5 | 167.9 | 197.2 | 235.8 | 272.7 |
| Heredia | 51.8 | 85.1 | 133.8 | 165.6 | 223.3 | 290.7 |
| Heredia | 12.0 | 19.2 | 26.1 | 31.1 | 38.8 | 46.6 |
| Remainder | 39.8 | 65.8 | 107.8 | 134.5 | 184.6 | 244.1 |
| Limón | 41.4 | 68.4 | 115.1 | 143.9 | 199.2 | 265.3 |
| Puerto Limón | 11.3 | 19.4 | 29.6 | 36.9 | 49.5 | 63.8 |
| Remainder | 30.1 | 49.0 | 85.5 | 107.0 | 149.7 | 201.4 |
| Puntarenas | 88.2 | 156.5 | 218.2 | 272.6 | 359.3 | 457.8 |
| Puntarenas | 13.3 | 19.6 | 26.3 | 30.3 | 36.5 | 42.4 |
| Remainder | 74.9 | 136.9 | 191.9 | 242.3 | 322.9 | 415.4 |
| San José | 281.8 | 487.7 | 695.2 | 863.1 | 1,137.6 | 1,448.9 |
| San José | 146.1 | 257.2 | 401.0 | 507.8 | 696.4 | 919.6 |
| Remainder | 135.7 | 230.4 | 294.1 | 355.3 | 441.2 | 529.3 |

Net international migration is not assumed to be a factor in Costa Rica's population growth by the CELADE projection.

## Provincial Projections

The population of each province as projected to midyear 1980, 1990, and 2000 is presented in Table 60. No change in the ranking of the provinces is projected. The province of San Jose is projected to slightly increase its dominance in terms of size by surpassing one million by 1990 and 1.4 million by the year 2000. San Jose Province's share of the national population is projected to increase from 37 per cent in 1973 to 39 per cent in 2000. Besides San Jose, only the province of Alajuela is projected to reach the half million population mark by the end of the century. Virtually no change is projected in the distribution of the population between the inland provinces (San Jose, Alajuela, Heredia, and Cartago) and the coastal provinces.

Limon, the smallest province, is projected to increase the fastest between 1973 and 2000 by maintaining an average growth rate of over three per cent a year (Table 61). Heredia, Puntarenas, and San Jose are

Table 61

**Observed and projected population growth rates of provinces and urbanized areas in Costa Rica, 1950 to 2000**

| Province and urbanized area | Average annual growth rate (%) of enumerated population | | Average annual growth rate (%) of projected population | | |
|---|---|---|---|---|---|
| | 1950–1963 | 1963–1973 | 1973–1980 | 1980–1990 | 1990–2000 |
| **National total** | **3.98** | **3.33** | **2.80** | **2.57** | **2.24** |
| Alajuela | 3.74 | 3.00 | 2.53 | 2.26 | 1.93 |
| Alajuela | 2.68 | 5.53 | 2.38 | 2.84 | 2.47 |
| Remainder | 3.84 | 2.74 | 2.55 | 2.20 | 1.86 |
| Cartago | 3.37 | 2.72 | 2.19 | 1.94 | 1.61 |
| Cartago | 2.60 | 6.41 | 2.36 | 2.45 | 2.50 |
| Turrialba | 3.57 | 3.38 | 2.54 | 2.34 | 1.98 |
| Remainder | 3.47 | 2.02 | 2.13 | 1.67 | 1.33 |
| Guanacaste | 3.73 | 2.23 | 2.32 | 1.89 | 1.56 |
| Liberia | 4.55 | 5.67 | 3.22 | 3.28 | 2.76 |
| Remainder | 3.70 | 2.05 | 2.26 | 1.79 | 1.45 |
| Heredia | 3.86 | 4.48 | 2.98 | 2.99 | 2.64 |
| Heredia | 3.70 | 3.01 | 2.47 | 2.20 | 1.84 |
| Remainder | 3.91 | 4.87 | 3.11 | 3.17 | 2.79 |
| Limón | 3.91 | 5.15 | 3.13 | 3.25 | 2.87 |
| Puerto Limón | 4.21 | 4.17 | 3.08 | 2.93 | 2.55 |
| Remainder | 3.74 | 5.51 | 3.14 | 3.36 | 2.97 |
| Puntarenas | 4.46 | 3.28 | 3.12 | 2.76 | 2.42 |
| Puntarenas | 3.02 | 2.93 | 1.98 | 1.85 | 1.50 |
| Remainder | 4.69 | 3.33 | 3.27 | 2.87 | 2.52 |
| San José | 4.26 | 3.50 | 3.03 | 2.76 | 2.42 |
| San José | 4.40 | 4.39 | 3.31 | 3.16 | 2.78 |
| Remainder | 4.12 | 2.41 | 2.65 | 2.16 | 1.82 |

Source: Table 60.

expected to increase at greater than the national rate of growth, while Alajuela, Cartago, and Guanacaste grow more slowly than the national rate.

**Urbanized Area Projections**

Table 60 presents the projected population of the eight urbanized areas with over 10,000 people in 1973. The population of these areas, collectively, is projected to more than double from 575,000 in 1973 to 1.26 million in the year 2000. These eight areas would comprise 34.1 per cent of the national population in 2000 compared with 30.7 per cent in 1973 (Table 60). The projected rate of increase of the urbanized area population is 2.89 per cent per annum between 1973 and 2000, and the rate for the remainder of the population is 2.32 per cent.

The Heredia urbanized area is projected to surpass Puntarenas in population before 1980 to become the fifth largest city in Costa Rica. Liberia's population is projected to exceed that of Turrialba by 1990. The population of the urbanized area of San Jose will increase by a factor of 2.3 between 1973 and 2000, when it will be nearly 920,000 and will represent about one-fourth (24.9 per cent) of the national population and nearly three-fourths of the urbanized area population. San Jose is projected to be the fastest growing city through the year 2000 (Table 61). By the end of the century it is expected to be 13 times larger than than Cartago and 4.5 times larger than the cities of Cartago, Alajuela, and Puerto Limon, combined. Only these three cities (besides San Jose) will have populations of 50,000 or more in 2000.

The smaller urbanized areas of Heredia, Puntarenas, and Turrialba will increase at less than the national rate, according to the projection. In fact, the rural population in the provinces of Heredia and Puntarenas is projected to grow at a more rapid pace than the respective urbanized populations. Much of the Puntarenas rural growth, however, is in an industrialized area adjacent to the city.

In summary, the above data indicate rather moderate rates of growth of the eight urbanized areas between now and 2000. The proportion of the national population which is projected to live in these areas increases only nominally. The indicated future populations of the urbanized areas are conservative projections because of the method employed. Since the projected population of an urbanized area is determined by the trend of that area's proportion of its province's population during the latest two intercensal periods, the slow pace of urbanization between 1950 and 1963 is incorporated into the projection. If the projection of city populations were based only the 1963–73 period, the resulting figures could be significantly larger. This conservative feature of the projections methodology probably more than offsets the upward bias of the CELADE projection discussed in previous paragraphs.

If the projections are borne out in Table 60, three general conclusions regarding future population growth in Costa Rica may be drawn: (1) the population of the country will continue to increase at a rate of over two per cent a year and reach nearly 3.7 million by the year 2000; (2) the population of the eight largest urbanized areas will comprise only a slightly greater proportion of the national population in 2000 than in 1973; (3) and the San Jose urbanized area will slowly increase its dominance of the other cities and contain a quarter of Costa Rica's population in the year 2000.

## Appendix A

### Component parts of the San Jose metropolitan region

| Province, Canton and District | 1973 Population | Province, Canton and District | 1973 Population |
|---|---|---|---|
| | (in thousands) | | (in thousands) |
| **Province of San Jose** | | **Province of Cartago** | |
| **Canton Central** | **215.4** | **Canton Central** | |
| **Canton Escazu** | **25.0** | Parte Oriental | 13.5 |
| **Canton Desamparados** | | Parte Occidental | 8.3 |
| Desamparados | 30.7 | Carmen | 7.4 |
| San Miguel | 8.2 | San Nicolas | 9.4 |
| San Juan de Dios | 6.5 | San Francisco | 5.2 |
| San Rafael Arriba | 5.5 | Guadalupe | 7.7 |
| San Antonio | 5.1 | Dulce Nombre | 3.4 |
| Patarra | 2.0 | **Canton La Union** | **23.4** |
| Damas | 4.3 | **Canton Oreamuno** | |
| San Rafael Abajo | 5.8 | San Rafael | 10.4 |
| **Canton Aserri** | | **Canton el Guarco** | |
| Aserri | 11.7 | Tejar | 6.4 |
| **Canton Goicoechea** | **61.6** | | |
| **Canton Santa Ana** | **14.5** | **Province of Heredia** | |
| **Canton Alajuelita** | **23.0** | **Canton Central** | **36.5** |
| **Canton Coronado** | | **Canton Barba** | |
| San Isidro | 6.3 | Barba | 3.1 |
| Patalillo | 3.5 | San Roque | .9 |
| **Canton Tibas** | **35.6** | Santa Lucia | 1.6 |
| **Canton Moravia** | | **Canton Santo Domingo** | |
| San Vicente | 15.6 | Santo Domingo | 5.1 |
| La Trinidad | 2.7 | San Vicente | 1.6 |
| **Canton Montes de Oca** | **33.7** | San Miguel Sur | 2.1 |
| **Canton Curridabat** | **15.6** | Paracito | .9 |
| | | Santo Tomas | 2.3 |
| | | Santa Rosa | 3.1 |
| | | Tures | 1.3 |
| | | **Canton Santa Barbara** | |
| | | Santa Barbara | 2.5 |
| | | San Pedro | 1.3 |
| **Province of Alajuela** | | San Juan | 1.8 |
| **Canton Central** | | **Canton San Rafael** | |
| Alajuela | 33.1 | San Rafael | 4.7 |
| San José | 9.5 | San Josecito | 6.0 |
| San Antonio | 7.5 | Santiago | 1.0 |
| Santiago Oeste | 4.3 | **Canton San Isidro** | |
| San Isidro | 7.2 | San Isidro | 3.7 |
| San Rafael | 5.5 | **Canton Belen** | **8.5** |
| Santiago Este | 4.4 | **Canton Flores** | **6.5** |
| Desamparados | 6.7 | **Canton San Pablo** | **6.7** |

## Appendix B

Costa Rica: Population projections by sex and quinquennial age groups, 1975-2000. Recommended hypothesis

| Age groups | 1975 | 1980 | 1985 | 1990 | 1995 | 2000 |
|---|---|---|---|---|---|---|
| | | | males | | | |
| **Total** | **1,005.342** | **1,152.968** | **1,317.529** | **1,491.370** | **1,671.902** | **1,866.245** |
| 0- 4 | 149.363 | 168.738 | 188.380 | 201.078 | 212.118 | 230.975 |
| 5- 9 | 140.165 | 148.059 | 167.646 | 187.408 | 200.191 | 211.276 |
| 10-14 | 138.536 | 139.833 | 147.742 | 167.333 | 187.084 | 199.861 |
| 15-19 | 121.639 | 138.177 | 139.540 | 147.466 | 167.040 | 186.766 |
| 20-24 | 97.467 | 121.197 | 137.762 | 139.164 | 147.092 | 166.629 |
| 25-29 | 75.204 | 96.973 | 120.679 | 137.228 | 138.652 | 146.565 |
| 30-34 | 59.147 | 74.730 | 96.438 | 120.061 | 136.555 | 137.988 |
| 35-39 | 47.678 | 58.637 | 74.167 | 95.770 | 119.272 | 135.685 |
| 40-44 | 40.494 | 47.086 | 57.984 | 73.401 | 94.829 | 118.136 |
| 45-49 | 35.470 | 39.720 | 46.256 | 57.024 | 72.240 | 93.378 |
| 50-54 | 28.501 | 34.290 | 38.479 | 44.887 | 55.413 | 70.279 |
| 55-59 | 22.209 | 27.045 | 32.599 | 36.642 | 42.807 | 52.913 |
| 60-64 | 18.435 | 20.395 | 24.887 | 30.056 | 33.843 | 39.602 |
| 65-69 | 12.670 | 16.100 | 17.850 | 21.827 | 26.411 | 29.794 |
| 70-74 | 8.742 | 10.232 | 13.027 | 14.471 | 17.727 | 21.489 |
| 75-79 | 5.386 | 6.592 | 7.749 | 9.909 | 11.055 | 13.600 |
| 80+ | 4.236 | 5.164 | 6.344 | 7.645 | 9.573 | 11.309 |
| | | | females | | | |
| **Total** | **988.471** | **1,132.753** | **1,293.409** | **1,462.999** | **1,639.254** | **1,829.058** |
| 0- 4 | 143.886 | 162.198 | 180.770 | 192.716 | 203.199 | 221.182 |
| 5- 9 | 134.897 | 142.788 | 161.349 | 180.067 | 192.113 | 202.653 |
| 10-14 | 134.376 | 134.689 | 142.620 | 161.187 | 179.903 | 191.947 |
| 15-19 | 118.096 | 134.189 | 134.544 | 142.486 | 161.045 | 179.748 |
| 20-24 | 94.767 | 117.880 | 133.992 | 134.368 | 142.308 | 160.849 |
| 25-29 | 74.476 | 94.512 | 117.620 | 133.723 | 134.110 | 142.040 |
| 30-34 | 58.832 | 74.178 | 94.194 | 117.258 | 133.330 | 133.725 |
| 35-39 | 47.553 | 58.467 | 73.796 | 93.759 | 116.750 | 132.770 |
| 40-44 | 40.433 | 47.100 | 57.996 | 73.266 | 93.132 | 116.001 |
| 45-49 | 35.480 | 39.859 | 46.511 | 57.335 | 72.481 | 92.175 |
| 50-54 | 28.856 | 34.688 | 39.052 | 45.638 | 56.318 | 71.249 |
| 55-59 | 22.912 | 27.868 | 33.578 | 37.869 | 44.315 | 54.742 |
| 60-64 | 19.460 | 21.647 | 26.404 | 31.885 | 36.026 | 42.222 |
| 65-69 | 13.760 | 17.678 | 19.735 | 24.144 | 29.231 | 33.100 |
| 70-74 | 9.736 | 11.659 | 15.049 | 16.870 | 20.715 | 25.161 |
| 75-79 | 5.912 | 7.302 | 8.783 | 11.387 | 12.820 | 15.809 |
| 80+ | 5.039 | 6.051 | 7.416 | 9.041 | 11.458 | 13.685 |
| | | | both sexes | | | |
| **Total** | **1,993.813** | **2,285.721** | **2,610.938** | **2,954.369** | **3,311.156** | **3,695.303** |
| 0- 4 | 293.249 | 330.936 | 369.150 | 393.794 | 415.317 | 452.157 |
| 5- 9 | 275.062 | 290.847 | 328.995 | 367.475 | 392.304 | 413.929 |
| 10-14 | 272.912 | 274.522 | 290.362 | 328.520 | 366.987 | 391.808 |
| 15-19 | 239.735 | 272.366 | 274.084 | 289.952 | 328.085 | 366.514 |
| 20-24 | 192.234 | 239.077 | 271.754 | 273.532 | 289.400 | 327.478 |
| 25-29 | 149.680 | 191.485 | 238.299 | 270.951 | 272.762 | 288.605 |
| 30-34 | 117.979 | 148.908 | 190.632 | 237.319 | 269.885 | 271.713 |
| 35-39 | 95.231 | 117.104 | 147.963 | 189.529 | 236.022 | 268.455 |
| 40-44 | 80.927 | 94.186 | 115.980 | 146.667 | 187.961 | 234.137 |
| 45-49 | 70.950 | 79.579 | 92.767 | 114.359 | 144.721 | 185.553 |
| 50-54 | 57.357 | 68.978 | 77.531 | 90.525 | 111.731 | 141.528 |
| 55-59 | 45.121 | 54.913 | 66.177 | 74.511 | 87.122 | 107.655 |
| 60-64 | 37.895 | 42.042 | 51.291 | 61.941 | 69.869 | 81.824 |
| 65-69 | 26.430 | 33.778 | 37.585 | 45.971 | 55.642 | 62.894 |
| 70-74 | 18.478 | 21.891 | 28.076 | 31.341 | 38.442 | 46.650 |
| 75-79 | 11.298 | 13.894 | 16.532 | 21.296 | 23.875 | 29.409 |
| 80+ | 9.275 | 11.215 | 13.760 | 16.686 | 21.031 | 24.994 |

Source: CELADE, Boletín Demográfico 7:13 (January 1974). Table 2, p. 21.

# EL SALVADOR

This chapter examines the literature on demographic growth patterns and urbanization in El Salvador in the context of national and city population projections to the year 2000.

The published results of El Salvador's 1971 census population are incomplete. As of mid-1977 only the first of two volumes containing extensive data had been released. The information in Volume I relates to population numbers, geographic distribution (urban and rural) and the characteristics of age, sex, marital condition, education and fertility.[1] Applicable portions of the volume are included in this study.

Volume II, if it is issued, will focus on the labor force, occupational structures, and related economic characteristics of the population, cross-tabulated with such key variables as age, sex, and urban or rural place of residence. This would represent the most detailed information ever assembled on these topics in El Salvador.

### Population and Growth Rate

The population of El Salvador increased from 1.9 million inhabitants in 1950 to 4.1 million in 1975. It is projected to increase to 8.8 million by the year 2000. Thus, it has doubled and is projected to more than double again in each of two 25 year intervals. The national population growth rates underlying these increases are quite high—averaging 3.1

---

[1] El Salvador, Dirección General de Estadística y Censos, *Cuarto Censo Nacional de Población* 1971, Volume 1, San Salvador, 1974.

per cent per annum in the 1950-71 interval, and a projected 3.2 per cent between 1971-2000.

The total population enumerated in El Salvador's four censuses of this century and the implied average annual growth rates for the inter-censal periods are presented in Table 62. The results of the latter three censuses appear to be rather reliable, but there is no consensus about the path of population growth prior to 1950.

Published estimates agree on a figure of 1,168,000 for the mid-year population in 1920, but diverge after that date. Two series of estimates shown in Table 63 diverge substantially between 1920 and 1930, then gradually converge through 1950. The less variable series of vital rates calculated by Collver might seem more plausible, but his total population figure for 1930 implies that the census overcounted the population by nearly eight per cent.[1] The CELADE series accepts the 1930 census as accurate, but implies an undercount of 3.8 per cent in 1950, while Collver's 1950 estimate indicates an underenumeration only half as great.

It is difficult to evaluate the growth rate presented by CELADE since the component crude birth and death rates are not given. Furthermore, comparison of these estimates with vital rates based on registration data is tenuous because registration of deaths in El Salvador during this period was incomplete. Collver concludes that birth registration has been nearly complete since 1900, but that death registration is only 75 per cent complete. In the preparation of his estimates, he applies a constant adjustment of 33 per cent to the registered number of deaths.

Despite the ambiguity of the above estimates, it may be concluded that the population of El Salvador increased by over 60 per cent from 1920 to 1950. The average annual growth rate for that period was approximately 1.6 per cent.

The vital rates obtained from the registration system for the period since 1950 are presented in Table 64. The rate of natural increase derived from the registration data is considerably greater than that indicated by census results (Table 62). The discrepancy is largely attributable to the consistent underregistration of deaths.

The series of population totals and vital rates for 1950 and after, prepared for El Salvador by CELADE (Table 65) shows growth rates close to those computed from census totals. The series is actually a projection of the adjusted 1961 census population, but one which takes into account the recorded vital rates following that date. The CELADE series implies that the 1950 census underenumerated the population by

---

[1]O. Andrew Collver, *Birth Rates in Latin America: New Estimates of Historical Trends and Fluctuations*, Berkeley: Institute of International Studies, University of California, 1965.

**Table 62**

**Enumerated population and intercensal growth rates of El Salvador; 1930, 1950, 1961, and 1971.**

| Date | Enumerated population | Average annual rate of increase (%) during intercensal period |
|---|---|---|
| May 10, 1930 | 1,437,157 | |
| June 13, 1950 | 1,855,917 | 1.27 |
| May 2, 1961 | 2,510,984 | 2.78 |
| June 27, 1971 | 3,549,260 | 3.41 |

Source: El Salvador census reports.

**Table 63**

**Estimates by Collver and CELADE of the population and growth rate of El Salvador, 1920 to 1950**

| | Collver estimates | | | | CELADE estimates [a] | |
|---|---|---|---|---|---|---|
| Period | Starting population (thousands) | Crude birth rate | Crude death rate | Rate of natural increase (%) | Starting population (thousands) | Annual rate of increase (%) |
| 1920–24 | 1,161 | 46.6 | 32.8 | 1.38 | 1,168 | 2.16 |
| 1925–29 | 1,244 | 47.1 | 34.1 | 1.30 | 1,301 | 2.07 |
| 1930–34 | 1,328 | 46.5 | 32.7 | 1.38 | 1,443 | 1.18 |
| 1935–39 | 1,423 | 45.4 | 29.6 | 1.58 | 1,531 | 1.29 |
| 1940–44 | 1,540 | 45.2 | 28.5 | 1.67 | 1,633 | 1.42 |
| 1945–49 | 1,674 | 44.8 | 22.8 | 2.20 | 1,753 | 1.93 |
| 1950 | 1,869 | — | — | — | 1,931 | — |

[a] The CELADE estimates refer to periods beginning at midyear; hence they refer to 1920-25, 1925-30, etc.

Sources: O. Andrew Collver, *Birth Rates in Latin America: New Estimates of Historical Trends and Fluctuations.* Berkeley: Institute of International Studies, University of California, 1965, p. 122.

Centro Latinoamericano de Demografía (CELADE), *Boletín Demográfico.* 7:13 (January 1974).

**Table 64**

**Registered crude birth rate, crude death rate, and rate of natural increase of El Salvador, 1950-1972**

| Year(s) | Crude birth rate | Crude death rate | Rate of natural increase (%) |
|---|---|---|---|
| 1950–54 | 49.0 | 15.4 | 3.36 |
| 1955–59 | 49.0 | 13.7 | 3.53 |
| 1960–64 | 48.7 | 11.2 | 3.75 |
| 1965–69 | 44.4 | 9.8 | 3.46 |
| 1970 | 40.0 | 9.9 | 3.01 |
| 1971 | 43.5 | 8.1 | 3.54 |
| 1972 | 40.7 | 8.6 | 3.21 |

Sources: 1950-69: Carlos A. Rodriguez and Ricardo Castañeda Rugamas, *El Salvador Perfil Demográfico.* San Salvador: Asociación Demográfica Salvadoreña, September 1971, p. 14.

1970-72: *Population Index* 40:3 (July 1974) 597, 601.

3.8 per cent, the 1961 census undercounted by 3.2 per cent, and the 1971 census by 2.1 per cent.

The crude birth rate (CBR) given with the CELADE series closely parallels the rate based on vital registration. After experiencing a slight decline through the 1940's, the birth rate increased and peaked at about 49 per thousand population for the 1955-60 period. Since 1960 the birth rate has declined steadily, and was recorded as 40.7 in 1972 (Table 64). The decrease of the CBR has been substantial—about nine points in the ten years from 1960 to 1970.

The decline of the birth rate has been partially offset by a decreasing crude death rate (CDR). The decline of the CDR began earlier and has been more gradual (Table 63 and 65). The death rate was estimated by Collver to be 34.1 in 1925-29, but had fallen to 21.3 by 1950-55, and is projected to be 11.1 during 1970-75. The CDR since 1950 estimated by CELADE is roughly one-third greater than that calculated from registration data, as was also true of Collver's estimates for the period prior to 1950.

Since about 1950 a significant number of Salvadoreans have migrated to neighboring countries. The CELADE population series (Table 65) assumes a net out-migration of 3,500 people a year from 1950 to 1965. This may be a conservative figure since in 1969 there were an estimated 12,000 Salvadoreans in Nicaragua, 30,000 in Guatemala, and 300,000 in Honduras.[1] About 250,000 of the migrates to Honduras were farmers who mostly settled on undeveloped tracts in sparsely populated areas of the north coast and the interior.

The government of Honduras in 1969 began to enforce its Agrarian Reform Law which allows only native-born citizens to own land. Blutstein reports that 61,000 Salvadoreans had returned to El Salvador by November 1969.[2] The migration rate estimated by CELADE for the 1965-70 period would account for a net total of 55,000 immigrants up to midyear 1970. International migration is assumed to be negligible after 1970.

Because the crude birth rate remained at about 48 per thousand while the crude death rate was declining, the rate of natural increase peaked in the 1960-65 period at 3.25 per cent per annum. The current descent of the CBR, which began after 1965, has lowered the rate of natural increase slightly. The reversal from net emigration to net immigration from 1960-65 to 1965-70, however, caused the national population to increase at a greater rate during the latter period.

On average, over the past 50 years the population of El Salvador has

[1]Howard I. Blutstein, et al., Area Handbook for El Salvador, DA PAM 550-150, Washington, D.C.: U.S. Government Printing Office, 1971, pp. 53-54.
[2]Ibid.

**Figure 16**
**Age-specific fertility rates, El Salvador; 1961–1971.**

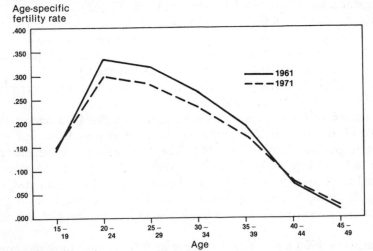

Age-specific fertility rate

grown at a high rate. Between 1920 and 1970 the population tripled, growing at an average rate of 2.2 per cent a year. Since 1950 the increase has been more rapid: the population grew at a rate of 3.0 per cent a year from 1950 to 1970 and increased by over 80 per cent during that span.

**Table 65**

**CELADE Estimates of population, crude birth rate, crude death rate, migration rate, and rate of increase of El Salvador, 1950 to 1975**

| Period | Population at beginning of period | Crude birth rate | Crude death rate | Migration rate (per 1,000) | Average annual rate of increase (%) |
|---|---|---|---|---|---|
| 1950–55 | 1,930,829 | 48.1 | 21.3 | −1.7 | 2.51 |
| 1955–60 | 2,189,681 | 48.8 | 18.8 | −1.5 | 2.86 |
| 1960–65 | 2,526,589 | 48.0 | 15.5 | −1.3 | 3.12 |
| 1965–70 | 2,953,680 | 44.2 | 13.0 | 3.4 | 3.47 |
| 1970–75 | 3,516,110 | 42.2 | 11.1 | 0.0 | 3.11 |
| 1975 | 4,108,402 | — | — | — | — |

Source: Centro Latinoamericano de Demografía (CELADE), *Boletín Demográfico* 7:13 (January 1974).

**Fertility Rates**

The decrease in the level of fertility since 1961 is reflected in the age-specific fertility rates (Figures 16). The women age group 20-39 has been responsible for the fertility decline. The family planning program of the Salvadorean Demographic Association has probably contributed to the lowering of fertility, but its impact cannot have been large since it began operations only in 1967. Although fertility has decreased since 1961, its present level is still high. The population growth rate remains above three per cent a year. The age-specific fertility rates graphed in Figure 16 correspond to a total fertility rate of 6.16 in 1971, compared with a rate of 6.67 in 1961.

**Age Distribution**

Despite the decrease in the fertility level between 1961 and 1971, the census of the latter date yielded a somewhat younger population (Table 66). The percentage of the population under age 15 increased from 44.8 in 1961 to 46.4 in 1971. The increase was in the age cohorts not affected by the lower fertility, those aged 5-14 in 1971. The 0-4 age group was slightly smaller in 1971 (16.8 per cent) than in 1961 (17.2 per cent) as a proportion of the total population. The dependency ratio has not yet been affected by the decrease in fertility. The ratio increased from 92.3 to 99.6 between 1961 and 1971.

A longer life expectancy for the population in general, and a moderate fall in the crude birth rate (from 42 to 33)—one falling slightly faster than the still declining death rate (see Table 73)—will produce significant shifts in the age structure of the population as projected to the year 2000. The distribution, according to CELADE projections, is given in Table 67, and shown in further detail in Appendix A of this chapter.

As in Costa Rica and Panama, El Salvador's population under age 15 will also decline in proportional terms between 1970-2000, but not at the speed projected for those two countries; nor will it attain the "low" level reached in them. Table 68 shows that Costa Rica's population under age 15 is projected to decline by a full 10 per cent between 1970-2000, and that of Panama by 6.2 per cent. The decline for El Salvador is 5.1 per cent. Another feature is the still very high proportion of those under age 15 projected for El Salvador by the year 2000—41.3 per cent. This is a level that will have been attained by the other two countries roughly 20 years earlier.

The reciprocal of these trends is a proportional increase among those 15-64 conventionally known as the "productive age" population. Those 65 and older are discounted from this discussion since the total numbers waiver in a rather limited range—roughly 3.2 to 5.0 per cent of the entire population. Accordingly, these trends will be accompanied by

**Table 66**

**Percentage of population in broad age groups, and dependency ratios for El Salvador; 1961 and 1971**

| Age | 1961 | | | 1971 | | |
|---|---|---|---|---|---|---|
| | Total | Urban | Rural | Total | Urban | Rural |
| all ages | 100.0% | 100.0% | 100.0% | 100.0% | 100.0% | 100.0% |
| 0-14 | 44.8 | 41.4 | 46.9 | 46.4 | 41.3 | 49.8 |
| 15-64 | 52.0 | 54.8 | 50.3 | 50.1 | 54.5 | 47.2 |
| 65+ | 3.2 | 3.8 | 2.8 | 3.5 | 4.2 | 3.0 |
| Dependency ratio[a] | 92.3 | 82.5 | 98.8 | 99.6 | 83.5 | 111.9 |

[a] The dependency ratio is P(0-14) P(65+)/P(15-64) X 100, where P(a) is the population age "a".

Source: Albert J. Struyk, "Ajuste de la Población Censal de 1971, por Sexo, según Grupos de Edades Quinquenales (Estudio Preliminar)," San Salvador: Dirección General de Estadística y Censos, January 1974, pp. 29-31.

**Table 67**

**Population in broad age groups, and dependency ratios for El Salvador, 1980-2000 as projected by CELADE.**

| Age group | Population | | | Percentage distribution | | |
|---|---|---|---|---|---|---|
| | 1980 | 1990 | 2000 | 1980 | 1990 | 2000 |
| Total | 4,812,688 | 6,594,675 | 8,802,651 | 100.0 | 100.0 | 100.0 |
| 0-14 | 2,172,941 | 2,891,075 | 3,635,189 | 45.2 | 43.8 | 41.3 |
| 15-64 | 2,483,450 | 3,480,770 | 4,856,590 | 51.6 | 52.8 | 55.2 |
| 65+ | 156,297 | 222,830 | 310,872 | 3.2 | 3.4 | 3.5 |
| Dependency ratios | 94 | 89 | 81 | | | |

Source: Centro Latinoamericano de Demografía (CELADE): Boletín Demografico, 7:13 (January 1974).

a decline in the dependency ratio for El Salvador, but once again the decline will neither be as sharp nor will it reach the low level to be attained in Costa Rica and Panama (Table 69).

## Urban-Rural Fertility Differentials

One child/woman ratio commonly used is the number of children under age one per 1,000 women ages 15-44. This ratio in 1961 and 1971 in El Salvador is shown in Table 70. By this measure fertility decreased by 6 per cent during the latest intercensal period. However, the decline was confined to the urban population. Urban fertility dropped 16.5 per cent while rural fertility remained approximately constant. The 60 per cent of the population which lives in rural areas has not reduced its fertility. Urban fertility is now about 60 per cent as great as rural fertility.

The urban population in El Salvador is not as young as the rural counterpart because of lower urban fertility and migration by persons ages 15-30 to urban areas (Table 66). The dependency ratio in 1971 was 83.5 in urban areas, compared with 111.9 in rural areas. Declining mortality and constant or slightly increasing fertility among the rural

**Table 68**

**El Salvador, Costa Rica, Panama. Enumerated and projected population for those in age group 0-14 as proportion of total population, 1970-2000**

| Country | Percentage of total population | | | | |
|---|---|---|---|---|---|
| | 1960 | 1970 | 1980 | 1990 | 2000 |
| El Salvador | 44.8 (1961) | 46.4 (1971) | 45.2 | 43.8 | 41.3 |
| Costa Rica | 47.7 (1963) | 44.0 (1973) | 39.2 | 36.9 | 34.0 |
| Panama | 43.5 | 43.4 | 41.4 | 39.8 | 37.2 |

Source: For Costa Rica and Panama see those country chapters, for El Salvador see source note, Table 66, and CELADE, *Boletín Demográfico*, 7:13 (January 1974).

**Table 69**

**Dependency Ratios, 1960-70, and Projected to 2000: El Salvador, Panama and Costa Rica**

| Country | Dependency Ratios | | | | |
|---|---|---|---|---|---|
| | 1960 | 1970 | 1980 | 1990 | 2000 |
| El Salvador | 91(1961) | 100(1971) | 94 | 89 | 81 |
| Costa Rica | 104 | 91 | 75 | 69 | 63 |
| Panama | 89 | 89 | 84 | 79 | 72 |

Source: See source note, Table 68.

**Table 70**

**Number of Children Under Age One per 1,000 Women Ages 15-44 by Urban and Rural Areas, El Salvador; 1961 and 1971**

| Residence | 1961 | 1971 | Per cent Change |
|---|---|---|---|
| Urban | 148.8 | 124.3 | − 16.5 |
| Rural | 204.7 | 206.7 | + 1.0 |
| Total | 180.9 | 170.0 | − 6.0 |

Source: William P. McGreevey, "Population Dynamics and Policies: El Salvador," Washington, D.C.: Interdisciplinary Communications Program, Smithsonian Institution, May 1974, p. 15.

population continued to produce a younger age distribution between 1961 and 1971. The rural dependency ratio increased substantially, from 99 to 112, during this period.

As is true in other Latin American nations, a greater proportion of females than of males migrate from rural to urban areas. The percentage of females living in urban areas in 1971 increased more steeply by age group than the male percentage (Figure 17). The urban residence ratio (URR) for females peaks earlier and at a higher level than the male ratio. The decline in the URR between ages 20-24 and 35-39 is much less pronounced for females than for males. After age 40 the females URR increased steadily while the male ratio shows only a slight in-

**Figure 17**
**Urban Residence Ratios by Age and Sex, El Salvador, 1971.**

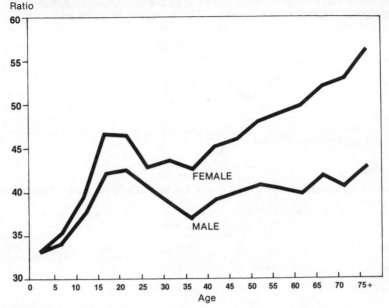

**Figure 18**
**Sex Ratios by Age Group for the Total, Urban and Rural**
**Populations of El Salvador, 1971.**

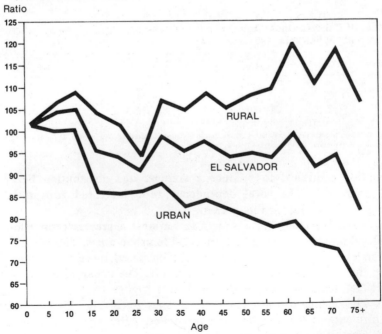

92

crease. The observed decline in the URR for each sex between the approximate ages of 25 and 40 could result from each younger cohort being more urban at each age than the older cohorts. However, it is more likely that the major cause of the decline is that some persons of both sexes return to rural areas after a period in the cities. The return might be prompted by the completion of one's education, failure to find employment, or the accumulation of a desired amount of savings.

The number of males per 100 females in the urban and rural population (Figure 18) also demonstrates the greater urbanization of females. The sharp drop in the sex ratio between ages 15 and 30 in El Salvador indicates a greater underenumeration of males than of females between these ages.

## Occupational Structure, Labor Force Participation, by Age and Sex

In 1961, some 807,092 persons comprised the labor force of El Salvador—or 47.6 per cent of the population 10 years of age and older. This number represents 32.1 per cent of the total population of the country. Modification of the dependency ratio from one which simply states the relationship between those in various age groupings to one that considers the working vs. non-working population, yields an index number of 211—or roughly two dependents per each person in the labor force. Children under 10 numbered 815,211, or 33 per cent of the national population. The next largest category of "economic inactives" consists of "personas al cuidado del hogar", a group comprised of 611,082 females—essentially housewives.

For the male population of El Salvador the occupational structure is of particular interest because of the very high proportion engaged in agriculture. A comparison between El Salvador, Costa Rica, Panama, and Guatemala appears in Table 71. The census years represented vary considerably, but there is comparability on key points; only males over 10 are considered in each case, and the sub-categories comprising the agriculture sector are identical (farm owner-operators, agricultural workers, farm machine operators, etc.). Only Guatemala, with 63 per

Table 71

**Percentage of Males in the Labor Force Engaged in Agricultural Activities**

| Country | Percentage |
|---|---|
| El Salvador (1961) | 70% |
| Costa Rica (1973) | 43% |
| Guatemala (1973) | 63% |
| Panama (1970) | 49% |

Source: Population Census volumes for each country.

**Table 72**

**Rural to Urban Percentage Shift for 10 Latin American Countries, 1960 and Projected to 1980**[a]

| | 1960<br>Percent Urban | 1980<br>Percent Urban | Net Urban Increase<br>1960–1980 |
|---|---|---|---|
| Country | | | |
| El Salvador | 19 | 23 | + 4 |
| Argentina | 60 | 71 | +11 |
| Brazil | 31 | 47 | +16 |
| Chile | 50 | 65 | +15 |
| Costa Rica | 26 | 31 | + 5 |
| Guatemala | 16 | 23 | + 7 |
| Mexico | 52 | 62 | +10 |
| Panama | 40 | 51 | +11 |
| Peru | 31 | 48 | +17 |
| Venezuela | 53 | 69 | +16 |

[a] "Urban" is considered to be the population in cities of 20,000 and more inhabitants as reported by each country in the 1970 census reports. The population of those *same cities* were then traced back to 1960, and their projected population traced forward to 1980. In two cases, Costa Rica and Guatemala because of irregular census years, census totals are interpolated for 1960, based on 1950–63 and 1950–64 rates of increase, respectively.

Source: The respective country chapters in this study, and Fox, Robert W., *Urban Population Growth Trends in Latin America*, Inter-American Development Bank, Washington, D.C., 1975.

cent and a very large rural indigenous population, is in the same range with El Salvador at 70 per cent.

The new census volume is expected to reveal a decline in proportional (not absolute) terms of males in agriculturally-related activities. Confirmation of a decline and its magnitude is of vital interest because of the very high male proportion already engaged in agriculture in 1961 in combination with three other known elements. First, El Salvador has the highest population density of all Latin American countries. This is estimated for 1974 at 487 persons per square mile and compares with 23 persons for Argentina, 52 for Colombia, 127 for Guatemala, 39 for Nicaragua, and 421 for Haiti, its nearest competitor. Second, new agricultural frontiers simply do not exist in El Salvador. Even the most casual observer will note while flying over the country that virtually all land suitable for agriculture is presently under cultivation. But third, of all countries studied, El Salvador shows and is projecting the highest rural population increases. By rural is meant all population *outside* cities and towns of 20,000 and more inhabitants.

The rural population percentage increase observed and projected for El Salvador (1961–80) is 82 per cent; for Brazil, 34 per cent; Mexico, 53 per cent; Peru, 29 per cent; Venezuela, 29 per cent; Panama, 47 per cent; and Guatemala, 58 per cent. Only Costa Rica, where a 76 per cent rural increase is expected for the 1960–80 interval, approaches the Salvadorean level, but in this country the pressures on available farmland are much less severe. In Argentina and Chile, incidentally, rural population numbers have and are projected to continue to remain stable in *absolute terms*.

Thus, given a rapid build-up of rural population pressures in what is a very small and crowded country, and a projected national growth rate yielding extraordinarily high population totals of 3.5 million in 1971, 4.8 million in 1980 and 8.8 million by 2000, a search for possible rural remedies takes on considerable importance. Two alternatives besides a rapid reduction in fertility are rapid urbanization in order to drain off The redundant rural labor force to the cities, and occupational diversification away from agricultural pursuits among males in the rural areas. The first alternative can be dismissed rather quickly, because a rapid, or even moderate pace of urbanization, is simply not occurring in El Salvador. Table 72, which presents data on the transition from rural to urban-based societies in the ten Latin American countries thus far studied, shows that the percentage gain of the urban over the rural sector (1960 and projected to 1980) is least in El Salvador.

The other alternative is implicit in a phenomenon taking place throughout Latin America in varying degrees which, as yet, has received little attention: greater numbers of rural males who leave farming or never begin farming in the first place are acquiring other occupational skills. Except for a few countries, the extent of this has not been quantified. Reliable information is available for Costa Rica that may provide a basis for a later comparison with El Salvador, since the urbanization trends for both countries are quite similar. In the 1963–1973 interval, the number of rural Costa Rican males engaged in agriculture increased from 179,613 to 195,273—a jump of just 9 per cent. But in the industrial categories there is a remarkable gain from 50,063 to 102,246 rural males, or an increase of 104 per cent. The industrial categories include mining and quarry exploitation; manufacturing industries; electricity, gas and water related; construction; commerce, restaurants and hotels; transportation, communications, and storage; financial establishments, insurance, and real estate; and classifications pertaining to the provision of community and social services.

The question to be answered by the as yet unpublished volume of El Salvador's census is whether this same trend has developed in the rural sector of that country since 1961.

Labor force participation rates in 1961 by age and sex, and separately for the urban and rural sectors, are shown in Figure 19. The pattern for urban and rural males is quite similar to those in Costa Rica and Panama. Rural males participate in greater numbers in the labor force than do their urban counterparts, and they remain in it longer. For El Salvador, the proportions of urban females by age group in the work force are similar to the Costa Rican and Panamanian experience, but

**Figure 19**
**Economically active population, urban and rural,
by sex, in El Salvador, 1961.**

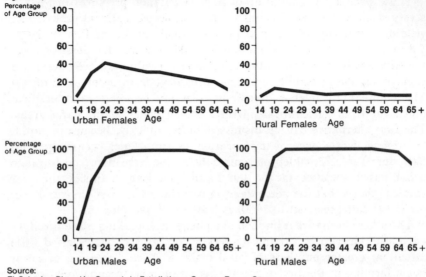

Source:
El Salvador, Dirección General de Estadística y Censos, *Tercer Censo
Nacional de Población, 1961,* San Salvador, 1965. Table 20.

rural participation rates, low in the two aforementioned countries, are even lower in El Salvador.

Information on specific occupations for urban vs. rural males and females unfortunately is not available from the 1961 census report. This added disaggregation is expected in the new document and will permit a close examination of the occupational *roles* that have developed in the republic for both men and women.

**Population Projections**

The total population of urbanized areas in El Salvador is projected to the years 1980, 1990, and 2000 by allocating the projected national population first to departments then to urbanized areas using the ratio-trend methodology as elaborated by Jerome P. Pickard.[1] Since this method progresses from a population projection for the country as a whole, to regional projections and to urbanized area projections, it is termed a "step-down" system. The detailed projection methodology is explained on pages 207–11.

---

[1]Pickard, *Dimensions to Metropolitanism,* pp. 53–56.

## National Projection

The population of El Salvador has been projected to the year 2000 by CELADE (Table 73). This projection is based on the age and sex distribution of the 1961 census but takes into account the total population figure reported by the census of 1971. As was mentioned earlier the crude birth rate of the CELADE series closely parallels that recorded by the vital registration system. The CELADE total population figure for 1971 implies an underenumeration of 2.1 per cent by the census of that year.

The CELADE projection is based on the assumption that the total fertility rate will decline by 29 per cent from 6.19 in 1970-75 to 4.39 in 1995-2000 and that life expectancy at birth will increase by 20 per cent from 57.83 years in 1970-75 to 69.25 years in 1995-2000. The decline in mortality will offset the gradual fertility decline, so that the growth rate of the population will remain at its 1970-75 level until 1990 (Table 73).

According to the CELADE projection, the population of El Salvador in the year 2000 will be 2.5 times as large as the 1970 total. The decline in both fertility and mortality would produce a population in 2000 with approximately the age structure of the urban population in 1971. The population at the end of the century would be 41.3 per cent in the ages 0-14, 55.2 per cent in the ages 15-64, and 3.5 per cent ages 65 and above (compare with Table 66). The dependency ratio would be reduced from 100 in 1971 to 81 in the year 2000. Net international migration is assumed to be negligible.

## Department Projections

The population of each department is projected to mid-year 1980, 1990, and 2000 by continuing the trend of the ratio of each department's population to the national population observed for 1950, 1961, and 1971.

Table 73

**Projected Population, Crude Birth Rate, Crude Death Rate, and Rate of Increase; El Salvador; 1970 to 2000**

| Period | Population at beginning of period (in thousands) | Crude birth rate | Crude death rate | Average annual rate of increase (%) |
|--------|--------------------------------------------------|------------------|------------------|-------------------------------------|
| 1970-1975 | 3,516 | 42.2 | 11.1 | 3.11 |
| 1975-1980 | 4,108 | 41.1 | 9.5 | 3.16 |
| 1980-1985 | 4,813 | 40.0 | 8.2 | 3.18 |
| 1985-1990 | 5,643 | 38.3 | 7.2 | 3.11 |
| 1990-1995 | 6,595 | 36.1 | 6.3 | 2.97 |
| 1995-2000 | 7,654 | 33.5 | 5.6 | 2.79 |
| 2000 | 8,803 | | | |

Source: Centro Latinoamericano de Demografía (CELADE), *Boletín Demográfico* 7:13 (January 1974).

The projection results are shown in Table 75. The department of San Salvador is projected to increase its dominance by reaching one million by 1980 and 2.3 million in the year 2000. Its percentage of the national population is expected to increase from 20.6 in 1971 to 26.4 in 2000. San Miguel department is projected to surpass Santa Ana by 2000. At the end of the century, seven of El Salvador's 13 departments are projected to contain over a half million inhabitants, but only San Salvador will exceed one million.

Between 1971 and 2000 the department of San Salvador and La Union are projected to grow at rates above the national average (Table 76). La Libertad, La Paz, and Sonsonate are expected to increase at near the national rate, while the remaining departments would grow at lower rates.

### Urban Population Growth

The urban population discussed in prior sections is that defined by the *Dirección General de Estadística y Censos*. By the national definition 1,405,544 persons, or 39.5 per cent of the total population, lived in urban areas in 1971. The following sections examine population projections for the major urbanized areas of El Salvador under a different definition of "urbanized area" which includes only cities of 10,000 or more inhabitants in 1971. The urbanized area of San Salvador is comprised of the urban population (as defined for each census) of the ten municipalities which constitute the metropolitan area of San Salvador. These municipalities are San Salvador, Mejicanos, Soyapango, Delgado, Cuscatancingo, Ayutextepeque, Ilopango and San Marcos in the Department of San Salvador; and Nueva San Salvador and Antiguo Cuscatlan in the Department of La Libertad. The municipality of San Salvador is considered to be 95, 97, and 99 per cent urban in 1950,

Table 74

**Enumerated and Projected Population of El Salvador, Thirteen Urbanized Areas, and Non-urbanized Areas, 1950 to 2000**

| | | Thirteen urbanized areas[a] | | Non-urbanized areas | |
|---|---|---|---|---|---|
| Year | El Salvador | Population in thousands | Per cent of total | Population in thousands | Per cent of total |
| 1950 | 1,855.9 | 385.8 | 20.8 | 1,470.1 | 79.2 |
| 1961 | 2,511.0 | 583.7 | 23.2 | 1,927.3 | 76.8 |
| 1971 | 3,549.3 | 908.9 | 25.6 | 2,640.4 | 74.4 |
| 1980 | 4,812.7 | 1,329.8 | 27.6 | 3,482.9 | 72.4 |
| 1990 | 6,594.7 | 1,969.2 | 29.9 | 4,625.5 | 70.1 |
| 2000 | 8,802.7 | 2,820.4 | 32.0 | 5,982.3 | 68.0 |

[a] The thirteen urbanized areas included are listed in Table 75.

Source: Table 75.

1961, and 1971, respectively.[1] There are twelve other cities of 10,000 or more inhabitants. The population of each of these cities is the urban population of its respective municipality as reported for each census.

The total population of the thirteen urbanized areas in 1971 was 908,900, or 25.6 per cent of the national population (Table 74). The population of all urbanized areas as enumerated by the last three censuses is presented in Table 75. San Salvador is a primate city among El Salvador's cities. The San Salvador urbanized area is 5.7 times as large as Santa Ana; and 2.9 times the size of Santa Ana, San Miguel, and Sonsonate added together. Sixteen per cent of the national population lives in the San Salvador urbanized area. No other city exceeded 100,000 population in 1971, although Santa Ana has passed that mark by now. The third largest city, San Miguel, had 61,900 people, and Sonsonate 33,300 in 1971. San Salvador grew the most rapidly of the four largest urbanized areas between 1961 and 1971—at a rate of 4.9 per cent a year (Table 76). San Miguel grew 4.3 per cent; Sonsonate increased at the same rate as the national population (3.4 per cent); and Santa Ana grew at a rate of 3.0 per cent a year.

Following the four largest cities is a group of seven cities of similar size, all between 16 and 20 thousand population at the 1971 census. The fastest-growing of these during the 1961–71 period were Cojutepeque (5.5 per cent a year) and Usulutan (4.6 per cent). San Vicente (1.8 per cent) and Ahuachapan (2.0 per cent) werc the slowest-growing. Among the smaller cities, Acajutla increased at a rate of 10.1 per cent a year from a small base of 3,700 in 1961.

The growth of the population of El Salvador, the thirteen urbanized areas listed in Table 75, non-urbanized areas, (essentially rural), and the urbanized area of San Salvador is graphed in Figure 20. Although the urban population as defined here is increasing at a greater rate than the non-urban population, the latter is growing by a larger number annually. The true rate of increase of the urbanized population is underrepresented by Figure 20 because of the use of a cohort of urbanized areas which excludes growth due to the reclassification of other areas to urbanized areas.

## Urbanized Area Projections

The projected population of the 13 urbanized areas with over 10,000 population in 1973 is presented in Table 75. Although the population of these areas, collectively, is projected to more than triple from 909,000

---

[1] El Salvador, Dirección General de Estadística y Censos, "Comentarios acerca del Volumen y Comportamiento de la Población Urbana del Area Metropolitana de El Salvador, Para los Años 1950, 1961, 1971, y 30 de agosto de 1974", (mimeo), San Salvador, 1974.

# Table 75

## Enumerated and Projected Population of Departments and Urbanized Areas in El Salvador, 1950 to 2000

| Department and Urbanized Area | Enumerated Population in thousands | | | Projected Population in thousands (midyear) | | |
|---|---|---|---|---|---|---|
| | June 13 1950 | May 2 1961 | June 27 1971 | 1980 | 1990 | 2000 |
| National Total | 1,855.9 | 2,511.0 | 3,549.3 | 4,812.7 | 6,594.7 | 8,802.7 |
| **Ahuachapán** | **94.6** | **130.7** | **179.8** | **241.9** | **327.8** | **432.3** |
| Ahuachapán | 10.3 | 13.3 | 16.3 | 20.3 | 25.0 | 30.1 |
| Remainder | 84.4 | 117.4 | 163.5 | 221.7 | 302.7 | 402.1 |
| **Cabañas** | **77.6** | **94.6** | **129.2** | **165.9** | **214.3** | **269.4** |
| **Cuscatlán** | **90.1** | **113.0** | **152.2** | **195.9** | **253.4** | **319.0** |
| Cojutepeque | 10.0 | 11.4 | 20.0 | 28.0 | 39.8 | 54.7 |
| Remainder | 80.1 | 101.6 | 132.2 | 167.9 | 213.5 | 264.3 |
| **Chalatenango** | **105.9** | **129.9** | **172.1** | **218.0** | **277.0** | **342.6** |
| **La Libertad** | **144.0** | **203.5** | **282.8** | **385.4** | **529.4** | **707.9** |
| Antiguo Cuscatlán Nueva San Salvador[a] | 19.7 | 28.6 | 41.4 | 58.2 | 82.5 | 113.7 |
| Quezaltepeque | 6.4 | 9.4 | 12.6 | 17.1 | 23.3 | 30.8 |
| Remainder | 117.9 | 165.5 | 228.7 | 310.1 | 423.7 | 563.4 |
| **La Paz** | **96.8** | **130.7** | **184.4** | **249.4** | **340.5** | **452.6** |
| Zacatecoluca | 9.2 | 12.2 | 16.8 | 22.2 | 29.6 | 38.5 |
| Remainder | 87.7 | 118.4 | 167.7 | 227.2 | 310.9 | 414.1 |
| **La Unión** | **109.7** | **148.1** | **220.0** | **305.3** | **429.3** | **587.2** |
| La Unión | 7.9 | 11.4 | 17.2 | 24.6 | 35.6 | 50.1 |
| Remainder | 101.8 | 136.7 | 202.8 | 280.7 | 393.7 | 537.2 |
| **Morazán** | **96.7** | **119.4** | **158.0** | **200.4** | **255.0** | **315.8** |
| **San Miguel** | **171.2** | **231.8** | **323.0** | **434.5** | **589.3** | **778.0** |
| San Miguel | 26.7 | 39.9 | 61.9 | 89.9 | 131.7 | 186.6 |
| Remainder | 144.5 | 191.9 | 261.1 | 344.6 | 457.6 | 591.3 |
| **San Salvador** | **296.5** | **463.2** | **731.7** | **1,081.7** | **1,614.1** | **2,323.7** |
| San Salvador[b] | 193.6 | 316.0 | 523.5 | 799.6 | 1,232.5 | 1,825.5 |
| Remainder | 102.8 | 147.2 | 208.2 | 282.1 | 381.7 | 498.1 |
| San Salvador Metropolitan Area[c] | 213.4 | 344.6 | 565.0 | 857.8 | 1,315.0 | 1,939.3 |
| **San Vicente** | **87.6** | **112.9** | **156.2** | **205.9** | **273.3** | **353.2** |
| San Vicente | 11.0 | 15.4 | 18.5 | 23.3 | 29.1 | 35.5 |
| Remainder | 76.6 | 97.5 | 137.8 | 182.6 | 244.2 | 317.7 |
| **Santa Ana** | **202.5** | **259.2** | **333.0** | **421.2** | **533.0** | **656.5** |
| Chalchuapa | 9.9 | 13.3 | 18.9 | 25.4 | 34.2 | 44.8 |
| Santa Ana | 51.7 | 72.8 | 98.4 | 131.1 | 174.8 | 225.9 |
| Remainder | 140.9 | 173.0 | 215.7 | 264.7 | 324.0 | 385.9 |
| **Sonsonate** | **120.3** | **166.9** | **233.6** | **317.6** | **435.4** | **581.1** |
| Ajacutla | 2.0 | 3.7 | 10.3 | 17.6 | 30.4 | 48.8 |
| Sonsonate | 17.9 | 23.7 | 33.3 | 44.7 | 60.4 | 79.6 |
| Remainder | 100.4 | 139.6 | 190.0 | 255.2 | 344.6 | 452.8 |
| **Usulután** | **162.3** | **207.1** | **293.3** | **389.8** | **523.0** | **683.3** |
| Usulután | 9.5 | 12.5 | 19.8 | 28.0 | 40.1 | 55.8 |
| Remainder | 152.9 | 194.6 | 273.5 | 361.8 | 482.9 | 627.4 |

[a] The combined urban population of Antiguo Cuscatlán and Nueva San Salvador are included in the San Salvador Metropolitan Area.
[b] The total urban population of the municipios of San Salvador, Mejicano, Soyapongo, Delgado, Cuscatancingo, Ayutuxtepeque, Ilopango, and San Marcos.
[c] The San Salvador Metropolitan Area is comprised of population in the departments of both San Salvador (note b) and La Libertad (note a).

100

# Table 76

## Observed and Projected Population Growth Rates of Departments and Urbanized Areas in El Salvador, 1950 to 2000

| Department and Urbanized Area | Average Annual Growth Rate (%) of Enumerated Population | | Average Annual Growth Rate (%) of Projected Population | | |
|---|---|---|---|---|---|
| | 1950–1961 | 1961–1971 | 1971–1980 | 1980–1990 | 1990–2000 |
| National Total | 2.78 | 3.41 | 3.38 | 3.15 | 2.89 |
| Ahuachapán | 2.97 | 3.14 | 3.29 | 3.04 | 2.77 |
| Ahuachapán | 2.33 | 2.05 | 2.39 | 2.12 | 1.85 |
| Remainder | 3.04 | 3.26 | 3.38 | 3.12 | 2.84 |
| Cabañas | 1.82 | 3.07 | 2.77 | 2.56 | 2.29 |
| Cuscatlán | 2.08 | 2.93 | 2.80 | 2.57 | 2.30 |
| Cojutepeque | 1.20 | 5.53 | 3.72 | 3.53 | 3.17 |
| Remainder | 2.19 | 2.59 | 2.65 | 2.40 | 2.13 |
| Chalatenango | 1.88 | 2.77 | 2.62 | 2.40 | 2.13 |
| La Libertad | 3.18 | 3.24 | 3.44 | 3.18 | 2.91 |
| Antiguo Cuscatlán Nueva San Salvador[a] | 3.42 | 3.65 | 3.76 | 3.49 | 3.21 |
| Quezaltepeque | 3.48 | 2.91 | 3.37 | 3.08 | 2.81 |
| Remainder | 3.12 | 3.19 | 3.38 | 3.12 | 2.85 |
| La Paz | 2.75 | 3.39 | 3.35 | 3.11 | 2.84 |
| Zacatecoluca | 2.63 | 3.10 | 3.13 | 2.88 | 2.61 |
| Remainder | 2.76 | 3.42 | 3.37 | 3.14 | 2.87 |
| La Unión | 2.76 | 3.90 | 3.63 | 3.41 | 3.13 |
| La Unión | 3.41 | 4.02 | 3.96 | 3.70 | 3.42 |
| Remainder | 2.70 | 3.89 | 3.61 | 3.38 | 3.11 |
| Morazán | 1.93 | 2.76 | 2.64 | 2.41 | 2.14 |
| San Miguel | 2.78 | 3.27 | 3.29 | 3.05 | 2.78 |
| San Miguel | 3.70 | 4.32 | 4.13 | 3.82 | 3.48 |
| Remainder | 2.60 | 3.03 | 3.08 | 2.83 | 2.56 |
| San Salvador | 4.10 | 4.50 | 4.34 | 4.00 | 3.64 |
| San Salvador[b] | 4.50 | 4.97 | 4.70 | 4.33 | 3.93 |
| Remainder | 3.30 | 3.41 | 3.37 | 3.02 | 2.66 |
| San Salvador Urbanized Area[c] | 4.40 | 4.89 | 4.63 | 4.27 | 3.89 |
| San Vicente | 2.33 | 3.20 | 3.06 | 2.83 | 2.51 |
| San Vicente | 3.15 | 1.76 | 2.57 | 2.25 | 1.98 |
| Remainder | 2.21 | 3.41 | 3.13 | 2.91 | 2.63 |
| Santa Ana | 2.27 | 2.47 | 2.61 | 2.35 | 2.08 |
| Chalchuapa | 2.78 | 3.41 | 3.29 | 3.00 | 2.69 |
| Santa Ana | 3.15 | 2.97 | 3.18 | 2.87 | 2.56 |
| Remainder | 1.88 | 2.17 | 2.27 | 2.02 | 1.75 |
| Sonsonate | 3.01 | 3.31 | 3.41 | 3.16 | 2.89 |
| Ajacutla | 5.56 | 10.14 | 6.02 | 5.44 | 4.72 |
| Sonsonate | 2.54 | 3.36 | 3.26 | 3.02 | 2.75 |
| Remainder | 3.03 | 3.04 | 3.27 | 3.00 | 2.73 |
| Usulután | 2.23 | 3.43 | 3.16 | 2.94 | 2.67 |
| Usulután | 2.52 | 4.55 | 3.84 | 3.61 | 3.30 |
| Remainder | 2.22 | 3.35 | 3.10 | 2.89 | 2.62 |

[a] The combined urban populations of Antiguo Cuscatlán and Nueva San Salvador are included in the San Salvador Urbanized Area.
[b] The total urban population of the municipios of San Salvador, Mejicano, Soyapango, Delgado, Cuscatançingo, Ayutuxtepeque, Ilopango, and San Marcos.
[c] The San Salvador Urbanized Area is comprised of population in the departments of both San Salvador (note b) and La Libertad (note a).

Source: Table 75.

in 1971 to 2.8 million in the year 2000, the rate of urbanization in El Salvador is quite moderate. The population of these urbanized areas increased from 20.8 to only 25.6 per cent of the national total between 1950 and 1971. These projections indicate that the 13 urbanized areas will comprise 32.0 per cent of the national population in the year 2000 (Table 74). The projected rate of increase of the urbanized population is 3.9 per cent a year between 1971 and 2000, compared with a rate of 2.8 per cent for the remainder.

The projection for the urbanized area of San Salvador shows that it will increase by a factor of 3.4 between 1971 and 2000, when it will reach 1.9 million and will represent 22 per cent of the national total and over two-thirds (69 per cent) of the urbanized area population. San Salvador is projected to be the fastest-growing city through the year 2000 (Table 76), when it is expected to be 8.6 times the size of Santa Ana and 2.9 times as large as Santa Ana, San Miguel, and Sonsonate combined. Only these four cities will have over 75,000 people in 2000.

The nine smaller urbanized areas are projected to have populations of between 30 and 56 thousand in the year 2000, with Usulutan's population equalling 55,800 and Cojutepeque's 54,700. The growth of the larger urbanized areas may be at the expense of the smaller ones as well as the non-urbanized areas. The urbanized populations of Ahuachapan, Quezaltepeque, Zacatecoluca, and San Vicente are projected to increase at lower rates than the non-urbanized, or rural, populations of their respective departments.

The indicated future populations of the urbanized areas are conservative because of the method of projection. Since the projected population of an urbanized area is determined by the trend of that area's proportion of its department's population during the latest two intercensal periods, the projected rate of urbanization in El Salvador is dependent on the moderate pace of urbanization experienced between 1950 and 1971. Should the speed of urbanization increase during the remainder of this century, these projections will understate city populations.

From the projections presented in Table 75 three general conclusions regarding future population growth in El Salvador can be drawn: (1) national population growth will average above 3 per cent a year for the remainder of the century, reaching 8.8 million by the year 2000; (2) the proportion of the population living in the 13 largest urbanized areas will increase moderately to 32 per cent in 2000; and (3) the San Salvador urbanized area will increase its dominance over the other cities, and contain 22 per cent of El Salvador's population by the end of the century.

**Figure 20.**
**Enumerated and projected population of El Salvador,**
**thirteen urbanized areas, non-urbanized areas, and**
**San Salvador; 1950 to 2000.**
Population
in thousands

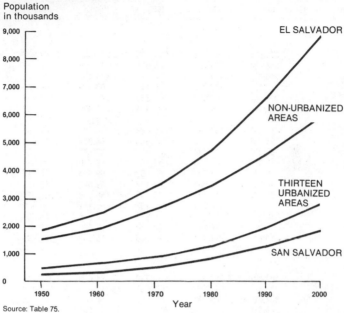

Source: Table 75.

## Appendix A

## El Salvador: Population projections by sex and quinquennial age groups, 1975-2000. Recommended hypothesis.

| Age Groups | Year | | | | | |
|---|---|---|---|---|---|---|
| | 1975 | 1980 | 1985 | 1990 | 1995 | 2000 |
| | | | males | | | |
| **Total** | **2,066.803** | **2,420.409** | **2,838.067** | **3,317.040** | **3,850.838** | **4,430.082** |
| 0- 4 | 371.353 | 430.967 | 499.127 | 565.913 | 627.833 | 680.377 |
| 5- 9 | 317.914 | 359.533 | 419.952 | 488.670 | 557.463 | 619.207 |
| 10-14 | 277.135 | 311.104 | 352.712 | 412.775 | 481.159 | 550.400 |
| 15-19 | 226.298 | 272.077 | 306.055 | 347.535 | 407.326 | 475.496 |
| 20-24 | 178.741 | 222.541 | 268.200 | 302.257 | 343.941 | 403.897 |
| 25-29 | 142.317 | 175.640 | 219.303 | 264.781 | 299.014 | 340.828 |
| 30-34 | 112.431 | 139.062 | 172.220 | 215.599 | 260.963 | 295.405 |
| 35-39 | 99.156 | 109.431 | 135.897 | 168.812 | 211.947 | 257.247 |
| 40-44 | 80.781 | 95.684 | 106.103 | 132.245 | 164.851 | 207.666 |
| 45-49 | 66.559 | 77.085 | 91.799 | 102.219 | 127.917 | 160.071 |
| 50-54 | 55.562 | 62.667 | 73.017 | 87.362 | 97.723 | 122.817 |
| 55-59 | 43.046 | 51.488 | 58.462 | 68.472 | 82.411 | 92.779 |
| 60-64 | 32.739 | 39.260 | 47.459 | 54.374 | 64.290 | 77.406 |
| 65-69 | 25.939 | 29.214 | 35.114 | 42.545 | 48.909 | 57.894 |
| 70-74 | 16.881 | 21.758 | 24.509 | 29.464 | 35.705 | 41.051 |
| 75-79 | 11.341 | 12.560 | 16.215 | 18.295 | 22.029 | 26.737 |
| 80+ | 8.610 | 10.338 | 11.923 | 14.722 | 17.357 | 20.804 |

103

**Appendix A cont.**

| Age Groups | Year | | | | | |
|---|---|---|---|---|---|---|
| | 1975 | 1980 | 1985 | 1990 | 1995 | 2000 |

|   | | | females | | | |
|---|---|---|---|---|---|---|
| **Total** | **2,041.599** | **2,392.279** | **2,805.073** | **3,277.635** | **3,802.907** | **4,372.569** |
| 0– 4 | 358.484 | 415.728 | 480.578 | 545.045 | 602.617 | 652.397 |
| 5– 9 | 310.332 | 350.357 | 408.531 | 474.153 | 539.262 | 597.170 |
| 10–14 | 272.523 | 305.252 | 345.445 | 403.519 | 469.535 | 535.638 |
| 15–19 | 221.814 | 268.902 | 301.839 | 342.129 | 400.254 | 466.408 |
| 20–24 | 175.119 | 219.276 | 266.444 | 299.606 | 340.189 | 398.609 |
| 25–29 | 140.727 | 172.953 | 217.136 | 264.389 | 297.871 | 338.767 |
| 30–34 | 111.999 | 138.546 | 170.789 | 214.921 | 262.290 | 296.119 |
| 35–39 | 98.862 | 109.492 | 135.930 | 168.021 | 211.990 | 259.381 |
| 40–44 | 80.853 | 95.738 | 106.457 | 132.570 | 164.353 | 207.958 |
| 45–49 | 66.372 | 77.478 | 92.124 | 102.770 | 128.386 | 159.659 |
| 50–54 | 56.313 | 62.900 | 73.762 | 88.023 | 98.545 | 123.540 |
| 55–59 | 44.139 | 52.636 | 59.117 | 69.627 | 83.445 | 93.813 |
| 60–64 | 34.068 | 40.594 | 48.749 | 55.058 | 65.227 | 76.427 |
| 65–69 | 27.461 | 30.813 | 37.193 | 45.171 | 51.243 | 60.975 |
| 70–74 | 18.617 | 23.893 | 26.919 | 32.616 | 39.764 | 45.278 |
| 75–79 | 13.285 | 14.812 | 19.034 | 21.462 | 26.031 | 31.768 |
| 80+ | 10.631 | 12.904 | 15.026 | 18.555 | 21.905 | 26.365 |

|   | | | both sexes | | | |
|---|---|---|---|---|---|---|
| **Total** | **4,108.402** | **4,812.688** | **5,643.140** | **6,594.675** | **7,653.745** | **8,802.651** |
| 0– 4 | 729.837 | 846.695 | 979.705 | 1,111.958 | 1,230.450 | 1,332.774 |
| 5– 9 | 628.246 | 709.890 | 828.483 | 962.823 | 1,096.725 | 1,216.377 |
| 10–14 | 549.658 | 616.356 | 698.157 | 816.294 | 950.694 | 1,086.038 |
| 15–19 | 448.112 | 540.979 | 607.894 | 689.664 | 807.580 | 941.904 |
| 20–24 | 353.860 | 441.817 | 534.644 | 601.863 | 684.130 | 802.506 |
| 25–29 | 233.044 | 348.593 | 436.439 | 529.170 | 596.885 | 679.595 |
| 30–34 | 224.430 | 277.608 | 343.009 | 430.520 | 523.253 | 591.524 |
| 35–39 | 198.018 | 218.923 | 271.827 | 336.833 | 423.937 | 516.628 |
| 40–44 | 161.634 | 191.422 | 212.560 | 264.815 | 329.204 | 415.624 |
| 45–49 | 132.931 | 154.563 | 183.923 | 204.989 | 256.303 | 319.730 |
| 50–54 | 111.875 | 125.567 | 146.779 | 175.385 | 196.268 | 246.357 |
| 55•59 | 87.185 | 104.124 | 117.579 | 138.099 | 165.856 | 186.592 |
| 60–64 | 66.807 | 79.854 | 96.208 | 109.432 | 129.517 | 156.130 |
| 65–69 | 53.400 | 60.027 | 72.307 | 87.716 | 100.152 | 118.869 |
| 70–74 | 35.498 | 45.656 | 51.428 | 62.080 | 75.469 | 86.329 |
| 75–79 | 24.626 | 27.372 | 35.249 | 39.757 | 48.060 | 58.505 |
| 80+ | 19.241 | 23.242 | 26.949 | 33.277 | 39.262 | 47.169 |

Source: CELADE, Boletín Demográfico 7:13 (January 1974), Table 2, p. 22.

# GUATEMALA

Guatemala has the largest population of the Central American nations. Its capital, Guatemala City, is the most populous city in the region, and its total urban population (by census definition) exceeds that of the other countries, although the percentage of the population living in cities of 10,000 and more inhabitants—about 25 per cent—is the second lowest, after Honduras.

In this study the Guatemalan data base was adjusted upward for the census years 1950, 1964, and 1973 in order to account for underenumerations. Had these undercounts been slight and more or less of equal magnitude, they could have been overlooked or a standard factor applied to bring the data into line with population estimates available from United Nations sources. But it was determined that the undercounts varied widely—7.1, 3.5, and 8.2 per cent, respectively—for each of the three census years.

Use of the original data would have led to the mistaken conclusion that the rate of population growth in Guatemala has slowed considerably between the two intercensal periods, dropping from an average annual level of 3.1 per cent (1950–64) to a rate of 2.2 per cent (1964–73). With the necessary adjustments, it turns out that the rate of population growth in Guatemala has remained stable, averaging 2.77 per cent throughout the 1950–1973 period.

The February 4, 1976 earthquake that devastated Guatemala claimed more than 24,000 lives. Entire towns in the central highlands were leveled, including Mixco, a suburb of Guatemala City, Zacatepequez, and Chimaltenango, a town midway between Guatemala City and Lake

Atitlan. It has not been possible in this study to take into account the effects of the earthquake, but since towns are rebuilding on the earlier sites, in the long run they should resume their former growth patterns.

## Growth Rate

The enumerated total population of Guatemala as reported by the General Bureau of Statistics (*Dirección General de Estadística*) for censuses since 1778, including the five censuses of this century, and the implied annual rates of growth are presented in Table 77. Collver states that the published population totals for 1893 through 1940 were "corrected" upward to correspond to the growth calculated on the basis of the registered increase.[1] He argues, however, that births were completely registered and that deaths were badly underregistered, hence the adjustments exaggerated the actual population totals. Collver concludes that the corrections were unwarranted and that the original census totals were reliable.

The 1940 figure has been corrected by about 900,000 "for a capricious alteration of the results."[2] Camisa estimates that the 1950 population was actually 3,005,700 at the census date and the 1964 population was 4,444,900. These estimates imply that the census underenumerated

Table 77

Guatemala: Enumerated Populations as Reported by the General Bureau of Statistics and by Collver, and Intercensal Growth Rates, 1778 to 1973.

| Date of Census | Reported by General Bureau of Statistics | | Reported by Collver | |
|---|---|---|---|---|
| | Population | Growth Rate | Population | Growth Rate |
| 1778 | 396,149 | — | — | — |
| 1880 | 1,224,602 | 1.11 | 1,224,602 | — |
| February 26, 1893 | 1,501,145 | 1.57 | 1,364,678 | 0.83 |
| August 28, 1921 | 2,004,900 | 1.02 | 1,743,391 | 0.86 |
| April 7, 1940 | 2,400,000 | 0.97 | 2,300,000 | 1.49 |
| April 18, 1950 | 2,790,868 | 1.50 | 2,790,868 | 1.93 |
| April 18, 1964 | 4,287,997 | 3.07 | — | — |
| March 26, 1973 | 5,211,929 | 2.18 | — | — |

Note: Collver argues that the published population totals of 1893 through 1940 were unnecessarily adjusted upward on the basis of increases shown by vital registration, but that the registration data were in fact in error.

Sources: Guatemala, Dirección General de Estadística, *VIII Censo de Población y III de Habitación. Población* (Cifras Preliminares), Series I, vol. 1, Guatemala City, September 1973, p. 9.

O. Andrew Collver, *Birth Rates in Latin America: New Estimates of Historical Trends and Fluctuations.* University of California, Berkeley, 1965, p. 125.

---

[1] Collver, *Birth Rates in Latin America,* p. 124.
[2] Guatemala, Dirección General de Estadística, *VII Censo de Población, 1964,* Vol. 1, Guatemala City, 1971, p. 5.

106

the population by 7.1 and 3.5 per cent, respectively, in 1950 and 1964.[1] The estimate for 1964 is based on the results of the Post-Enumeration Survey. The adjusted 1950 census population was derived by reverse survival of the 1964 adjusted age-sex distribution.

An analyst at the U.S. Bureau of the Census estimates the 1973 population to be 5,678,455, which implies an undercount of 8.2 per cent by the census.[2] The 1973 adjusted population, by sex, is derived by considering separately a) the population under age ten and b) the population aged ten and over. The population aged ten and over is estimated by subtracting the deaths which occurred to each age cohort between 1964 and 1973 from the adjusted 1964 population. The population under age ten is derived by considering the number of births during 1963-1973 and the deaths to those born during the same period. The registration of both births and deaths is accepted as complete.

According to Collver, the fluctuations in the growth rate of the population implied by the census results are due to unnecessary corrections of the census totals. His estimates of the growth rate during the first half of this century show a higher rate from each intercensal period to the next. Before 1920 both birth and death rates were high and the population grew at less than one per cent a year. Since 1920 the birth rate has remained high and the death rate has declined steadily to increase the growth rate of the population. The estimates of the actual population at the time of the latest three censuses made by Camisa and and the U.S. Bureau of the Census imply an intercensal growth rate of 2.79 per cent for 1950-1964 and 2.74 per cent for 1964-1973.

## Birth Rate

The crude birth rates as estimated by Collver for 1900-1959 and as recorded since 1960 are shown in Table 78. During most of the period prior to 1960 the birth rate fluctuated between 45 and 50 per thousand population. Since 1960 a slight decline in the birth rate has been observed. However, the data are not evidence of a long-term or substantial reduction in fertility. The crude birth rate in 1973 (43.4) was nearly the same as for the 1965-69 period (44.0). The modest decrease in fertility is also shown by the total fertility rate (TFR) and age-specific fertility rates (ASFR). The TFR was 6.66 in 1949-1951 and 6.42 in 1963-65. By 1973 the TFR was 5.89, which is still a high level of fertility since it indicates that Guatemalan women have nearly six births apiece on average.

---

[1] Zulma Camisa, *Guatemala: Proyecciones de la Población Total, 1965-2000,* Centro Latinoamericano de Demografía (CELADE), Series AS, No. 3, San José, Costa Rica, 1970, p. 6.

[2] Letter from Sylvia Quick, International Statistical Programs Center, U.S. Bureau of the Census, Washington, D.C., May 6, 1975.

**Table 78**

**Vital Rates in Guatemala, 1900 to 1973**

| Years | Crude Birth Rate | Crude Death Rate | Rate of Natural Increase (%) |
|---|---|---|---|
| 1900–04 | 45.8 | 35.4 | 1.04 |
| 1905–09 | 43.6 | 34.0 | 0.96 |
| 1910–14 | 46.6 | 33.0 | 1.36 |
| 1915–19 | 43.2 | 40.8 | 0.24 |
| 1920–24 | 48.3 | 33.7 | 1.46 |
| 1925–29 | 49.2 | 32.6 | 1.66 |
| 1930–34 | 46.2 | 31.7 | 1.45 |
| 1935–39 | 44.2 | 30.7 | 1.35 |
| 1940–44 | 45.2 | 28.5 | 1.67 |
| 1945–49 | 49.1 | 26.5 | 2.26 |
| 1950–54 | 50.9 | 23.4 | 2.75 |
| 1955–59 | 49.0 | 20.0 | 2.90 |
| 1960–64 | 47.6 | 18.0 | 2.96 |
| 1965–69 | 44.0 | 16.4 | 2.76 |
| 1970 | 41.6 | 14.9 | 2.67 |
| 1971 | 43.8 | 14.4 | 2.94 |
| 1972 | 44.2 | 13.3 | 3.09 |
| 1973 | 43.4 | 15.4 | 2.80 |

Sources: 1900–1959: O. Andrew Collver, *Birth Rates in Latin America: New Estimates of Historical Trends and Fluctuations,* University of California, Berkeley, 1965, p. 128.

1960–1973: *Population Index* 41:3 (July 1975) 546, 551.

**Figure 21**
**Age-specific fertility rates, Guatemala; 1949–1951, 1963–1965, and 1973.**

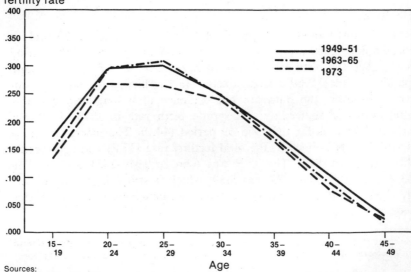

Sources:
1949–1951 and 1963–1965: Zulma C. Camisa, *Guatemala: Proyecciones de la Población Total, 1965–2000,* Centro Latinoamericano de Demografía (CELADE), Series AS, No. 3, San Jose, Costa Rica, 1970, p. 14.
1973: International Statistical Programs Center, U.S. Bureau of the Census, Washington, D.C., 1976.

108

The age-specific fertility rates of 1963-1965 differed little from those of 1949-1951 (see Figure 21). The rates for 1973 are estimated by distributing the total number of births in 1973 by the age-specific pattern of fertility of 1971. The rates estimated in this manner indicate that the slight decline in total fertility in Guatemala is attributable to lower fertility among women under age 30, particularly those aged 25-29. As yet the national family planning program can have had only a minor impact on fertility. The program was begun in 1969 and functions through 80 rural health centers and nine capital city clinics. It is estimated that 4.4 per cent of married women in the 15-44 age group were using family planning methods in 1974, and that about two-thirds of those were using supplies and services of the national program.[1]

## Death Rate

Table 78 presents the crude death rates (CDR) for 1900-1959 as estimated by Collver and for 1960-1973 as registered. The CDR declined slowly from 35.4 per thousand in 1900 to 20.0 per thousand in 1955-1959. The high rate of 40.8 during 1915-1919 is attributed to the incidence of influenza during that period.

The death rate has continued to decline steadily from 18.0 in 1960-1964 to 13.3 per thousand in 1972. The rate of 15.4 recorded for 1973 is probably a temporary increase and it can be anticipated that the Guatemalan death rate will resume its long-term decline.

## Age Distribution

The age distribution of Guatemala's population has not changed greatly since 1950 according to the corrected population figures derived by Camisa and the U.S. Bureau of the Census (see Table 79). In 1973, 44.7 per cent of the population was under age 15 and the dependency ratio was 91.9. The urban population is not as young because of lower fertility and the in-migration of young adults. In the urban population 40.4 per cent of the total is aged 0-14 and the dependency ratio is 78.9.

A very recent CELADE report containing revised population projections to year 2000 for Guatemala incorporates similarly revised age and sex structure information. This is presented in full at the end of this chapter (Appendix A) and is summarized in Table 80. CELADE's newly revised projections for year 2000 show 11,991,000 inhabitants, compared to 11,582,000 projected by the U.S. Bureau of the Census and used in this study. Population totals for the year 1973 are almost

---

[1]Dorothy Nortman and Ellen Hofstatter, "Population and Family Planning Programs: A Factbook," *Reports on Population/Family Planning,* No. 2 (7th edition), Population Council, New York, October 1975, pp. 29 and 75.

**Table 79**

**Percentage of Population in Broad Age Groups and Dependency Ratios for Guatemala; 1950, 1964, and 1973**

| Age | 1950 | 1964 | 1973 Total | 1973 Urban | 1973 Rural |
|---|---|---|---|---|---|
| All ages | 100.0% | 100.0% | 100.0% | 100.0% | 100.0% |
| 0–14 | 43.4 | 45.6 | 44.7 | 40.4 | 46.9 |
| 15–64 | 53.6 | 51.6 | 52.1 | 55.9 | 50.2 |
| 65+ | 3.0 | 2.8 | 3.2 | 3.7 | 2.9 |
| Dependency Ratio[a] | 86.6 | 93.8 | 91.9 | 78.9 | 99.2 |

[a] The dependency ratio is $(P(0-14) P(65+)/P(15-64))$ X 100, where P(a) is the population age "a".

Sources: 1950 and 1964: Zulma C. Camisa, *Guatemala: Proyecciones de la Población Total, 1965–2000*, Centro Latinoamericano de Demografía (CELADE), Series AS, No. 3, San José, Costa Rica, 1970, p. 6, corrected population.

1973: U.S. Bureau of the Census, International Statistical Programs Center, unpublished projections of the population of Guatemala, 1975.

**Table 80**

**Population in Broad Age Groups, 1980–2000 as Projected by CELADE**

| Age Group | Population 1980 | Population 1990 | Population 2000 | Percentage 1980 | Percentage 1990 | Percentage 2000 |
|---|---|---|---|---|---|---|
| Total | 7,006,019 | 9,200,754 | 11,991,462 | 100.0 | 100.0 | 100.0 |
| 0–14 | 2,999,704 | 3,767,890 | 4,695,417 | 42.8 | 41.0 | 39.1 |
| 15–64 | 3,786,638 | 5,108,699 | 6,806,214 | 54.1 | 55.1 | 56.8 |
| 65+ | 219,677 | 324,165 | 489,831 | 3.1 | 3.5 | 4.1 |

Source: Centro Latinoamericano de Demografía (CELADE), *Boletín Demográfico*, 9:17 (January, 1976).

**Table 81**

**Population Percentage under Age 15, Projected for 1980 and 2000 for Guatemala, El Salvador, Panama and Costa Rica.**

| Country | Population Age 0–14 as Percentage of total 1980 | Population Age 0–14 as Percentage of total 2000 |
|---|---|---|
| Guatemala | 42.8 | 39.1 |
| El Salvador | 45.2 | 41.3 |
| Panama | 41.4 | 37.2 |
| Costa Rica | 39.2 | 34.0 |

Source: Guatemala, see Source note, Table 80; for the remaining countries see the respective country chapters.

identical from the two sources. The divergencies are in the projections to year 2000.

The percentage distribution by age group is of interest here, regardless of the projected variance in total population numbers. Relative to three other countries in this study the percentages for Guatemala are similar, as expected for a region with one of the highest birth rates in the world. The age group distribution pattern for those under 15 for the four countries in 1980 and 2000 is shown in Table 81.

The very large percentage of population under age 15 is unquestionably placing a strain on the existing social and economic environment of Guatemala. This is attenuated, however, by the fact that the country is still largely rural, and many social and economic functions that would otherwise be supported by public institutions in a more urban setting are still maintained, if at all, by the family or community. As seen in Table 81, Guatemala's situation is little different from that of El Salvador or Panama, while Costa Rica's population percentage under age 15 is lower and should decline more rapidly owing to this country's sustained drop in the birth rate during the last decade.

In Table 82 Guatemala's age structure is compared with Latin America in general and with Argentina and the United States, two countries where a variety of factors have resulted in demographic profiles more typical of economically developed countries in temperate zones. The interest here is in the very large difference between Guatemala (and Latin America in general) on the one hand, and Argentina and the United States on the other. Among these countries and regional groupings, there are large proportional variations in the population group under age 15. In comparison to the United States, Latin America is projected to have doubled the proportion in this age bracket by the year 2000.

### Urban-Rural Fertility Differentials

Fertility in the urban areas of Guatemala is quite high, although it is somewhat lower than rural fertility. The U.S. Bureau of the Census places the urban total fertility rate at 5.32 and the rural TFR at 6.60 in 1973. Based on adjustments of the 1973 census population, it is estimated that there are 855 children aged 0-4 for every 1,000 females aged 15-44 in the total population. The ratio is 658 in the urban sector and 972 among the rural population.

The urban residence ratios graphed in Figure 22 are simply the percentage of the total population in each age-sex group which lives in urban areas. The ratios presented are calculated from a preliminary adjustment by the U.S. Bureau of the Census of a five per cent sample tabulation of the 1973 census results. The graphs of the ratios are similar to those observed for Costa Rica and El Salvador except that the salient features are much less pronounced. The degree of rural-urban migration indicated by the slope of the curves between ages 0-4 and 15-19 or 20-24 is substantially less in the case of Guatemala. The decline in the ratios centered on ages 35-39 and the increases at older ages are also more moderate in Guatemala. A greater percentage of females migrates to urban areas (as is true in the other Central

111

**Table 82**

**Percentage Distribution of the Population in Broad Age Groups for Guatemala, Argentina, the United States, and Latin America in 1950 and as Projected for 1980 and 2000**

| | Year and Age Groupings | | | | | | | | |
| --- | --- | --- | --- | --- | --- | --- | --- | --- | --- |
| | 1950 | | | 1980 | | | 2000 | | |
| Country | 0–14 | 15–64 | 65+ | 0–14 | 15–64 | 65+ | 0–14 | 15–64 | 65+ |
| Guatemala | 43.4 | 53.6 | 3.0 | 42.8 | 54.1 | 3.1 | 39.1 | 56.8 | 4.1 |
| Argentina | 30.5 | 65.3 | 4.2 | 28.2 | 63.2 | 8.6 | 25.0 | 64.5 | 10.5 |
| Latin America | 40.7 | 55.8 | 3.5 | 41.5 | 54.6 | 3.9 | 37.7 | 57.9 | 4.4 |
| United States | 26.9 | 65.0 | 8.1 | 24.0 | 65.1 | 10.9 | 19.1 | 68.4 | 12.5 |

Sources: CELADE, Boletín Demografíco, Issues 7:13 and 9:17. For the United States in 1950, see U.S. Bureau of the Census, *Estimates of Population of the United States by Single Years of Age, Color and Sex, 1900–59*, Report, p. 25–311, July, 1965.

For 1980 and 2000 see U.S. Bureau of the Census, *Projections of the Population of the United States, 1975–2050*, Report P 25, No. 601, October, 1975.

American countries) and the migration is at a younger age than among males. After age 40 females become increasingly more urbanized than males. The urban residence ratios calculated for 1973 are quite close to those calculated from the unadjusted 1964 census results (not shown)

**Figure 22**
**Urban residence ratios by age and sex, Guatemala, 1973.**

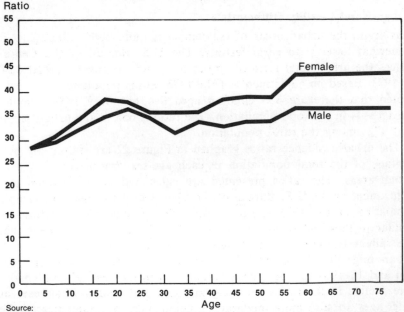

Source:
U.S. Bureau of the Census, International Statistical Programs Center, unpublished analysis of the 1973 Guatemalan population census, 1975.

except that the percentage of males ages 15-24 in urban areas is about three points greater in 1973.

## Occupational Structures and Labor Force Participation, by Age and Sex

The newly available 1973 final Guatemalan census report contains extensive data relating the occupational structures of the population by age and sex, cross-referenced by urban or rural place of residence.[1] Use of that information here requires explanation. First, the distinction between "urban" and "rural" employed here is that as defined by the census.[2] Accordingly, roughly 7 in every 20 inhabitants are considered urban and the remainder rural. Second, the final publication contains a newly revised population total of 5,160,000 which compares to 5,212,000 given in the preliminary count. The latter figure is used as the basis for calculating the projections. In considering this slight change, recalculations were not deemed necessary since the accuracy of any enumeration operates within certain tolerances. Still, it is important to note that references to absolute numbers in this section relate to the final Guatemalan census document, or to 5,160,000 inhabitants.

In 1973, 1,546,000 persons comprised the Guatemalan labor force. This represents 30 per cent of the total population, and 44 per cent of those 10 years of age and older. Modifying a dependency ratio from one that simply states the relationship between those in various age groups to one that considers the working vs. non-working population produces an index number of 234. Children under 10 number 1,648,000. The

---

[1] Guatemala, Dirección General de Estadística, *VIII Censo de Población 1973, Serie III, Tomo I,* Guatemala, 1975.

[2] Urban definitions in the census years 1950, 1964, and 1973 are:

1950—Urban area = (a) all localities whose population exceeds 2,000 inhabitants, and (b) all localities with a population between 1,500 and 2,000 inhabitants, having in addition potable water facilities.

1964-1973—Urban area = all populated localities officially designated as a city, village or town.

The number of urban areas in 1973 categorized by population size is as follows:

| 1973 Population Size | Number of Areas |
|---|---|
| 1- 1,999 | 181 |
| 2,000- 2,999 | 48 |
| 3,000- 4,999 | 46 |
| 5,000- 9,000 | 28 |
| 10,000- 49,999 | 19 |
| 50,000- 99,000 | 1 |
| 100,000-499,999 | 1 |
| 500,000+ | 1 |

Total 325

**Table 83**

**Males in the Labor Force, Numbers and Percentages in Agricultural Activities, 1973**

|  | Economically Active Males | Males in Agricultural Occupations | Percentage in Agriculture |
|---|---|---|---|
| Total | 1,328,730 | 862,438 | 65 |
| Urban | 436,178 | 112,447 | 26 |
| Rural | 892,352 | 749,991 | 84 |

Source: Guatemala, Dirección General de Estadística, *VIII Censo de Población. Serie III. Tomo I.* Tables 22 and 49, op. cit.

next largest category of "economic inactives" consists of "cuidan de su hogar," a group comprised of 1,301,000 females, essentially house-wives.[1]

A very high proportion of the male labor force is engaged in agricultural activities. (Table 83). The national average is 65 per cent, and in this respect it is similar to the 70 per cent for El Salvador (for 1961) which has the highest level in the region.

The population of Guatemala is largely indigenous. Considerable attention is given to this characteristic in the census report, permitting an examination of occupational pattern differences between the two major ethnic groups—the indigenous and European-derived population. A full 44 per cent of the population, or 2.3 million persons are classified as indigenous by the census.

Table 84 shows a comparison between the indigenous and non-indigenous male populations engaged in agricultural activities. The percentages between the two ethnic groupings in the rural sector are strikingly similar. Regardless of ethnic group, roughly 17 in every 20 rural economically-active males are engaged in agricultural pursuits.

A far different pattern exists in the urban sector. Half the urban indigenous males are agriculturalists, but only 16 per cent of the non-indigenous group falls in this category. Quite evidently, among thousands of European descendants this is related to opportunities and choices to enter into trade and commerce, as well as the location in Guatemala City of most of the non-indigenous male group. The high urban figure (54 per cent) in agriculture among the indigenous males is undoubtedly related to the fact that much of this population resides in small "urban" centers of fewer than 5,000 inhabitants that more realistically are large agricultural villages.

There is no earlier and comparable census information on this theme which would permit an examination of shifts in occupational trends

---

[1] This classification additionally includes 38,000 males, more than half of whom are in the age bracket 10-14.

114

over time,[1] particularly on whether the numbers in agriculture have kept pace with the general population increase. Figure 23 profiles the agricultural population by age group and is a reasonable substitute. It indicates that in rural Guatemala agriculture is retaining a strong grip on both indigenous and non-indigenous males. At least 80 per cent of all rural males above age 30 are farmers, and in the age category 15–30 the profile is about the same. Should a rural exodus from agriculture into other occupations occur, it would be found among young males. This has, in fact, occurred in rural Costa Rica, data for which are also shown in Figure 23.

Females in the labor force according to employment classification fall into a pattern similar to that observed in other regional countries (Table 85). The exception here is the very high number of women engaged in textile production, a largely indigenous occupation.

The proportion of economically active females (Figure 24) is sharply lower than for males, and in relative terms female opportunities for employment are far fewer in the rural than urban sector. This is a situation common to all countries of the region.

## Urban Population Growth

For the purposes of the 1964 and 1973 population censuses, urban areas were those defined by the Government Accord of April 7, 1938 as cities, towns, or villages (ciudad, villa, or pueblo). In 1950 the definition employed was "places of 2,000 or more inhabitants" and "places with 1,500 to 2,000 inhabitants which had running water".[2] The censuses reported that 25.0 per cent of the population lived in urban areas in 1950 and that 33.6 per cent did so in both 1964 and 1973. Some of the increase between 1950 and 1964 is accounted for by the use of a more comprehensive definition in 1964. The apparent lack of increase in urbanization between 1964 and 1973 is most likely explained by a change in census procedure which is described below.

Projections for major urbanized areas in Guatemala are based here on a minimum size of 10,000 inhabitants in 1973. Twenty areas in Guatemala meet this criterion. For most, the population of the urbanized area is taken to be the urban population reported by the censuses. In the Department of San Marcos the urban population of the towns of San Marcos and San Pedro Sacatepequez are considered to comprise a single urbanized area. The population of Guatemala City used here

---

[1]The U.S. Bureau of the Census does advise, however, that between 1964 and 1973, those in agriculture dropped from 73.6 to 66.5 per cent of the Guatemalan male labor force. See Table 88.

[2]Guatemala, Dirección General de Estadística, *VIII Censo de Población y III de Habitación, Población* (Cifras Preliminares), Series 1, vol. 1, Guatemala City, September 1973, p. 14. Also see footnote, page 113.

**Table 84**

**Guatemala, Males in the Labor Force, Numbers and Percentage in Agricultural Occupations, by Ethnic Grouping, 1973**

|  | Economically Active Males (a) | | Numbers in Agriculture (b) | | (b) as per cent of (a) | |
|---|---|---|---|---|---|---|
|  | Indigenous | Non-Indigenous | Indigenous | Non-Indigenous | Indigenous | Non-Indigenous |
| **Total** | **618,057** | **710,673** | **490,146** | **372,292** | **79** | **52** |
| Urban | 115,377 | 320,801 | 62,155 | 50,292 | 54 | 16 |
| Rural | 502,680 | 389,872 | 427,991 | 322,000 | 85 | 83 |

Source: Guatemala, Dirección General de Estadística, *III Censo de Población. Serie III. Tomo I.* Guatemala, 1975. Tables 21 and 49.

**Figure 23.**
**Percentage of economically active males in agriculture; Guatemala, by ethnic group, urban and rural, 1973; Costa Rica; rural 1973.**

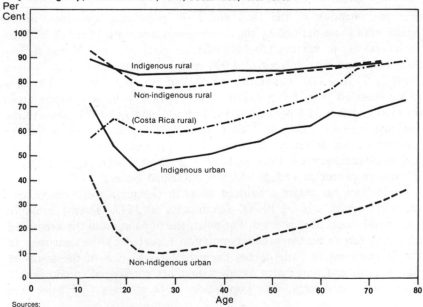

Sources:
Guatemala, Direccion General de Estadistica, *III Censo de Poblacion, Serie III, Tomo I,* Guatemala, 1975. Tables 21 and 49.
Costa Rica, Direccion General de Estadistica y Censos, *Censos Nacionales de 1973, Poblacion,* Tomo II, San Jose, 1975. Table 51.

116

**Table 85**

**Guatemala, Major Categories for Women in the Labor Force, 1973**

| Employment Category | Number | Percentage Distribution |
|---|---|---|
| Agricultural Workers | 14,702 | 7 |
| Retail Sales | 34,805 | 16 |
| Public and Private Instruction | 13,954 | 6 |
| Domestics | 69,644 | 32 |
| Sanitary and medical Services | 8,520 | 4 |
| Restaurant, Bar Employees | 6,428 | 3 |
| Textile Production | 31,092 | 14 |
| All Remaining Categories | 37,783 | 18 |
| **Total** | **216,928** | **100** |

Source: Guatemala, Dirección General de Estadística, *III Censo de Población. Serie III. Tomo 1.* Guatemala, 1975. Table 25.

**Figure 24.**
**Economically active population, urban and rural, by sex, in Guatemala, 1973**

Percentage of
Age Group

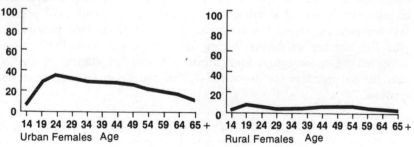

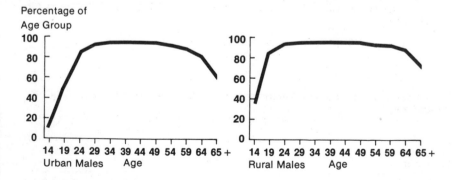

Source:
Guatemala Direccion General de Estadistica, *III Censo de Poblacion, Serie III, Tomo 1,* Guatemala, 1975. Table 22.

117

refs to the metropolitan area of the capital and is defined in more detail below. The population of these 20 urbanized areas as enumerated by the three most recent censuses is shown in Table 86. The arbitrary lower limit of 10,000 population seems to be a useful dividing line in Guatemala. In 1973 there were no cities with a population between 9,000 and 10,000 and only two between 8,000 and 9,000. However, Fahsen, et al., used 13,000 as the minimum size of urban areas.[1]

Before calculating the urbanized area populations given in Table 86 they were adjusted for census underenumeration and to take into account the shift from a *de facto* basis of residence in 1950 and 1964 to *de jure* basis in 1973. By methods explained earlier in this chapter Camisa adjusted the 1950 census total for a 7.15 per cent underenumeration, and the 1964 total for a 3.53 per cent undercount. The U.S. Bureau of the Census estimated the undercount in 1973 to be 8.22 per cent. All department and urbanized area populations have been adjusted for these presumed rates of underenumeration.

Department and urbanized area population totals in 1973 could be adjusted by the use of estimates prepared by the Guatemalan Census Office (DGE) as part of its census evaluation.[2] Corrected population totals are estimated for each department by sex and urban or rural area of residence by use of a balancing equation. The correct 1973 population for each department is estimated as its corrected 1964 population, plus the number or births during the 1964–1973 intercensal period (adjusted for underregistration), minus the adjusted number of deaths, plus the net increase (or decrease) due to migration (derived from the census).

---

[1] Federico Fahsen, Andrew J. Sherman, and Ricardo Goubaud, *Urbanización y Desarrollo Económico en Guatemala,* vol. 1, unpublished, Guatemala City, 1972.

[2] Guatemala, Dirección General de Estadística, *Evaluación del Censo de 1973 y Estimación de los Indices Vitales* (Documento de Trabajo para uso Interno), Guatemala City, May, 1976.

**Table 86**

**Enumerated Population of Departments and Urbanized Areas in Guatemala 1950, 1964 and 1973.**

| Department and Urbanized Area | Population in Thousands | | |
|---|---|---|---|
| | April 18 1950 | April 18 1964 | March 26 1973 |
| **National Total** | 2,790.9 | 4,288.0 | 5,211.9 |
| **Alta Verapaz** | 189.8 | 260.5 | 276.4 |
| Cobán | 7.9 | 9.9 | 11.9 |
| Remainder | 181.9 | 250.6 | 264.5 |

118

**Table 86 cont.**

| Department and Urbanized Area | Population in Thousands | | |
|---|---|---|---|
| | April 18 1950 | April 18 1964 | March 26 1973 |
| **Baja Verapaz** | **66.3** | **96.5** | **106.9** |
| **Chimaltenango** | **121.5** | **163.2** | **193.6** |
| Chimaltenango | 6.1 | 9.2 | 13.1 |
| Remainder | 115.3 | 154.0 | 180.4 |
| **Chiquimula** | **112.8** | **149.8** | **158.1** |
| Chiquimula | 8.8 | 14.7 | 16.2 |
| Remainder | 104.0 | 135.0 | 142.0 |
| **El Progreso** | **47.9** | **65.6** | **73.2** |
| **Escuintla** | **123.8** | **270.3** | **300.1** |
| Escuintla | 9.7 | 25.0 | 37.2 |
| Sta. Lucía Cotzumalguapa | 3.8 | 9.0 | 13.9 |
| Tiquisate | 4.6 | 9.8 | 10.8 |
| San José | 2.8 | 6.1 | 10.1 |
| Remainder | 102.8 | 220.3 | 228.1 |
| **Guatemala** | **438.9** | **810.9** | **1,127.9** |
| Guatemala City | 346.9 | 689.5 | 979.4 |
| Remainder | 92.0 | 121.3 | 148.4 |
| **Huehuetenango** | **200.1** | **288.1** | **368.8** |
| Huehuetenango | 6.2 | 10.1 | 11.8 |
| Remainder | 193.9 | 278.0 | 357.0 |
| **Izabal** | **55.0** | **116.7** | **170.9** |
| Puerto Barrios | 15.5 | 22.3 | 19.7 |
| Remainder | 39.5 | 94.4 | 151.2 |
| **Jalapa** | **75.2** | **99.2** | **118.1** |
| Jalapa | 6.6 | 10.3 | 13.8 |
| Remainder | 68.6 | 88.9 | 104.3 |
| **Jutiapa** | **138.9** | **194.8** | **231.0** |
| Jutiapa | 5.2 | 7.5 | 10.1 |
| Remainder | 133.7 | 187.3 | 220.9 |
| **Petén** | **15.9** | **26.6** | **64.5** |
| **Quetzaltenango** | **184.2** | **270.9** | **311.6** |
| Quetzaltenango | 27.7 | 44.3 | 46.0 |
| Coatepéque | 6.3 | 13.8 | 15.9 |
| Remainder | 150.2 | 212.9 | 249.7 |
| **Quiché** | **174.9** | **249.9** | **300.6** |
| **Retalhuleu** | **66.9** | **117.6** | **134.0** |
| Retalhuleu | 9.2 | 14.9 | 20.2 |
| Remainder | 57.7 | 102.6 | 113.8 |
| **Sacatepéquez** | **60.1** | **80.9** | **99.7** |
| Antigua Guatemala | 10.7 | 13.9 | 17.7 |
| Remainder | 49.4 | 67.0 | 82.0 |
| **San Marcos** | **232.6** | **337.0** | **388.1** |
| San Pedro Sacatepéquez & San Marcos | 10.8 | 14.9 | 16.7 |
| Remainder | 221.8 | 322.0 | 371.4 |
| **Santa Rosa** | **109.8** | **157.0** | **176.2** |

119

**Table 86 cont.**

| Department and Urbanized Area | Population in Thousands | | |
|---|---|---|---|
| | April 18 1950 | April 18 1964 | March 26 1973 |
| **Sololá** | **82.9** | **107.8** | **126.9** |
| Santiago Atitlán | 7.2 | 9.4 | 11.5 |
| Remainder | 75.7 | 98.4 | 115.4 |
| **Suchitepéquez** | **124.4** | **186.6** | **212.0** |
| Mazatenango | 11.0 | 10.5 | 24.2 |
| Remainder | 113.4 | 167.1 | 187.9 |
| **Totonicapán** | **99.4** | **141.8** | **166.6** |
| **Zacapa** | **69.5** | **96.6** | **106.7** |
| Zacapa | 8.3 | 11.2 | 12.7 |
| Remainder | 61.3 | 85.3 | 94.0 |

Source: Guatemala census reports.

DGE estimated the intercensal crude birth rate to have been 43.97 per thousand, the crude death rate to have been 13.07 per thousand, and the annual rate of increase to have been 3.09 per cent. The corrected 1973 population total is 5,879,690, which implies a census underenumeration of 12.2 per cent (using the final census figure of 5,160,221).

The estimated department totals are not used here as the base for departmental population projections because the intercensal growth rate of 3.1 per cent annually for the total population seems somewhat high. The average annual growth rate derived from vital statistics was 2.8 per cent[1] for 1965–1973, and the intercensal average estimated by the U.S. Bureau of the Census report employed here was 2.7 per cent.

However, the departmental populations as corrected for underenumeration by DGE are presented in Table 87. DGE does not provide estimated rates of underenumeration for individual cities but does give them for the urban population of each department. The estimated populations of urbanized areas shown in Table 87 are obtained by applying the DGE percentage of omission for the urban population of the appropriate department to the enumerated urbanized area population as given in Table 86.

The adjusted populations of departments and urbanized areas given in Table 87 may be compared with those in Table 89, which were estimated by an across-the-board adjustment of 1973 census totals by 8.2 per cent. The population of Guatemala City is the only urbanized area total which is adjusted by less than 8.2 per cent by DGE. The percent-

[1]*Population Index* 41:3 (July 1975) p. 546.

age of omission in this case is estimated to be just 0.98. On the other hand, the census underenumeration of the urban population of the Department of Solola (applied to Santiago Atitlan) is estimated to be 22.78 per cent; of Izabal (applied to Puerto Barrios), 33.09 per cent; of Zacapa, 24.58 per cent; and of Jutiapa, 24.94 per cent.

**Table 87**

**Guatemala: Total Population of Departments and Urbanized Areas[a] Adjusted for Census Underenumeration by the Dirección General de Estadística, March 26, 1973.**

| Department and Urbanized Area | Population in thousands | Department and Urbanized Area | Population in thousands |
|---|---|---|---|
| **National Total** | **5,879.7** | **Jutiapa** | **273.0** |
| | | Jutiapa | 13.4 |
| **Alta Verapaz** | **349.9** | Remainder | 259.6 |
| Cobán | 14.7 | **Petén** | **67.1** |
| Remainder | 335.2 | **Quezaltenango** | **360.4** |
| **Baja Verapaz** | **128.5** | Quezaltenango | 55.2 |
| **Chimaltenango** | **219.2** | Coatepéque | 19.1 |
| Chimaltenango | 14.9 | Remainder | 286.1 |
| Remainder | 204.3 | **Quiché** | **341.7** |
| **Chiquimula** | **200.1** | **Retalhuleu** | **149.5** |
| Chiquimula | 19.6 | Retalhuleu | 23.4 |
| Remainder | 180.5 | Remainder | 126.1 |
| **El Progreso** | **86.9** | **Sacatepéquez** | **109.3** |
| **Escuintla** | **331.0** | Antigua Guatemala | 19.6 |
| Escuintla | 43.4 | Remainder | 89.7 |
| Sta. Lucía Cotzumalguapa | 16.3 | **San Marcos** | **444.7** |
| Tiquisate | 12.6 | San Marcos and San Pedro | |
| San José | 11.8 | Sacatepéquez | 19.8 |
| Remainder | 246.9 | Remainder | 424.9 |
| **Guatemala** | **1,165.2** | **Santa Rosa** | **212.0** |
| Guatemala City | 989.1 | **Sololá** | **147.1** |
| Remainder | 176.1 | Santiago Atitlán | 14.8 |
| **Huehuetenango** | **397.3** | Remainder | 132.3 |
| Huehuetenango | 14.1 | **Suchitepéquez** | **241.9** |
| Remainder | 383.2 | Mazatenango | 29.1 |
| **Izabal** | **192.9** | Remainder | 212.8 |
| Puerto Barrios | 29.4 | **Totonicapán** | **195.4** |
| Remainder | 163.5 | **Zacapa** | **130.0** |
| **Jalapa** | **136.4** | Zacapa | 16.8 |
| Jalapa | 15.8 | Remainder | 113.2 |
| Remainder | 120.6 | | |

[a] The urbanized area totals are calculated by applying the percentage of omission estimated by DGE for the urban population of the appropriate department to the enumerated urbanized area population as given in Table 86.

Source: Guatemala, Dirección General de Estadística, *Evaluación del Censo de 1973 y Estimación de los Indices Vitales.*

Both the 1964 and 1973 censuses of Guatemala enumerated an urban population which was 33.6 per cent of the total population.[1] The lack of change in the urban percentage could be attributable to three influences: (1) the urban proportion in fact remained constant; (2) the urban areas experienced a greater degree of underenumeration than did the rural areas in 1973; and (3) the change from a *de facto* basis for enumeration of residence in 1964 to a *de jure* basis in 1973 explains the lack of increase in the urban percentage.

The first explanation seems unlikely since every other Central American country became more urban during the 1960's. There is no reason to expect a halt in the urbanization process in Guatemala. The second explanation is also unlikely since in 1964 the postenumeration survey indicated that underenumeration was greater in rural areas (4.1 per cent) than in urban areas (2.8 per cent).

The method employed below to estimate the urban population in 1973 consistent with the 1964 urban percentage does not involve an assumption concerning the cause of the discrepancy between the estimated and the enumerated urban population. However, once the estimate has been made, it is assumed that the discrepancy between it and the enumerated urban population is due entirely to the shift from a *de facto* to a *de jure* basis of enumeration. The *de facto* population of urban areas would be greater than the *de jure* population if people visit or live temporarily in urban areas but maintain their residence in rural areas. The urban population as determined from the 1973 census is taken as the base for the projections, and the urban population as enumerated in 1950 and 1964 are adjusted to a *de jure* base.

To estimate the proportion urban in 1973 based on the 1964 concept of urban (and a *de facto* basis), the change in the employment structure of the male labor force is used. Since urbanization is generally highly correlated (negatively) with the proportion of the labor force in agriculture, the change in the latter is taken to indicate a shift in the former. The ratio of the change in percentage urban to the change in the percentage of the male labor force in agriculture is assumed to be the same as for another Central American nation. The proportion of the population of Costa Rica living in urban areas increased from 34.5

---

[1]This study is based on the preliminary results of the 1973 census. Final results (which became available after the preparation of the urbanized area projections) indicate that 36.0 per cent of the population of Guatemala lived in urban areas at the time of the census. This figure is close to the 37.3 per cent estimated on a *de facto* basis in the succeeding paragraphs. Had the figure of 36.0 per cent been employed in the following adjustments, the urbanized area population in 1950 and 1964 would have been adjusted downward by a lesser amount, estimated growth between 1964 and 1973 would have been less, and the projected population of urbanized areas would have been slightly less than shown in Table 89.

per cent in 1963 to 40.6 per cent in 1973. The proportion of the male labor force in agriculture declined from 58.5 per cent to 46.9 per cent during the same period (Table 88). Hence, the first indicator changed by 6.1 percentage points while the second was changing by 11.6 percentage points. These figures are in a ratio of 0.526 to 1. If this ratio holds for Guatemala, the decrease of 7.1 percentage points in the proportion of the male labor force in agriculture (Table 88) indicates that the percentage urban figure should have increased by 3.7 points between the 1964 and 1973 censuses. From this point forward it is assumed that the percentage urban in 1973 on a *de facto* basis was 37.3 per cent, and on a *de jure* basis was 33.6 per cent. These figures indicated that the *de jure* urban population was 90.1 per cent the size of the *de facto* population. It is assumed that this relationship was the same in 1950 and 1964 and that it applies to each urbanized area equally. These assumptions are no doubt only approximations of the actual relationship but there are no data that permit more specific criteria.

The populations of urbanized areas in 1950 and 1964 (corrected for underenumeration) are adjusted to their size estimated as if those censuses had been conducted on a *de jure* basis by assuming that the *de jure* population of each urbanized area was 90.1 per cent as large as its *de facto* population. The populations of departments and urbanized areas, corrected as described, for 1950, 1964, and 1973 are given in Table 89. The populations of non-urbanized areas are calculated as residuals. Growth rates of departments and urbanized areas during the latest two intercensal periods based on the corrected population totals are shown in Table 90.

The geographical components of the metropolitan area of Guatemala City have been variously defined. In this chapter a hybrid of the other

## Table 88

**Percentage Distribution of the Male Labor Force by Industry for Guatemala and Costa Rica at the Latest Two Censuses.**

| Industry | Guatemala | | Costa Rica | |
|---|---|---|---|---|
| | 1964[a] | 1973[b] | 1963[a] | 1973[c] |
| Agriculture | 73.6% | 66.5% | 58.5% | 46.9% |
| Industry | 15.5% | 20.9% | 23.6% | 27.2% |
| Services | 10.8% | 12.7% | 17.9% | 25.9% |

Note: The category "not adequately specified" is proportionately distributed among the three industrial categories.

For this table the industry of agriculture comprises agriculture, hunting, fishing, and forestry; industry comprises mining, manufacturing, construction, the public utilities, and transport, storage, and communication; and services comprises commerce, banking, and services.

[a] International Labour Office, *Yearbook of Labour Statistics 1971.* Geneva, Table 2A.
[b] U.S. Bureau of the Census, International Statistical Programs Center.
[c] Costa Rica, Dirección General de Estadísticas y Censos, *Censos Nacionales de 1973. Población.* vol. 1, San José, December 1974.

definitions is used which is more comprehensive than any one of the others. The entire population of the municipalities of Guatemala, Santa Catarina Pinula, Mixco, Amatitlan, Villa Nueva, and Petapa is included in the Metropolitan Area of Guatemala City, as was done by Fahsen (Table 91).[1] Fahsen's inclusion 75 per cent of the population of the municipality of Chinautla and 30 per cent of the population of Villa Canales is also followed. The urban population of the municipalities of San Jose Pinula and San Pedro Sacatepequez as enumerated by the censuses is incorporated into the metropolitan area as suggested by a report of the *Banco Nacional de la Vivienda* (BANVI).[2] The metropolitan area delineated in this manner is not a unit which has been defined by the census organization. In fact, it includes some population which is classed as rural by the census.

The enumerated metropolitan area population of 347,000 in 1950 compares with totals of 313,000 and 342,000 defined by BANVI and Fahsen, respectively. The total of 690,000 in 1964 is somewhat larger than BANVI's definition of 616,000 and about the same as Fahsen's 686,000. The three population totals for the metropolitan area shown in Table 91 are then adjusted for the same degree of underenumeration as was the total population for each census year, and the 1950 and 1964 totals are further adjusted to an estimate of the *de jure* population. The population figures for Guatemala City given in Table 89 have been adjusted in this manner.

---

[1] Fahsen, *Urbanizacion y Desarrollo.*
[2] Banco Nacional de la Vivienda, "Poblacion," (mimeo) Guatemala City, no date.

Table 89

**Estimated and Projected Population of Departments and Urbanized Areas in Guatemala, 1950 to 2000.** [a]

| Department and Urbanized Area | Adjusted Population in Thousands | | | Projected Population in Thousands (midyear) | | |
|---|---|---|---|---|---|---|
| | April 18 1950 | April 18 1964 | March 26 1973 | 1980 | 1990 | 2000 |
| National Total | 3,005.7 | 4,444.9 | 5,678.5 | 6,939.8 | 9,107.9 | 11,582.4 |
| Alta Verapaz | 204.4 | 270.0 | 301.1 | 343.2 | 401.7 | 454.9 |
| Cobin | 7.7 | 9.3 | 12.9 | 14.6 | 18.1 | 21.7 |
| Remainder | 196.7 | 260.8 | 288.2 | 328.6 | 383.6 | 433.2 |
| Baja Verapaz | 71.4 | 100.0 | 116.5 | 137.0 | 167.6 | 198.5 |
| Chimaltenango | 130.8 | 169.1 | 210.9 | 242.4 | 296.1 | 349.9 |
| Chimaltenango | 6.0 | 8.6 | 14.3 | 17.4 | 24.1 | 31.8 |
| Remainder | 124.9 | 160.5 | 196.6 | 255.0 | 272.0 | 318.1 |
| Chiquimula | 121.5 | 155.2 | 172.3 | 193.5 | 222.9 | 248.3 |
| Chiquimula | 8.6 | 13.7 | 17.6 | 21.6 | 27.9 | 34.4 |
| Remainder | 113.0 | 141.5 | 154.7 | 171.9 | 195.0 | 213.9 |
| El Progreso | 51.6 | 68.0 | 79.7 | 91.5 | 109.6 | 126.9 |

# Table 89 cont.

| Department and Urbanized Area | Adjusted Population in Thousands | | | Projected Population in Thousands (midyear) | | |
|---|---|---|---|---|---|---|
| | April 18 1950 | April 18 1964 | March 26 1973 | 1980 | 1990 | 2000 |
| **Escuintla** | **133.3** | **280.2** | **327.0** | **448.2** | **634.8** | **864.2** |
| Escuintla | 9.5 | 23.3 | 40.5 | 59.3 | 97.5 | 150.6 |
| Sta. Lucia Cotzumalguapa | 3.7 | 8.4 | 15.2 | 21.9 | 36.0 | 55.7 |
| Tiquisate | 4.5 | 9.2 | 11.8 | 16.3 | 23.7 | 33.2 |
| San José | 2.7 | 5.7 | 11.0 | 15.6 | 25.6 | 39.5 |
| Remainder | 112.9 | 233.5 | 248.5 | 335.2 | 451.9 | 585.2 |
| **Guatemala** | **472.7** | **840.5** | **1,228.8** | **1,611.6** | **2,323.9** | **3,204.9** |
| Guatemala City | 336.6 | 644.0 | 1,067.1 | 1,430.0 | 2,137.2 | 3,021.3 |
| Remainder | 136.1 | 196.5 | 161.7 | 181.6 | 186.7 | 183.6 |
| **Huehuetenango** | **215.5** | **298.6** | **401.8** | **481.2** | **626.9** | **790.1** |
| Huehuetenango | 6.0 | 9.5 | 12.8 | 16.2 | 22.1 | 29.2 |
| Remainder | 209.5 | 289.2 | 389.0 | 465.1 | 604.8 | 760.8 |
| **Izabal** | **59.3** | **121.0** | **186.2** | **254.0** | **383.1** | **548.7** |
| Puerto Barrios | 15.1 | 20.9 | 21.5 | 37.3 | 47.8 | 58.2 |
| Remainder | 44.2 | 100.1 | 164.7 | 216.8 | 335.3 | 490.5 |
| **Jalapa** | **81.0** | **102.8** | **128.7** | **146.9** | **178.4** | **209.6** |
| Jalapa | 6.4 | 9.6 | 15.1 | 18.5 | 25.3 | 33.0 |
| Remainder | 74.6 | 93.2 | 113.6 | 128.4 | 153.1 | 176.6 |
| **Jutiapa** | **149.6** | **201.9** | **251.7** | **294.5** | **366.3** | **440.6** |
| Jutiapa | 5.0 | 7.0 | 11.0 | 13.3 | 18.2 | 23.8 |
| Remainder | 144.6 | 194.9 | 240.7 | 281.2 | 348.1 | 416.8 |
| **Petén** | **17.1** | **27.5** | **70.3** | **88.5** | **140.4** | **208.8** |
| **Quetzaltenango** | **198.4** | **280.8** | **339.5** | **403.4** | **504.6** | **610.6** |
| Quetzaltenango | 26.9 | 41.3 | 50.1 | 61.5 | 79.4 | 99.1 |
| Coatepéque | 6.1 | 12.8 | 17.4 | 23.5 | 33.9 | 46.3 |
| Remainder | 165.4 | 226.6 | 272.0 | 318.4 | 391.3 | 465.2 |
| **Quiché** | **188.4** | **259.1** | **327.6** | **387.3** | **488.6** | **596.4** |
| **Retalhuleu** | **72.0** | **121.9** | **146.0** | **186.4** | **249.6** | **323.2** |
| Retalhuleu | 8.9 | 13.9 | 22.0 | 28.1 | 40.6 | 56.3 |
| Remainder | 63.1 | 107.9 | 124.0 | 158.3 | 209.0 | 266.9 |
| **Sacatepéquez** | **64.8** | **83.9** | **108.6** | **125.7** | **156.4** | **188.3** |
| Antigua Guatemala | 10.4 | 13.0 | 19.3 | 22.4 | 29.0 | 36.3 |
| Remainder | 54.3 | 70.9 | 89.4 | 103.4 | 127.4 | 152.0 |
| **San Marcos** | **250.5** | **349.3** | **422.8** | **499.4** | **621.1** | **747.3** |
| San Pedro Sacatepéquez & San Marcos | 10.5 | 14.0 | 18.2 | 21.3 | 27.0 | 32.9 |
| Remainder | 240.0 | 335.3 | 404.6 | 478.0 | 594.1 | 714.4 |
| **Santa Rosa** | **118.3** | **162.8** | **192.0** | **224.6** | **274.4** | **324.4** |
| **Sololá** | **89.3** | **111.8** | **138.2** | **156.6** | **188.0** | **218.3** |
| Santiago Atitlán | 7.0 | 8.8 | 12.5 | 14.4 | 18.3 | 22.4 |
| Remainder | 82.3 | 103.0 | 125.8 | 142.2 | 169.7 | 195.9 |
| **Suchitepéquez** | **134.0** | **193.5** | **231.0** | **276.2** | **346.4** | **420.3** |
| Mazatenango | 10.7 | 18.2 | 26.3 | 33.8 | 47.3 | 63.4 |
| Remainder | 123.3 | 175.2 | 204.7 | 242.5 | 299.1 | 356.9 |
| **Totonicapan** | **107.0** | **147.0** | **181.5** | **213.7** | **266.6** | **321.8** |
| **Zacapa** | **74.9** | **100.1** | **116.3** | **134.0** | **160.7** | **186.4** |
| Zacapa | 8.0 | 10.5 | 13.8 | 16.1 | 20.1 | 24.3 |
| Remainder | ·66.9 | 89.6 | 102.4 | 118.0 | 140.6 | 162.0 |

[a] The population of departments and urbanized areas as enumerated in the censuses of 1950, 1964 and 1973 (see Table 86) is adjusted for an estimated underenumeration of 7.15 per cent, 3.53 per cent, and 8.22 per cent in the respective years (notes 1 and 2 of the text, p. 107). The adjusted population of urbanized areas in 1950 and 1964 is further adjusted to a *de jure* basis by the assumption that the *de jure* population of urbanized areas equals 90.1 per cent of the *de facto* population, as elaborated in the text of this report. The non-urban, or "remainder," totals are calculated as residuals of the adjusted department and urbanized area totals.

# Table 90

## Estimated and Projected Population Growth Rates of Departments and Urbanized Areas of Guatemala, 1950 to 2000.

| Department and Urbanized Area | Estimated Average Annual Growth Rate (per cent) | | Projected Average Annual Growth Rate (per cent) | | |
|---|---|---|---|---|---|
| | 1950–1964 | 1964–1973 | 1973–1980 | 1980–1990 | 1990–2000 |
| **National Total** | **2.79** | **2.74** | **2.76** | **2.72** | **2.40** |
| **Alta Verapaz** | **1.99** | **1.22** | **1.80** | **1.57** | **1.24** |
| Cobán | 1.35 | 3.73 | 1.69 | 2.14 | 1.78 |
| Remainder | 2.01 | 1.12 | 1.81 | 1.55 | 1.22 |
| **Baja Verapaz** | **2.41** | **1.71** | **2.23** | **2.02** | **1.69** |
| **Chimaltenango** | **1.83** | **2.47** | **1.92** | **2.00** | **1.67** |
| Chimaltenango | 2.62 | 5.72 | 2.69 | 3.25 | 2.77 |
| Remainder | 1.79 | 2.27 | 1.86 | 1.90 | 1.57 |
| **Chiquimula** | **1.75** | **1.17** | **1.60** | **1.41** | **1.08** |
| Chiquimula | 3.39 | 1.78 | 2.80 | 2.55 | 2.09 |
| Remainder | 1.61 | 1.00 | 1.45 | 1.26 | 0.93 |
| **El Progreso** | **1.98** | **1.78** | **1.90** | **1.80** | **1.47** |
| **Escuintla** | **5.31** | **1.73** | **4.34** | **3.48** | **3.09** |
| Escuintla | 6.45 | 6.18 | 5.24 | 4.98 | 4.34 |
| Sta. Lucía Cotzumalguapa | 5.90 | 6.61 | 5.03 | 4.98 | 4.36 |
| Tiquisate | 5.09 | 2.83 | 4.42 | 3.78 | 3.37 |
| San José | 5.37 | 7.29 | 4.76 | 4.97 | 4.36 |
| Remainder | 5.19 | 0.70 | 4.12 | 2.99 | 2.58 |
| **Guatemala** | **4.11** | **4.25** | **3.73** | **3.66** | **3.21** |
| Guatemala City | 4.63 | 5.65 | 4.03 | 4.02 | 3.46 |
| Remainder | 2.63 | −2.18 | 1.60 | 0.28 | −0.17 |
| **Huehuetenango** | **2.33** | **3.32** | **2.48** | **2.64** | **2.31** |
| Huehuetenango | 3.25 | 3.41 | 3.18 | 3.14 | 2.79 |
| Remainder | 2.30 | 3.32 | 2.46 | 2.63 | 2.30 |
| **Izabal** | **5.10** | **4.82** | **4.28** | **4.11** | **3.59** |
| Puerto Barrios | 2.31 | 0.32 | 7.59 | 2.49 | 1.97 |
| Remainder | 5.84 | 5.57 | 3.78 | 4.36 | 3.80 |
| **Jalapa** | **1.70** | **2.51** | **1.82** | **1.94** | **1.61** |
| Jalapa | 2.91 | 5.01 | 2.80 | 3.14 | 2.66 |
| Remainder | 1.59 | 2.22 | 1.69 | 1.76 | 1.43 |
| **Jutiapa** | **2.14** | **2.47** | **2.16** | **2.18** | **1.85** |
| Jutiapa | 2.38 | 5.07 | 2.63 | 3.12 | 2.71 |
| Remainder | 2.13 | 2.36 | 2.14 | 2.13 | 1.80 |
| **Petén** | **3.40** | **10.48** | **3.17** | **4.62** | **3.97** |
| **Quetzaltenango** | **2.48** | **2.12** | **2.37** | **2.24** | **1.91** |
| Quetzaltenango | 3.08 | 2.15 | 2.82 | 2.56 | 2.21 |
| Coatepéque | 5.34 | 3.38 | 4.17 | 3.64 | 3.12 |
| Remainder | 2.25 | 2.04 | 2.17 | 2.06 | 1.73 |
| **Quiché** | **2.28** | **2.62** | **2.30** | **2.32** | **1.99** |
| **Retalhuleu** | **3.76** | **2.67** | **3.36** | **2.92** | **2.58** |
| Retalhuleu | 3.18 | 5.12 | 3.35 | 3.67 | 3.27 |
| Remainder | 3.84 | 1.55 | 3.36 | 2.78 | 2.44 |
| **Sacatepéquez** | **1.85** | **2.89** | **2.01** | **2.18** | **1.85** |
| Antigua Guatemala | 1.57 | 4.41 | 2.04 | 2.60 | 2.25 |
| Remainder | 1.90 | 2.59 | 2.01 | 2.09 | 1.76 |

126

**Table 90 cont.**

| Department and Urbanized Area | Estimated Average Annual Growth Rate (per cent) | | Projected Average Annual Growth Rate (per cent) | | |
|---|---|---|---|---|---|
| | 1950–1964 | 1964–1973 | 1973–1980 | 1980–1990 | 1990–2000 |
| **San Marcos** | **2.37** | **2.14** | **2.29** | **2.18** | **1.85** |
| San Pedro Sacatepéquez & San Marcos | 2.06 | 2.97 | 2.19 | 2.33 | 2.00 |
| Remainder | 2.39 | 2.10 | 2.29 | 2.17 | 1.84 |
| **Santa Rosa** | **2.28** | **1.85** | **2.16** | **2.00** | **1.67** |
| **Sololá** | **1.60** | **2.38** | **1.71** | **1.83** | **1.50** |
| Santiago Atitlán | 1.62 | 3.93 | 1.95 | 2.39 | 2.03 |
| Remainder | 1.60 | 2.24 | 1.69 | 1.77 | 1.44 |
| **Suchitapéquez** | **2.62** | **1.98** | **2.46** | **2.26** | **1.93** |
| Mazatenango | 3.81 | 4.10 | 3.43 | 3.38 | 2.92 |
| Remainder | 2.51 | 1.74 | 2.33 | 2.10 | 1.77 |
| **Totonicapán** | **2.27** | **2.36** | **2.25** | **2.21** | **1.88** |
| **Zacapa** | **2.07** | **1.68** | **1.96** | **1.81** | **1.48** |
| Zacapa | 1.90 | 3.10 | 2.05 | 2.25 | 1.90 |
| Remainder | 2.09 | 1.50 | 1.94 | 1.75 | 1.42 |

Source: Table 89.


**Table 91**

**Enumerated Population of the Components of the Metropolitan Area of Guatemala City; 1950, 1964, and 1973**

| Municipio | Note | 1950 | 1964 | 1973 |
|---|---|---|---|---|
| Total Metropolitan Area | | 346,912 | 689,538 | 979,430 |
| Guatemala | A | 294,344 | 572,671 | 717,322 |
| Sta. Catarina Pinula | A | 5,187 | 9,500 | 12,968 |
| Mixco | A | 11,784 | 36,940 | 129,627 |
| Amatitlán | A | 11,616 | 19,727 | 26,436 |
| Villa Nueva | A | 7,428 | 17,477 | 42,045 |
| Petapa | A | 2,146 | 3,373 | 8,067 |
| Chinautla | B | 3,672 | 15,287 | 24,682 |
| Villa Canales | B | 5,993 | 8,059 | 9,557 |
| San José Pinula | C | 2,034 | 2,554 | 3,806 |
| San Pedro Sacatepéquez | C | 2,708 | 3,950 | 4,920 |

A. Total population of the municipio.
B. Based on Fahsen's assumption that 75 per cent of the population of Chinautla and 80 per cent of the population of Villa Canales is in the Guatemala City Metropolitan Area.
C. The urban population of the municipio as reported by the census.

Sources: Banco Nacional de la Vivienda, *Población*. (mimeo), Guatemala City, no date.

Federico Fahsen, Andrew J. Sherman, and Ricardo Goubaud, *Urbanización y Desarrollo Económico en Guatemala*. vol. 1, Guatemala City, 1972.

Guatemala, Dirección General de Estadística, *VII Censo de Población 1964*. vol. 1, Guatemala City, 1971.

Guatemala, Dirección General de Estadística, *VIII Censo de Población y III Censo de Habitación, 26 de Marzo de 1973, Población*. (Cifras Preliminares) series 1, vol. 1, Guatemala City, 1973.

The Guatemala City metropolitan area is an increasingly primate city. In 1950 it was 12.5 times as large as Quezaltenango and 6.4 times greater than the combined population of the next three cities in size (Quezaltenango, Puerto Barrios, and Mazatenango). In 1973 the Metropolitan Area was 21.3 times the size of Quezaltenango and 9.1 times as large as the next three cities (Quezaltenango, Escuintla, and Mazatenango). Guatemala City has increased from 11.2 per cent of the national population in 1950 to 18.8 per cent in 1973.

The total population of the twenty urbanized areas (adjusted for underenumeration and to a *de jure* basis) nearly tripled between 1950 and 1973 while growing from 16.6 per cent of the total population to 25.2 per cent (Table 92).

In 1950 only Guatemala City and Quezaltenango exceeded 20,000 in population (adjusted for underenumeration and to a *de jure* basis). Four other cities contained at least 10,000 inhabitants. By 1964 Escuintla and Puerto Barrios had also passed the 20,000 mark and there were seven cities with populations of 10–20,000. During the 1950–1964 intercensal period Escuintla grew at a rate of nearly 6.5 per cent per annum while the other three urbanized areas in the department of Escuintla increased at rates of over five per cent a year (Table 90). Coatepeque, in the Department of Quezaltenango, increased by 5.3 per cent a year and Guatemala City's growth rate was 4.6 per cent during 1950–1964.

Guatemala City reached a population of one million by 1973; Quezaltenango, 50,000; and Escuintla, 40,000. Only three other cities exceeded 20,000. Guatemala City continued to grow at a rapid pace (5.65 per cent a year) between 1964 and 1973. Although the population of the non-urbanized area of the Department of Guatemala as enumerated increased by 27,000 between 1964 and 1973 (Table 86), when the population is adjusted for underenumeration and the urban population in 1964 is adjusted to a *de jure* basis, the non-urbanized population shows a decline of 35,000 during the 1964–1973 intercensal period (Table 89). The cities of Escuintla, Santa Lucia Cotzumalguapa, and San Jose in the Department of Escuintla all increased at rates greater than 6 per cent per annum. Chimaltenango, Jalapa, Jutiapa, and Retalhuleu grew by more than 5 per cent and Antigua Guatemala and Mazatenango by more than 4 per cent. Because of a hurricane in early 1973 which destroyed portions of Puerto Barrios, the urban population enumerated in 1973 was actually 2,500 less than that in 1964 (Table 86).

The growth of the population of Guatemala, the 20 urbanized areas shown in Table 89, non-urbanized areas, and the Guatemala City Metropolitan Area since 1950 is graphed in Figure 25. Although the growth rate of the non-urbanized population was lower in 1964–1973 than in 1950–1964, the annual increment was slightly larger for the

**Figure 25**

**Estimated and projected population of Guatemala, twenty urbanized areas, remaining population (or non-urbanized areas) and Guatemala City, 1950 to 2000.**

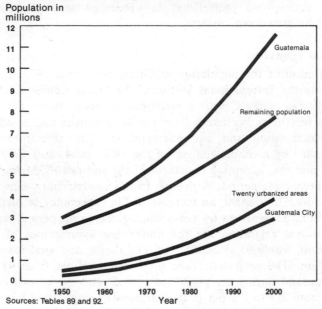

Sources: Tables 89 and 92.

latter period. This increment was also greater than that for the 20 urbanized areas.

## Population Projections

The total population of urbanized areas is projected to the years 1980, 1990, and 2000 by allocating the projected national population first

Table 92

**Estimated and Projected Population of Guatemala, Twenty Urbanized Areas, and Remaining Population, 1950 to 2000.**

| Year | Guatemala | Twenty Urbanized Areas [a] | | Remaining Population | |
|------|-----------|---------------------------|----------------------|---------------------|----------------------|
| | | Population in thousands | Per Cent of total | Population in thousands | Per Cent of total |
| 1950 | 3,005.7 | 500.3 | 16.6 | 2,505.4 | 83.4 |
| 1964 | 4,444.9 | 901.7 | 20.3 | 3,543.2 | 79.7 |
| 1973 | 5,678.5 | 1,430.4 | 25.2 | 4,248.1 | 74.8 |
| 1980 | 6,939.8 | 1,903.1 | 27.4 | 5,036.7 | 72.6 |
| 1990 | 9,107.9 | 2,799.1 | 30.7 | 6,308.8 | 69.3 |
| 2000 | 11,582.4 | 3,913.4 | 33.8 | 7,669.0 | 66.2 |

[a] The twenty urbanized areas are those listed in Table 89.

129

to departments then to urbanized areas using a modification of the ratio-trend methodology elaborated by Jerome P. Pickard.[1] Since this method progresses from a population projection for the country as a whole, to regional projections, to urbanized area projections, it is termed a "step-down" system.

## National Projection

A projection of the population of Guatemala from 1973 to 2000 prepared by the International Statistical Programs Center (ISPC) of the U.S. Bureau of the Census is employed in this section.[2] The base population for the projection is from the 1973 census and is adjusted for underenumeration and age misreporting. The adjustments are accomplished by a cohort analysis of the 1950, 1964, and 1973 censuses, by age and sex, accepting registered births and deaths during the 1964–1973 intercensal period. A decline in the total fertility rate from 5.89 in 1973 to 3.75 in 2000, an increase in life expectancy at birth for both sexes from 52 years to 64 years during the same period, and nil net international migration are the underlying assumptions of the ISPC projection. Table 93 gives the total population and vital rates from the projection. The projected crude birth rate declines from 41.5 to 29.6 per thousand during the projection period, and the annual growth rate drops from 2.7 to 2.2 per cent. Guatemala's population is projected to be nearly 11.6 million in the year 2000. The ISPC projection may be compared with those prepared by Camisa[3] and by CELADE[4] which are based on the adjusted 1964 census population. Both projections yield similar totals for midyear 1973 ((5,751,000 and 5,744,000, respectively) but somewhat greater populations for the year 2000 (12,354,500 and 11,991,000) than the ISPC projection. Each of the other projections assumes a slower decline in fertility and a more rapid drop in mortality than does the ISPC projection. The Camisa and CELADE projections assume a total fertility rate in 1995–2000 of 4.39 and 4.31, respectively, and a life expectancy at birth of 67.2 and 67.0 years in the same time interval.

The ISPC projection yields an older population in the year 2000 then in 1973 due to declining fertility and mortality. In the year 2000, 38.1 per cent of the population would be ages 0–14, 58.6 per cent would be 15–64, and 3.3 per cent would be 65 or older (compare with Tables 79 and 80). The projection dependency ratio is 70.6.

---

[1] Pickard, *Dimensions to Metropolitanism,* p. 53–56.

[2] Materials mailed by Sylvia Quick, U.S Bureau of the Census, International Statistical Programs Center, Washington, D.C. July 3, 1975.

[3] Camisa, *Guatemala: Proyecciones.* Medium Projection.

[4] Centro Latinoamericano de Demografía (CELADE), *Boletín Demográfico* 9:17, Santiago, Chile (January, 1976).

**Table 93**

**Projected Population, Crude Birth Rate, Crude Death Rate, and Rate of Increase; Guatemala; Midyear 1973 to 2000.**

| Period | Population at beginning of period (in thousands) | Crude birth rate | Crude death rate | Average annual rate of increase (%) |
|--------|------|------|------|------|
| 1973–1975 | 5,720 | 41.5 | 14.5 | 2.73 |
| 1975–1980 | 6,039 | 39.9 | 11.8 | 2.80 |
| 1980–1985 | 6,940 | 37.5 | 10.0 | 2.75 |
| 1985–1990 | 7,975 | 34.9 | 9.0 | 2.59 |
| 1990–1995 | 9,108 | 32.3 | 8.0 | 2.43 |
| 1995–2000 | 10,318 | 29.6 | 7.3 | 2.23 |
| 2000 | 11,582 | | | |

Source: U.S. Bureau of the Census, International Statistical Programs Center, Washington, D.C., 1975.

## Department Projections

The observed trend of each department's proportion of the national population is extrapolated to 1980, 1990, and 2000, and the Guatemalan population projected for these years is allocated to the departments on this basis. Table 89 presents the projected departmental populations. The Department of Guatemala is projected to grow at an average of 3.5 per cent a year for the remainder of the century, and to reach a population of two million by 1990 and three million by 2000. No other department is projected to contain a population as great as one million during this century, although six others will exceed 500,000.

The population of the Department of Escuintla increased at an annual rate of 5.3 per cent during 1950–1964 but only at 1.7 per cent during 1964–1973. However, the projection takes the growth of both periods into account and yields a growth rate of 3.56 per cent for the remainder of the century. Since the projection implies a much greater rate for 1973–1980 than was observed for 1964–1973, one should be quite wary of the results. If the results are accurate, Escuintla will be the second-fastest growing department from 1973 to 2000, after Izabal (Table 90). Escuintla would move from its position as the sixth most populous department in 1973 to fourth in 1980, and to second in 1990.

Other departments projected to grow at rates above the national average are Peten and Retalhuleu. From its small size of 70,300 in 1973, Peten, with increases averaging 4.0 per cent a year, is expected to nearly triple to 208,800 by the year 2000. The population of Retalhuleu is projected to increase at an average of 2.9 per cent a year and to reach 323,000 by 2000. The most slowly growing departments between 1973 and 2000 are projected to be Chiquimula (1.34 per cent a year) and Alta Verapaz (1.51 per cent).

## Urbanized Area Projections

Urbanized area populations were projected by extrapolating the observed trend of their proportion of the appropriate departmental population. The projected population of the 20 urbanized areas with over 10,000 population in 1973 is given in Table 89. Their combined population is expected to increase by a factor of 2.7 from 1973 to 2000, when it will reach 3.9 million. Its share of the national population will grow from 25 per cent in 1973 to 34 per cent in 2000 (Table 92). The projection methodology contains built-in conservative biases which prevent areas of observed rapid growth from expanding without limit during the period of the projection.

The Guatemala City metropolitan area is expected to increase its share of the national population but not its degree of primacy among cities. The metropolitan area is projected to contain three million inhabitants in the year 2000, an increase by a factor of 2.8 over 1973. Its population in the year 2000 will be 26 per cent of the national total and 77 per cent of that in the 20 urbanized areas. At the end of this century Guatemala City is expected to be 20.1 times as large as Escuintla, and 9.6 times as large as Escuintla, Quezaltenango, and Mazatenango combined. This is a conservative projection of the population of the metropolitan area. BANVI presents four possible figures for Guatemala City in the year 2000 ranging from 3.0 to 3.9 million depending on the degree of decentralization of Guatemala's urban system by then.[1]

Escuintla is the only other city projected to contain a population of over 100,000 in the year 2000. Of course, Escuintla's projected rapid growth of 4.8 per cent a year for 1973–2000 is a direct result of its observed growth. From less than 10,000 in 1950 it has increased at over 6 per cent a year to exceed 40,000 in 1973 (using adjusted population totals). Whether a rate of growth which would more than triple its size before the year 2000 can be sustained is open to question. However, under the assumption of partial decentralization, BANVI shows Escuintla continuing to grow at 6.6 per cent per annum and reaching a population of 270,000 at the end of the century. Since Escuintla may become Guatemala's second largest city in the 1980's, its size has great bearing on the primacy index of Guatemala City calculated above.

The population of the urbanized area of Quezaltenango is projected to increase at an average rate of 2.5 per cent and to equal 99,000 in the year 2000. This is also a conservative projection. BANVI projects that Quezaltenango's population will reach 164,000 in the year 2000, with an annual growth of 3.8 per cent. By either projection, Quezaltenango will fall one rank to become the nation's third largest city in the 1980's.

---

[1]Banco Nacional de la Vivienda, "Poblacion."

The population of Mazatenango is expected to increase by an annual average rate of 3.2 per cent and reach 63,400 by the end of the century. These figures are also substantially below BANVI's projected rate of 4.3 per cent and of a population total of 89,000 in the year 2000.

The enumerated population of Puerto Barrios was smaller in 1973 (19,700) than in 1964 (22,300) as a result of a devastating hurricane in early 1973. When the 1964 total is adjusted to a *de jure* basis and both figures are corrected for underenumeration, the population registered an increase of 600 during the intercensal period. It is assumed here that the reduced population figure in 1973 represents only a temporary setback to the growth of Puerto Barrios. For the purposes of the projection, the 1973 Puerto Barrios population (corrected for underenumeration) is taken to be 32,094, which would have been its population had it increased by the same percentage as did the Department of Izabal during the 1964–1973 intercensal period. The corrected total implies an annual growth rate of 4,8 per cent for the period. The resultant projection is of an average growth rate of 3.7 per cent and a population of 58,200 in the year 2000. This would make Puerto Barrios Guatemala's fifth largest city, compared with its rank of sixth in 1973. Assuming partial decentralization of Guatemala's urban system, BANVI's projected total for Puerto Barrios is 63,600 in the year 2000.

The urbanized areas of Santa Lucia Cotzumalguapa and San Jose, both in Escuintla Department, are projected to grow at annual rates of over 4 per cent in the remainder of the century. The projection indicates that four additional cities will experience growth averaging at least 3 per cent a year between 1973 and 2000—Tiquisate, Huehuetenango, Coatepeque, and Retalhuleu. The urbanized areas of Coban, Chiquimula, Antigua Guatemala, San Pedro Sacatepequez-San Marcos, Santiago Atitlan, and Zacapa are expected to increase at rates below that of the national population.

The features of the projection methodology which restrain rapid urban growth also have the effect of raising the population totals of the "remaining," or non-urbanized areas. This effect is most notable when it produces a reversal in the trend of growth rates of a non-urbanized area. Examples of this reversal occur in the projections for Escuintla, Guatemala, and Retalhuleu. Between 1964 and 1973 the non-urbanized population (corrected) of Guatemala declined by 2.2 per cent a year (Table 90), but the projection for 1973-1980 indicates that the population will increase by 1.6 per cent a year. The non-urbanized population of Escuintla and Retalhuleu increased at rates of 0.7 and 1.6 per cent, respectively, during 1964-1973, but are projected to grow at rates of 4.1 and 3.4 per cent during 1973-1980.

The population projections presented in Table 89 suggest these general conclusions: (1) the population of Guatemala will double between

133

1973 and the year 2000, when it will be nearly 11.6 million; (2) the proportion of the national population in the 20 largest urbanized areas will increase from 25.2 per cent in 1973 to 33.8 per cent in the year 2000; (3) the Guatemala City metropolitan area will reach three million and comprise 26 per cent of the national total at the end of the century; and (4) the four fastest-growing urbanized areas will be in the department of Escuintla. The city of Escuintla is projected to grow at an average annual rate of 4.8 per cent and to equal 150,600 population in year 2000.

### Appendix A

Guatemala: Population projections by sex and quinquennial age groups, 1975–2000. Recommended hypothesis.

| Age groups | year | | | | | |
|---|---|---|---|---|---|---|
| | 1975 | 1980 | 1985 | 1990 | 1995 | 2000 |
| | males | | | | | |
| **Total** | **3,082.244** | **3,550.393** | **4,075.042** | **4,661.832** | **5,323.940** | **6,074.684** |
| 0– 4 | 534.229 | 598.789 | 661.883 | 729.929 | 811.998 | 909.610 |
| 5– 9 | 436.753 | 500.316 | 566.466 | 632.105 | 703.148 | 788.126 |
| 10–14 | 379.208 | 428.808 | 492.521 | 559.040 | 625.260 | 696.946 |
| 15–19 | 328.191 | 374.988 | 424.653 | 488.423 | 555.093 | 621.539 |
| 20–24 | 280.961 | 323.514 | 370.304 | 420.058 | 483.891 | 550.691 |
| 25–29 | 229.313 | 275.735 | 318.263 | 365.127 | 415.055 | 479.008 |
| 30–34 | 183.136 | 224.053 | 270.240 | 312.831 | 359.858 | 410.029 |
| 35–39 | 153.605 | 178.197 | 218.797 | 264.800 | 307.497 | 354.691 |
| 40–44 | 136.316 | 148.733 | 173.243 | 213.526 | 259.329 | 302.069 |
| 45–49 | 118.088 | 131.437 | 143.532 | 167.899 | 207.748 | 253.178 |
| 50–54 | 91.554 | 112.114 | 125.406 | 137.585 | 161.634 | 200.747 |
| 55–59 | 68.173 | 84.962 | 104.666 | 117.736 | 129.842 | 153.197 |
| 60–64 | 50.581 | 61.521 | 77.153 | 95.608 | 108.130 | 119.812 |
| 65–69 | 37.316 | 43.609 | 53.404 | 67.404 | 84.020 | 95.513 |
| 70–74 | 27.622 | 29.907 | 35.205 | 43.406 | 55.129 | 69.094 |
| 75–79 | 15.455 | 19.875 | 21.654 | 25.640 | 31.784 | 40.558 |
| 80 + | 11.243 | 13.835 | 17.652 | 20.175 | 24.524 | 29.876 |
| | females | | | | | |
| **Total** | **2,999.395** | **3,455.626** | **3,966.923** | **4,538.922** | **5,184.372** | **5,916.788** |
| 0– 4 | 514.188 | 575.286 | 636.187 | 700.905 | 778.347 | 871.761 |
| 5– 9 | 421.434 | 482.298 | 544.428 | 608.207 | 676.976 | 757.542 |
| 10–14 | 367.217 | 414.207 | 475.204 | 537.704 | 602.022 | 671.432 |
| 15–19 | 318.022 | 363.328 | 410.421 | 471.530 | 534.247 | 599.090 |
| 20–24 | 271.941 | 314.104 | 359.451 | 406.694 | 467.947 | 530.897 |
| 25–29 | 222.205 | 267.702 | 309.857 | 355.307 | 402.762 | 464.203 |
| 30–34 | 177.603 | 217.765 | 263.060 | 305.274 | 350.890 | 398.617 |
| 35–39 | 149.437 | 173.397 | 213.275 | 258.411 | 300.716 | 346.518 |
| 40–44 | 133.673 | 145.411 | 169.296 | 208.907 | 253.879 | 296.242 |
| 45–49 | 116.113 | 129.487 | 141.356 | 165.133 | 204.409 | 249.116 |
| 50–54 | 91.034 | 111.575 | 124.911 | 136.869 | 160.445 | 199.223 |
| 55–59 | 68.901 | 85.831 | 105.768 | 119.024 | 131.045 | 154.281 |
| 60–64 | 51.437 | 62.784 | 78.863 | 97.957 | 111.045 | 123.066 |
| 65–69 | 38.423 | 44.909 | 55.386 | 70.263 | 88.071 | 100.655 |
| 70–74 | 28.628 | 31.251 | 36.990 | 46.174 | 59.226 | 74.975 |
| 75–79 | 16.280 | 21.008 | 23.232 | 27.840 | 35.149 | 45.544 |
| 80 + | 12.859 | 15.283 | 19.238 | 22.723 | 27.196 | 33.616 |

**Appendix A cont.**

| Age groups | year | | | | | |
|---|---|---|---|---|---|---|
| | 1975 | 1980 | 1985 | 1990 | 1995 | 2000 |
| | both sexes | | | | | |
| Total | 6,081.689 | 7,006.019 | 8,041.965 | 9,200.754 | 10,508.312 | 11,991.462 |
| 0– 4 | 1,048.417 | 1,174.075 | 1,298.070 | 1,430.834 | 1,590.345 | 1,781.371 |
| 5– 9 | 858.187 | 982.614 | 1,110.894 | 1,240.312 | 1,380.312 | 1,545.668 |
| 10–14 | 746.425 | 843.015 | 967.725 | 1,096.744 | 1,227.282 | 1,368.378 |
| 15–19 | 646.213 | 738.316 | 835.074 | 959.953 | 1,089.340 | 1,220.629 |
| 20–24 | 552.902 | 637.618 | 729.755 | 826.752 | 951.838 | 1,081.588 |
| 25–29 | 451.518 | 543.437 | 628.120 | 720.434 | 817.817 | 943.211 |
| 30–34 | 360.739 | 441.818 | 533.300 | 618.105 | 710.748 | 808.646 |
| 35–39 | 303.042 | 351.594 | 432.072 | 523.211 | 608.213 | 701.209 |
| 40–44 | 270.489 | 294.144 | 342.539 | 422.433 | 513.208 | 598.311 |
| 45–49 | 234.201 | 260.924 | 284.888 | 333.032 | 412.157 | 502.294 |
| 50–54 | 182.588 | 223.689 | 250.317 | 274.454 | 322.079 | 399.970 |
| 55–59 | 137.074 | 170.793 | 210.434 | 236.760 | 260.887 | 307.478 |
| 60–64 | 102.018 | 124.305 | 156.016 | 193.565 | 219.175 | 242.878 |
| 65–69 | 75.739 | 88.518 | 108.790 | 137.667 | 172.091 | 196.168 |
| 70–74 | 56.250 | 61.158 | 72.195 | 89.580 | 114.355 | 144.069 |
| 75–79 | 31.735 | 40.883 | 44.886 | 53.480 | 66.933 | 86.102 |
| 80 + | 24.102 | 29.118 | 36.890 | 43.434 | 51.720 | 63.492 |

Source: CELADE, Boletín Demográfico 7:13 (January, 1974), Table 2, p. 23.

# HONDURAS

Honduras, with a 1975 population of 3.0 million, is the fastest-growing country in Central America. The annual average rate of growth is estimated at 3.47 per cent for the 1970–75 period, which results from a crude birth rate of 49.3 and a crude death rate of 14.6 per thousand[1] Honduras is also the least-urbanized country in the region (31.0 per cent in 1974) although its urban population grew at a rate of five per cent a year between 1961 and 1974.

The census data for 1961 are insufficiently disaggregated to adequately differentiate between those in employment categories (agriculture, services, etc.) in the urban vs. rural sectors and between male and female, therefore it is not possible to review trends in labor force participation rates and shifting occupational structures. Data for such review will become available once the complete results of the 1974 census are published.

## Growth Rate

The population of Honduras as enumerated in its 12 censuses and as estimated by CELADE for census dates since 1926 is shown in Table 94. Before 1940, and particularly before 1930, the census seriously undercounted the total population. The four censuses between 1940 and 1961 were quite accurate. However, the CELADE population estimate for March, 1974 implies that the census of that year underenumerated

---

[1] Centro Latinoamericano de Demografía (CELADE), *Boletín Demográfico* 7:13 (January 1974) pp. 31–34.

the population by 8.4 per cent. The National Demographic Survey of Honduras found the crude birth rate to be 49.2[1] and the crude death rate 14.2[2] per thousand population for the period from December 7, 1970 to October 21, 1972. The rate of natural increase of 3.5 per cent found by the survey indicates that the 1961-74 intercensal growth rate estimated by CELADE (3.2 per cent) is more accurate than the rate implied by the 1961 and 1974 censuses (2.7 per cent). The intercensal growth rate estimated by CELADE indicates that the rate of natural increase, 1961-1974, was about 3.3 percent a year because net international emigration equalled 0.13 per cent a year. The series of estimated population growth rates provided by Collver for Honduras (Table 95) is generally somewhat higher than the corresponding rates from the CELADE population series (Table 94). However, the two series indicate that the population of Honduras has grown at an annual rate exeeding 1.5 per cent at least since 1910 (with the exception of the 1915-19 period). The growth rate reached 2.0 per cent a year after 1940, and 3.0 per cent after 1955. The population doubled between 1950 and 1974, and will double again in 20 years if the current growth rate of 3.47 per cent is maintained.

## Birth Rate

The birth rate in Honduras has been the highest in Latin America for at least the past 25 years.[3] According to Collver the crude birth rate (CBR) was near 44 per thousand population from 1910 to 1949 (Table 95), and his estimates are conservative. The CELADE estimates place the CBR at 54.6 in 1950-55 and 49.3 in 1970-75. These estimates are confirmed by the National Demographic Survey of Honduras which measured the CBR at 49.2 over a 23 month period from 1970 to 1972.[4] The average CBR derived from the vital statistics registry for 1970 and 1971 is 44.0, or 10.6 per cent less than found by the survey. Compared with the CELADE estimates, the CBR based on vital registration was 10.6 per cent too low in 1961 and 17.7 per cent too low in 1951.[5]

The very high fertility in Honduras is reflected in other measures derived from the national survey. The general fertility rate, or annual

---

[1] Zulma C. Camisa, *Fecundidad y Nupcialidad,* Encuesta Demográfica Nacional de Honduras, part 3; Honduras, Dirección General de Estadística y Censos and Centro Latinoamericano de Demografía, series A, no. 129, San José, Costa Rica, May 1975, p. 15.

[2] Antonio Ortega and Manuel Rincón, *Mortalidad,* Encuesta Demográfica Nacional de Honduras, part 4; Honduras, Dirección General de Estadística y Censos and Centro Latinoamericano de Demografía, series A, no. 129, San José, Costa Rica, August 1975, p. 13.

[3] CELADE, *Boletín Demográfico* 7:13. p. 31.

[4] Camisa, *Fecundidad y Nupcialidad.* p. 15.

[5] *Ibid.,* p. 25.

**Table 94**

**Population and Intercensal Growth Rates of Honduras: from Censuses, 1881-1974; and as Estimated, 1926-1974**

| | Censuses | | CELADE Estimates[a] | | |
|---|---|---|---|---|---|
| Date of Census | Population | Annual Growth Rate (%) | Population (1,000's) | Annual Growth Rate (%) | Implied Census Under-enumeration |
| 1881 | 307,289 | — | | | |
| 1887 | 337,917 | 1.28 | | | |
| December 18, 1910 | 553,446 | 2.18 | | | |
| December 17, 1916 | 605,997 | 1.51 | | | |
| December 26, 1926 | 700,811 | 1.45 | 887 | — | 21.0 |
| June 29, 1930 | 854,184 | 5.64 | 948 | 1.90 | 9.9 |
| June 30, 1935 | 962,000 | 2.38 | 1,027 | 1.60 | 6.3 |
| June 30, 1940 | 1,107,859 | 2.82 | 1,119 | 1.72 | 1.0 |
| June 24, 1945 | 1,200,542 | 1.61 | 1,236 | 2.00 | 2.8 |
| June 18, 1950 | 1,368,605 | 2.64 | 1,389 | 2.34 | 1.4 |
| April 17, 1961 | 1,884,765 | 2.95 | 1,923 | 3.00 | 2.0 |
| March 1974 | 2,653,857 | 2.66 | 2,898 | 3.19 | 8.4 |

[a] The CELADE estimates are adjusted to the census dates.

Sources: 1881-1961 censuses: Honduras, Dirección General de Estadística y Censos, *Anuario Estadística 1963,* Tegucigalpa, July 1964, p. 25.

1974 census: Honduras, Dirección General de Estadística y Censos, *Censo Nacional de Población y Vivienda, Marzo 1974, Cifras Preliminares,* Tegucigalpa, January 1975, p. 1.

Estimates: Centro Latinoamericano de Demografía (CELADE), *Boletín Demográfico* 7:13 (January 1974) p. 7.

number of births per one thousand females 15-49, was 230.9; and the total fertility rate was 7.5 children per woman. Rural women bear an average of 3.4 more children during their lifetime (8.7) than do urban women (5.3). The substantial difference between urban and rural age-specific fertility rates is graphed in Figure 26.

Among the geographical regions of Honduras, delineated for the purposes of the National Demographic Survey, fertility varies little, except in the 'urban centers' region (Table 96). The total fertility rate (TFR) is 8.4 in the Northeast and West, and 8.2 in the South. The TFR is measured at 4.7 in the urban centers region which included six of the country's eight largest cities: Tegucigalpa, San Pedro Sula, El Progreso, Puerto Cortes, Tela, and La Lima (see Figure 27). In each of the four regions, fertility is lower among the urban than the rural population. Fertility in both the urban and rural areas of the urban centers region is lower than those areas of the other regions. With regard to fertility by area of residence, there is no apparent consistency among the other three regions. The highest rural TFR (9.0) is observed in the Northeast, while the greatest urban TFR (7.3) occurs in the West. The South has the lowest urban fertility of the three regions, but has intermediate rural fertility.

Fertility in Honduras varies inversely with socio-economic status as determined by the level of education and the occupation of the head of the household (Table 96). The results of the national survey indicate

138

## Figure 26
**Age-specific fertility rates in Honduras, by urban and rural residence, 1971–1972.**

Age-specific
fertility rate

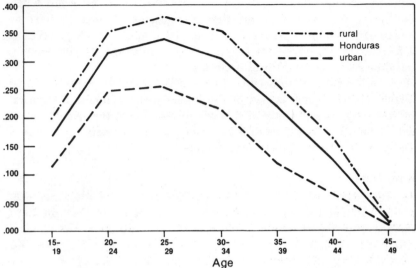

Source:
Zulma C. Camisa, *Fecundidad y Nupcialidad*, Encuesta Demográfica Nacional de Honduras, part 3; Honduras, Dirección General de Estadística y Censos and Centro Latinoamericano de Demografía, series A, no. 129, San Jose, Costa Rica, May 1975, pp. 17, 33.

## Table 95
### Estimated Vital Rates in Honduras, 1910–1975

| Period | Crude Birth Rate | Crude Death Rate | Rate of Net International Migration | Annual Rate of Growth (%) |
|---|---|---|---|---|
| 1910–14 | 43.7 | 24.5 | — | 1.92 |
| 1915–19 | 41.7 | 27.4 | — | 1.43 |
| 1920–24 | 44.3 | 23.1 | — | 2.12 |
| 1925–29 | 44.1 | 23.1 | — | 2.10 |
| 1930–34 | 42.0 | 21.7 | — | 2.03 |
| 1935–39 | 41.9 | 22.1 | — | 1.98 |
| 1940–44 | 43.8 | 23.9 | — | 2.00 |
| 1945–49 | 44.5 | 19.0 | — | 2.56 |
| 1950–55 | 54.6 | 28.5 | 2.34 | 2.84 |
| 1955–60 | 53.3 | 24.4 | 2.02 | 3.09 |
| 1960–65 | 51.8 | 20.7 | 1.72 | 3.28 |
| 1965–70 | 51.1 | 17.5 | −4.68 | 2.89 |
| 1970–75 | 49.3 | 14.6 | — | 3.47 |

Sources: 1910-1949: O. Andrew Collver, *Birth Rates in Latin America: New Estimates of Historical Trends and Fluctuations.* Berkeley: University of California, 1965, p. 136.

1950-1975: Centro Latinoamericano de Demografía (CELADE), *Boletín Demográfico* 7:13 (January 1974) 31-34.

that the TFR is 5.8 for the combined upper, upper-middle, and middle categories; 7.9 for the lower-middle category; and 8.1 for the lower category. The greatest urban fertility (a TFR of 6.1)is found among women of the lower category, while the highest rural fertility (TFR equal to 9.3) occurs in the lower-middle category. In no residence-status group is fertility low. Urban women of the first socio-economic category bear an average of 4.7 children. In 1975 only 40,000 women, or 6.6 per cent of all females 15–44, were contraceptive acceptors at the 34 government-sponsored maternal/child health clinics.[1]

If overall fertility is to decline, that decline would be expected to be initiated among urban women of the higher socio-economic categories. The relatively lower fertility of this group may signal the beginnings of such a trend, but as yet there is no evidence that the very high level of fertility is on a path of long-term decline.

### Death Rate

The crude death rate (CDR) of 14.2 per thousand population measured by the National Demographic Survey[2] is one of the highest in Latin America, with the exception of the rate of 18.0 in Bolivia. Even so, the CDR has been halved from its level of 28.5 in 1950–1955 (Table 95). The CDR computed from vital registration, 1971–1972, is 8.0, indicating that death registration is less than 60 per cent complete.

Mortality varies substantially by region, area of residence, and socio-economic category (Table 97). Both the CDR and the infant mortality rate (IMR), or the number of deaths to infants of less than one year of age per 1,000 births in a given year, are much lower in the surveyed urban centers than in the other geographic regions. Mortality is the greatest in the Western region where the CDR equals 19.7, and the IMR is 132.7. The CDR in all urban areas of the survey is 9.0, compared with a rate of 16.5 in rural areas; and the urban IMR is 85.6, compared with 127.2 in rural areas. Mortality is significantly lower among the three middle to upper socio-economic categories than among the lower-middle and lower categories. The lower socio-economic category experiences higher mortality than the lower-middle category, but the difference is not great.

### Migration

The overall low population density of 23 persons per square kilometer and the undeveloped land areas of the north coast and parts of the in-

---

[1] Population Reference Bureau, *World Population Growth and Response, 1965–1975: A Decade of Global Action,* Washington, D.C., April, 1976, p. 146.

[2] Ortega and Rincón, *Mortalidad.*

**Figure 27**
**Honduras: Departments, principal cities, and regions**
**(Defined for the National Demographic Survey).**

Regions defined for the National Demographic Survey:

1. (shaded) Urban centers
2. Northeast
3. West
4. South
ns. not surveyed

Source:

Zulma C. Camisa, *Fecundidad y Nupcialidad,* Encuesta Demográfica Nacional de Honduras, part 3; Honduras, Dirección General de
Estadística y Censos and Centro Latinoamericano de Demografía,
series A, no. 129, San José, Costa Rica, May 1975, p. 62.

**Table 96**

**Total Fertility Rates for Regions and Socio-economic Categories in Honduras,
By Urban and Rural Residence, 1971–1972.**

|  |  |  | Region[a] |  |  |
|---|---|---|---|---|---|
|  | Honduras | Urban Centers | Northeast | West | South |
| Honduras | 7.5 | 4.7 | 8.4 | 8.4 | 8.2 |
| Urban | 5.3 | 4.0 | 6.8 | 7.3 | 5.4 |
| Rural | 8.7 | 6.8 | 9.0 | 8.6 | 8.8 |

|  |  | Socio-economic Category |  |  |
|---|---|---|---|---|
|  | Total | Upper, Upper-middle, and Middle | Lower-Middle | Lower |
| Honduras | 7.5 | 5.8 | 7.9 | 8.1 |
| Urban | 5.3 | 4.7 | 5.6 | 6.1 |
| Rural | 8.7 | 8.0 | 9.3 | 8.5 |

[a] The regions are illustrated in Figure 28.

Source: Zulma C. Camisa, *Fecundidad y Nupcialidad,* Encuesta Demográfica Nacional de Honduras, part 3; Honduras,
Dirección General de Estadística y Censos and Centro Latinoamericano de Demografía, series A, no. 129, San José,
Costa Rica, May 1975, pp. 56, 63.

terior have attracted migrants to Honduras from other Central American countries. El Salvador's population density in 186 persons per square kilometer and its land holding pattern favors large landowners. Blutstein[1] estimates that 250,000 Salvadoreans had become farmers in Honduras, migrating principally between the Second World War and 1969. An additional 50,000 Salvadorean laborers had moved to provincial towns in Honduras where they competed for employment with Hondurans. CELADE assumes that net immigration to Honduras equalled 3,500 persons per year from 1950 to 1965 (Table 95), for a net total of 52,500 immigrants during the period.

In 1969 Honduras began requiring aliens to leave under a provision of the Agrarian Reform Law which allows only native-born citizens to own land. Blutstein states that 61,000 Salvadoreans returned to their country in that year alone. The CELADE population series assumes that net outmigration from Honduras equalled 55,000 people during the 1965-1970 period. International migration is assumed to be negligible after 1970.

## Age Distribution

Continuing high fertility and decreasing mortality, especially among infants and children, have caused Honduras' population to become

**Table 97**

**Honduras: Crude Death Rate (CDR) and Infant Mortality Rate (IMR) by Region, Area of Residence, and Socio-economic Category, 1971-1972**

| | | | Region | | |
|---|---|---|---|---|---|
| | Honduras | Urban Centers | Northeast | West | South |
| CDR | 14.2 | 8.2 | 15.2 | 19.7 | 12.4 |
| IMR | 117.0 | 84.8 | 108.8 | 132.7 | 131.2 |

| | | Area of Residence | |
|---|---|---|---|
| | Honduras | Urban | Rural |
| CDR | 14.2 | 9.0 | 16.5 |
| IMR | 117.0 | 85.6 | 127.2 |

| | | Socio-economic Category | |
|---|---|---|---|
| | Honduras | Upper, Upper-middle, and Middle | Lower-Middle | Lower |
| CDR | 14.2 | 8.8 | 14.8 | 16.1 |
| IMR | 117.0 | 95.2 | 114.1 | 126.3 |

Source: Antonio Ortega and Manuel Rincón, *Mortalidad.* Encuesta Demográfica Nacional de Honduras, part 4; Honduras, Dirección General de Estadística y Censos and Centro Latinoamericano de Demografía, series A, no. 129, San José, Costa Rica, August 1975, pp. 32–38.

---

[1]Blutstein; *et. al., Handbook for El Salvador.* pp. 53–54.

somewhat younger in 1975 than it was in 1950, according to the CELADE population series which adjusts for census age-misreporting (Table 98). The percentage of the population under age 15 has risen from 44.6 in 1950 to 46.9 in 1975. The dependency ratio has also increased, from 90 to 99, during the same period.

In the projections to the year 2000, a very large proportion of Honduras' population will continue to be under age 15. These age structures are detailed in Appendix A of this chapter. The estimated proportions in this age bracket should shift only slightly between 1950–2000 as noted in Tables 98 and 99. Approximately 44.6 per cent of the population was under age 15 in 1950 and 43.2 per cent is projected for the year 2000. These percentages, however, take on a far different meaning when converted to absolute numbers. Honduras had approximately 620,000 children (under age 15) in 1950, but this group will number roughly three million in the year 2000. Thus,extremely heavy and continuing burdens will be placed on the society to provide basic social services to this growing number during their formative years, while yet another set of difficulties will be encountered to provide sufficient employment in this traditional agrarian society.

The proportion of Honduran children to the total population is high even in comparison to the remaining countries of the region (Table 100), and the country will maintain this position through the close of the century.

Because of the rural-to-urban migration of young adults, particularly ages 15 to 24, and lower urban fertility rates, the urban population is considerably older than the rural population. Based on 1961 census results unadjusted for age-misreporting, 43.9 per cent of the urban population is under age 15, compared with 49.0 per cent of the rural population. The dependency ratio is 105 among the rural population and 88 in urban areas.

**Table 98**

**Honduras: Percentage of Population in Broad Age Groups and Dependency Ratios; Adjusted for 1950, 1960, and 1975; and Unadjusted from the Census of 1961.**

| Age | Adjusted | | | 1961 Census | | |
|---|---|---|---|---|---|---|
| | 1950 | 1960 | 1975 | Total | Urban | Rural |
| All ages | 100.0% | 100.0% | 100.0% | 100.0% | 100.0% | 100.0% |
| 0–14 | 44.6 | 46.0 | 46.9 | 47.8 | 43.9 | 49.0 |
| 15–64 | 52.7 | 51.6 | 50.3 | 49.7 | 53.3 | 48.7 |
| 65 | 2.7 | 2.5 | 2.8 | 2.4 | 2.8 | 2.3 |
| Dependency Ratio[a] | 89.7 | 93.8 | 98.8 | 101.1 | 87.6 | 105.5 |

[a] The dependency ratio is $(P(0\text{-}14) + P(65)/P(15\text{-}64)) \times 100$, where P(a) is the population age "a".

Sources: Adjusted: Centro Latinoamericano de Demografía (CELADE), *Boletín Demográfico* 7:13 (January 1974) 24.

Unadjusted: Honduras, Dirección General de Estadística y Censos, *Censos Nacional de Honduras. Características Generales y Educativas de la Población. Abril 1961.* Tegucigalpa, December 1964, p. 5.

A ten per cent sample drawn from the 1974 census results confirms that the age distribution has become slightly younger and that the rural population is significantly younger than the urban population.[1] The sample indicates that 48.2 per cent of the population is aged 0-14, 48.9 per cent is 15-64, and 2.9 per cent is 65 plus. The dependency ratio was 104.4 in 1974. In urban areas 44.3, 52.7, and 3.0 per cent of the population is in the respective age groups and the dependency ratio is 89.8. Among the rural population the respective percentages are 50.3, 46.9, and 2.8, and the dependency ratio is 113.4.

As is true in other Latin American countries, many teenagers and young adults migrate from rural to urban places and a majority of the migrants are females. The percentage of each sex-age group which lives in urban areas (graphed in Figure 28) indicates that this migration is greatest among both males and females ages 10-19. Figure 28 is based not on final census results but on the ten per cent sample. In the sample, 35.3 per cent of the population lives in urban areas, compared with the 31.1 per cent indicated by the preliminary census results. Until

Table 99

Population in Broad Age Groups, 1980-2000 as Projected by CELADE.

| Age Group | Population | | | Percentage | | |
|-----------|-----------|-----------|-----------|-----------|-----------|-----------|
| | 1980 | 1990 | 2000 | 1980 | 1990 | 2000 |
| Total | 3,594,728 | 4,996,614 | 6,881,452 | 100.0 | 100.0 | 100.0 |
| 0-14 | 1,686,939 | 2,253,778 | 2,972,279 | 46.9 | 45.1 | 43.2 |
| 15-64 | 1,804,202 | 2,585,760 | 3,677,223 | 50.2 | 51.8 | 53.4 |
| 65+ | 103,587 | 157,076 | 231,950 | 2.9 | 3.1 | 3.4 |

Source: Centro Latinoamericano de Demografía (CELADE), *Boletín Demográfico* 7:13 (January 1974).

Table 100

Percentage of Population under Age 15, Projected for 1980 and 2000 for Central America Countries and Panama.

| Country | Population Age 0-14 as Percentage of Total | |
|---------|-----------|-----------|
| | 1980 | 2000 |
| Honduras | 46.9 | 43.2 |
| Costa Rica | 39.2 | 34.0 |
| El Salvador | 45.2 | 41.3 |
| Guatemala | 42.8 | 39.1 |
| Nicaragua | 45.9 | 39.4 |
| Panama | 41.4 | 37.2 |

Source: Honduras, see note, Table 99; for the remaining countries see those country chapters in this report.

---

[1] Honduras, Dirección General de Estadística y Censos, *Censos de Población y Vivienda, 1974, Resultados Muestra*, Tegucigalpa, July 1975, Table 1.

**Figure 28**
**Urban residence ratios by age and sex, Honduras, 1974.**

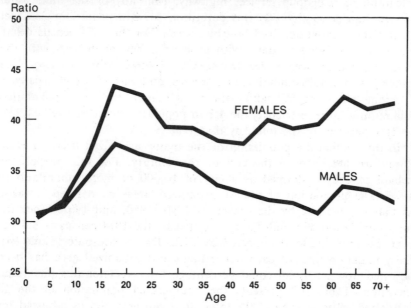

Source:
Honduras, Direccion General de Estadistica y Censos, *Censo de Poblacion y Vivienda, 1974, Resultados Muestra*, Tegucigalpa, July 1975, Table 1.

final census figures are published, all observations pertaining to the 1974 population should be regarded as tentative. For this reason, the importance of Figure 28 lies not in the height of the curves but rather in their changes from one age group to another. The decline in urban residence ratios (URR) at ages over 20 for males and females is the result of both cohort effect (a return to rural areas by previous migrants) and a period effect (a continuing urbanization trend such that younger persons are more urban than their elders). The rise in the URR for females over age 45 is evidence of the cohort effect. The gradual urbanization of older women does not occur among males. The curves in Figure 28 are much steeper between ages 0 and 19 than are similar graphs of the 1961 population (not shown). This change reflects an upsurge in recent rural-to-urban migration relative to that in the period preceding 1961.

## Urban Population Growth

The discussions of the urban population in preceding sections have been based on the urban definition employed by the *Dirección de Estadística y Censos*. In 1940 and 1950 urban places were designated by an administrative order and not defined by a minimum population or other characteristics. In 1961 a place was classified as urban if it

145

had a population of at least 1,000 persons plus a primary school; mail, telegraph or telephone service; highway, rail, air, or sea link; water service; and electricity.[1] By this definition 437,818 people, or 23.2 per cent of the population, lived in urban areas. For the 1974 census urban places were defined as those with at least 2,000 inhabitants with the following four services: water, transportation links, primary school, and either postal or telecommunication service; and with either electricity, a sewerage plant, or a health center.[2] Although the 1974 population minimum is more restrictive, the urban population increased to 824,994, or 31.1 per cent of the total, by that year.

In this section the population of the major urbanized areas of Honduras are projected to the end of the century. For this purpose an urbanized area is defined as a city of 10,000 or more inhabitants in 1974. The population of the 13 urbanized areas so defined is taken as that enumerated by the census in 1940, 1950, and 1961. Since the total population of Honduras as counted by the 1974 census is 8.4 per cent less than the total projected by CELADE for the date (Table 94), the population total of each department and urbanized area has been adjusted upward by an equal percentage to correct for this underenumeration. Table 102 presents the enumerated population of the 13 urbanized areas at each of the latest four censuses and as adjusted for underenumeration in 1974.

The total population of the 13 urbanized areas has more than tripled since 1950 to 686,000 in 1974, equivalent to 23.7 per cent of the

Table 101

**Enumerated and Projected Population of Honduras, Thirteen Urbanized Areas, and Non-urbanized Areas, 1940 to 2000**

| | | 13 Urbanized Areas[a] | | Non-Urbanized Areas | |
|---|---|---|---|---|---|
| Year | Honduras | Population in thousands | Per Cent of Total | Population in Thousands | Per Cent of Total |
| 1940 | 1,107,859 | 129.8 | 11.7 | 978.0 | 88.3 |
| 1950 | 1,368,605 | 181.1 | 13.2 | 1,187.6 | 86.8 |
| 1961 | 1,884,765 | 319.3 | 16.9 | 1,565.4 | 83.1 |
| 1974[b] | 2,897,504 | 686.3 | 23.7 | 2,211.2 | 76.3 |
| 1980 | 3,594,728 | 935.4 | 26.0 | 2,659.3 | 74.0 |
| 1990 | 4,996,614 | 1,467.7 | 29.4 | 3,528.9 | 70.6 |
| 2000 | 6,881,452 | 2,250.2 | 32.7 | 4,631.3 | 67.3 |

[a] The thirteen urbanized areas included are listed in Table 102.
[b] The 1974 totals have been adjusted to correspond to the CELADE projection for that year.

Source: Table 102.

---

[1] Honduras, Dirección General de Estadística y Censos, *Censo Nacional de Honduras, Caracteristicas Generales y Educativas de la Población, Abril 1961*, Tegucigalpa, December 1964, pp. xxxii–xxvii.
[2] Honduras, Dirección General de Estadística y Censo, *Censo Nacional de Población y Vivienda. Marzo 1974, Cifras Preliminares*, Tegucigalpa, January 1975, introduction.

nation's population (Table 101). Urbanization in Honduras progressed slowly between 1940 and 1961, but the urban population as a proportion of the total increased by nearly seven percentage points in the 1961–1974 period.

Although Tegucigalpa is the largest city in Honduras, its population is less than one-third of a million. It is the only capital in Central America which is not a primate city, and it has not been the country's fastest-growing city over the past 24 years. In 1950 Tegucigalpa's population was still under 100,000, but it has since reached about 300,000. Tegucigalpa was 2.3 times the size of San Pedro Sula in 1940, but only 1.8 times as large in 1974. The only three cities with 10,000 or more inhabitants in 1940 were Tegucigalpa, San Pedro Sula, and La Ceiba. By 1950 Tela and Puerto Cortes had joined this group, and by 1961 El Progreso and Choluteca had also passed this mark. San Pedro Sula is the only urbanized area other than the capital with a population greater 100,000.

San Pedro Sula has also been the fastest-growing city in Honduras since 1950. Its rate of increase was 9.4 per cent a year during the 1950–1961 intercensal period and 7.9 per cent in 1961–1974 (Table 103). Tegucigalpa grew at annual rates of 5.7 per cent and 6.1 per cent during the two most recent intercensal periods, and Choluteca at rates of 4.5 per cent and 6.8 per cent. The urbanized areas of Comayagua, Siguatepeque, Danli, Juticalpa, and El Progreso have also expanded at average annual rates above 4.0 per cent during the 1950–1974 period.

The population size of Honduras, of the 13 urbanized areas listed in Table 102, of rural areas and of Tegucigalpa are graphed in Figure 29. Both the rate of growth and the absolute growth of the population of Honduras and of Tegucigalpa have increased successively in the three past intercensal periods. Although the combined population of the 13 urbanized areas is growing at a faster rate than the non-urbanized population, the annual increments to the non-urbanized populations are greater.

**Tables 102**

**Honduras: Enumerated Population, 1940 to 1974; Estimated Population, 1974; and Projected Population, 1980 to 2000.**

| Department and Urbanized Area | Enumerated Population in Thousands | | | | CELADE[a] estimate for March 1974 | Projected Population, Thousands (midyear) | | |
|---|---|---|---|---|---|---|---|---|
| | June 30 1940 | June 8 1950 | Apr. 17 1961 | March 1974 | | 1980 | 1990 | 2000 |
| **National Total** | 1,107.9 | 1,368.6 | 1,884.8 | 2,653.9 | 2,897.5 | 3,594.7 | 4,996.6 | 6,881.5 |
| **Atlántida** | 43.9 | 63.6 | 92.9 | 148.4 | 162.1 | 208.4 | 309.5 | 451.1 |
| La Ceiba | 11.3 | 16.6 | 24.9 | 38.6 | 42.1 | 54.1 | 80.0 | 116.0 |
| Tela | 9.0 | 12.6 | 13.6 | 19.3 | 21.0 | 23.7 | 30.5 | 38.3 |
| Remainder | 23.6 | 34.3 | 54.4 | 90.6 | 98.9 | 130.5 | 198.9 | 296.9 |

147

**Table 102 cont.**

| Department and Urbanized Area | Enumerated Population in Thousands | | | | CELADE[a] estimate for March 1974 | Projected Population, Thousands (midyear) | | |
|---|---|---|---|---|---|---|---|---|
| | June 30 1940 | June 8 1950 | Apr. 17 1961 | March 1974 | March 1974 | 1980 | 1990 | 2000 |
| **Choluteca** | **88.2** | **107.3** | **149.2** | **192.1** | **209.8** | **256.6** | **343.1** | **453.1** |
| Choluteca | 5.1 | 7.1 | 11.5 | 25.1 | 27.4 | 35.8 | 54.9 | 81.9 |
| Remainder | 83.2 | 100.2 | 137.7 | 167.0 | 182.4 | 220.8 | 288.3 | 371.2 |
| **Colón** | **30.6** | **35.5** | **41.9** | **77.2** | **84.3** | **109.5** | **161.8** | **236.7** |
| **Comayagua** | **54.0** | **68.2** | **96.4** | **135.5** | **147.9** | **184.9** | **257.8** | **355.0** |
| Comayagua | 4.8 | 5.2 | 8.5 | 13.4 | 14.6 | 19.4 | 28.2 | 40.7 |
| Siguatepeque | 2.4 | 4.6 | 6.0 | 12.0 | 13.1 | 16.7 | 26.2 | 40.1 |
| Remainder | 46.9 | 58.4 | 82.0 | 110.1 | 120.2 | 148.8 | 203.3 | 274.2 |
| **Copán** | **82.1** | **95.9** | **126.2** | **151.3** | **165.2** | **195.5** | **248.6** | **312.1** |
| Santa Rosa de Copán | 6.0 | 6.4 | 7.9 | 12.1 | 13.2 | 15.9 | 20.8 | 27.1 |
| Remainder | 76.0 | 89.5 | 118.2 | 139.2 | 152.0 | 179.6 | 227.8 | 284.9 |
| **Cortés** | **87.3** | **125.7** | **200.1** | **373.6** | **407.9** | **538.9** | **828.0** | **1,243.9** |
| La Lima[c] | (4.3) | (6.2) | 9.9 | 14.3 | 15.6 | 19.8 | 28.1 | 38.7 |
| Puerto Cortés | 7.0 | 12.2 | 17.0 | 25.7 | 28.0 | 34.1 | 49.5 | 69.1 |
| San Pedro Sula | 20.4 | 21.1 | 58.6 | 148.1 | 161.7 | 238.9 | 401.9 | 657.6 |
| Remainder | 55.6 | 86.2 | 114.5 | 185.6 | 202.7 | 246.1 | 348.6 | 478.4 |
| **El Paraíso** | **67.7** | **82.6** | **106.8** | **140.8** | **153.8** | **184.0** | **242.4** | **315.2** |
| Danlí | 3.2 | 4.2 | 6.3 | 11.4 | 12.4 | 15.9 | 23.4 | 33.6 |
| Remainder | 64.5 | 78.4 | 100.5 | 129.5 | 141.4 | 168.1 | 219.1 | 281.6 |
| **Francisco Morazán** | **158.9** | **190.4** | **284.4** | **451.8** | **493.3** | **637.0** | **920.1** | **1,315.1** |
| Tegucigalpa | 47.2 | 72.4 | 134.1 | 270.6 | 295.5 | 405.6 | 637.4 | 974.2 |
| Remainder | 111.7 | 118.0 | 150.4 | 181.1 | 197.8 | 231.4 | 282.7 | 340.9 |
| **Gracias a Dios** [b] | — | — | 10.9 | 21.1 | 23.0 | 30.6 | 46.5 | 69.6 |
| **Intibucá** | **52.6** | **59.4** | **73.1** | **81.7** | **89.2** | **101.7** | **122.7** | **145.9** |
| **Islas de la Bahía** | **7.0** | **8.1** | **9.0** | **13.2** | **14.4** | **16.8** | **21.7** | **27.8** |
| **La Paz** | **48.5** | **51.2** | **60.6** | **65.4** | **71.4** | **79.7** | **92.4** | **105.8** |
| **Lempira** | **79.0** | **90.9** | **111.5** | **127.5** | **139.2** | **159.0** | **194.0** | **233.3** |
| **Ocotepeque** | **46.0** | **45.7** | **52.5** | **51.2** | **55.9** | **60.6** | **66.4** | **71.9** |
| **Olancho** | **64.5** | **83.9** | **110.7** | **151.9** | **165.0** | **201.4** | **274.8** | **364.4** |
| Juticalpa | 3.8 | 3.2 | 7.2 | 10.1 | 11.0 | 15.4 | 22.0 | 31.5 |
| Remainder | 60.7 | 80.7 | 103.5 | 141.8 | 154.8 | 186.1 | 252.8 | 337.9 |
| **Santa Bárbara** | **80.4** | **96.4** | **146.9** | **185.2** | **202.2** | **253.9** | **345.6** | **464.8** |
| **Valle** | **53.7** | **65.3** | **80.9** | **91.0** | **99.3** | **113.5** | **140.1** | **170.0** |
| **Yoro** | **63.3** | **98.7** | **130.5** | **195.0** | **212.9** | **262.8** | **380.9** | **540.7** |
| El Progreso | 5.4 | 9.2 | 13.8 | 28.0 | 30.6 | 40.3 | 64.8 | 101.2 |
| Remainder | 57.9 | 89.5 | 116.7 | 166.9 | 182.3 | 222.5 | 316.2 | 439.5 |

[a] All department and urbanized area totals are adjusted to the national population total estimated by CELADE.
[b] Gracias a Dios formerly comprised part of the Department of Colón and was not established as a separate department until after the 1950 census.
[c] The population of the city of La Lima is not given in the census reports for 1940 and 1950. The figures shown here are approximations derived by assuming that La Lima grew at the same rate as the Department of Cortés during 1940-1950 and 1950-1961.

Sources: Enumerated totals: Honduras census reports.

1974 estimate: Centro Latinoamericano de Demografía (CELADE), *Boletín Demográfico* 7:13 (January 1974).

**Table 103**

**Observed and Projected Population Growth Rates of Departments and Urbanized Areas in Honduras, 1940 to 2000** [a]

| Department and Urbanized Area | Average Annual Growth Rate (%) of Observed Population | | | Average Annual Growth Rate (%) of Projected Population | | |
|---|---|---|---|---|---|---|
| | 1940–1950 | 1950–1961 | 1961–1974 | 1974–1980 | 1980–1990 | 1990–2000 |
| **National Total** | **2.13** | **2.95** | **3.34** | **3.40** | **3.29** | **3.20** |
| **Atlántida** | **3.74** | **3.49** | **4.32** | **3.97** | **3.96** | **3.77** |
| La Ceiba | 3.90 | 3.70 | 4.10 | 3.95 | 3.92 | 3.71 |
| Tela | 3.43 | 0.71 | 3.38 | 1.90 | 2.52 | 2.27 |
| Remainder | 3.77 | 4.25 | 4.64 | 4.38 | 4.21 | 4.00 |
| **Choluteca** | **1.96** | **3.04** | **2.65** | **3.18** | **2.91** | **2.78** |
| Choluteca | 3.38 | 4.46 | 6.76 | 4.20 | 4.28 | 4.00 |
| Remainder | 1.87 | 2.93 | 2.18 | 3.02 | 2.67 | 2.53 |
| **Colón** | **1.47** | **1.54** | **5.43** | **4.13** | **3.90** | **3.80** |
| **Comayagua** | **2.34** | **3.20** | **3.32** | **3.52** | **3.32** | **3.20** |
| Comayagua | 0.88 | 4.51 | 4.24 | 4.47 | 3.74 | 3.67 |
| Siguatepeque | 6.75 | 2.44 | 6.08 | 3.79 | 4.54 | 4.23 |
| Remainder | 2.19 | 3.13 | 2.97 | 3.38 | 3.12 | 2.99 |
| **Copán** | **1.57** | **2.53** | **2.09** | **2.65** | **2.41** | **2.27** |
| Santa Rosa de Copán | 0.64 | 1.98 | 3.95 | 2.88 | 2.73 | 2.65 |
| Remainder | 1.64 | 2.57 | 1.95 | 2.63 | 2.38 | 2.24 |
| **Cortés** | **3.67** | **4.28** | **5.53** | **4.40** | **4.29** | **4.07** |
| La Lima | (3.67) | (4.28) | 3.54 | 3.79 | 3.50 | 3.22 |
| Puerto Cortés | 5.58 | 3.06 | 3.86 | 3.11 | 3.72 | 3.34 |
| San Pedro Sula | 0.36 | 9.40 | 7.88 | 6.16 | 5.20 | 4.92 |
| Remainder | 4.42 | 2.62 | 4.43 | 3.07 | 3.48 | 3.17 |
| **El Paraíso** | **1.99** | **2.37** | **2.83** | **2.83** | **2.76** | **2.63** |
| Danlí | 2.72 | 3.76 | 5.24 | 3.93 | 3.84 | 3.63 |
| Remainder | 1.95 | 2.29 | 2.65 | 2.73 | 2.65 | 2.51 |
| **Francisco Morazan** | **1.82** | **3.70** | **4.28** | **4.04** | **3.68** | **3.57** |
| Tegucigalpa | 4.30 | 5.68 | 6.14 | 5.00 | 4.52 | 4.24 |
| Remainder | 0.55 | 2.23 | 2.13 | 2.48 | 2.00 | 1.87 |
| **Gracias a Dios** | — | — | **5.80** | **4.52** | **4.17** | **4.04** |
| **Intibucá** | **1.21** | **1.92** | **1.54** | **2.07** | **1.88** | **1.74** |
| **Islas de la Bahía** | **1.38** | **0.98** | **3.71** | **2.41** | **2.55** | **2.46** |
| **La Paz** | **0.55** | **1.55** | **1.27** | **1.73** | **1.48** | **1.35** |
| **Lempira** | **1.42** | **1.88** | **1.72** | **2.11** | **1.99** | **1.84** |
| **Ocotepeque** | **−0.08** | **1.29** | **0.48** | **1.28** | **0.92** | **0.79** |
| **Olancho** | **2.64** | **2.56** | **3.14** | **3.07** | **3.11** | **2.96** |
| Juticalpa | −1.81 | 7.47 | 3.30 | 5.23 | 3.61 | 3.58 |
| Remainder | 2.87 | 2.29 | 3.13 | 2.90 | 3.06 | 2.90 |
| **Santa Bárbara** | **1.83** | **3.88** | **2.48** | **3.60** | **3.08** | **2.96** |
| **Valle** | **1.98** | **1.97** | **1.59** | **2.11** | **2.11** | **1.93** |
| **Yoro** | **4.46** | **2.58** | **3.80** | **3.33** | **3.71** | **3.50** |
| El Progreso | 5.29 | 3.78 | 6.19 | 4.34 | 4.76 | 4.46 |
| Remainder | 4.38 | 2.44 | 3.46 | 3.15 | 3.51 | 3.29 |

[a] In making these calculations, census population totals are employed for 1940, 1950, and 1961; and population figures adjusted to the national total estimated by CELADE are used for 1974.

Source: Table 102.

149

**Figure 29**
**Enumerated and projected population of Honduras,**
**thirteen urbanized areas, non-urbanized areas, and**
**Tegucigalpa; 1940 to 2000.**

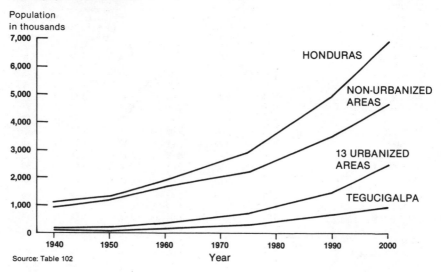

Source: Table 102

## Population Projections

The total population of urbanized areas in Honduras is projected to the years 1980, 1990, and 2000 by allocating the projected national population first to departments then to urbanized areas using a modification of the ratio-trend methodology as elaborated by Pickard.[1]

## National Projection

The projection of the population of Honduras to the year 2000 prepared by CELADE is employed in this report (Table 104). As was noted previously, CELADE'S projected vital rates for the 1970-75 period (CBR = 49.3, CDR = 14.6) correspond almost exactly to the rates obtained by the National Demographic Survey of Honduras for 1971–1972 (CBR = 49.2, CDR = 14.2). The CELADE projection rests on the assumptions that the total fertility rate will decline from 7.28 in 1970-1975 to 5.23 in 1995-2000 and that average expectation of life at birth will rise from 53.5 years to 67.0 years during the same period. These changes would yield a crude birth rate of 38.5 and a crude death rate of 6.9 in the 1995-2000 period, when the population would increase

[1]Pickard, *Dimensions to Metropolitanism.* pp. 53–56.

150

at an annual rate of 3.16 per cent. The total population is projected to more than double from 3.0 million in 1975 to 6.9 million in 2000. International migration is not assumed to affect Honduras' population growth in the 1970–2000 period.

The modest declines in fertility and mortality projected by CELADE would yield an age structure at the end of the century only slightly older than that in 1975. The 0–14 age group would comprise 43.2 per cent of the total population; the 15–64 age group, 53.4 per cent; and the 65 and over ages, 3.4 per cent (compare with Table 98). The dependency ratio in 2000 would be 87.1.

## Department Projections

The population of each of Honduras' 18 departments is projected to midyear 1980, 1990, and 2000 by continuing the trend of the ratio of a department's population to the national population observed in 1940, 1950, 1961, and 1974. The results of the projection are presented in Table 102. Gracias a Dios was not established as a department until after the 1950 census, and comprised part of the Department of Colon previously. The projection methodology requires a population total for each department at the date of the four latest censuses. In 1950 the area of Gracias a Dios contained 6,745 inhabitants. To estimate its population in 1940, it is assumed that Gracias a Dios experienced the same rate of growth in 1940–50 as did Colon. Hence, a figure of 5,828 persons is used as the 1940 population. The population assigned to Gracias a Dios in 1940 and 1950 is subtracted from the department of Colon in the calculations, but not in Table 102.

The Department of Francisco Morazan (containing Tegucigalpa) and Cortes (containing the urbanized areas of San Pedro Sula, Puerto Cortes, and La Lima) are both expected to have populations of over one million by the end of the century. Their combined populations will

Table 104

**Projected Population and Vital Rates for Honduras, 1970 to 2000**

| Period | Population at Beginning of Period (in Thousands) | Crude Birth Rate | Crude Death Rate | Average Annual Rate of Increase (%) |
|---|---|---|---|---|
| 1970–1975 | 2,553 | 49.3 | 14.6 | 3.47 |
| 1975–1980 | 3,037 | 46.3 | 12.7 | 3.36 |
| 1980–1985 | 3,595 | 44.0 | 11.0 | 3.30 |
| 1985–1990 | 4,241 | 42.2 | 9.5 | 3.27 |
| 1990–1995 | 4,997 | 40.5 | 8.2 | 3.23 |
| 1995–2000 | 5,875 | 38.5 | 6.9 | 3.16 |
| 2000 | 6,881 | | | |

Source: Centro Latinoamericano de Demografía (CELADE), *Boletín Demográfico* 7:13 (January 1974).

equal 37 per cent of the national total in the year 2000. The figures for the year 2000 represent a tripling of Cortes' population and an increase by a factor of 2.7 in Francisco Morazan's population over their 1974 levels. Only the department of Yoro (containing El Progreso) will also have more than one-half million inhabitants by the year 2000, although Santa Barbara, Choluteca, and Atlantida are projected to exceed 400,000 by then.

Cortes, the second largest department, and Gracias a Dios, the second smallest department, are expected to be the fastest-growing between 1974 and 2000, with each increasing at an average annual rate of 4.2 per cent over the 26-year period. The most populous department, Francisco Morazan, is projected to increase at an annual rate of 3.7 per cent during 1974–2000. Colon (3.9 per cent), Atlantida (3.9 per cent), Yoro (3.5 per cent), and Comayagua (3.3 per cent) are also expected to grow at rates above the national rate of 3.28 per cent a year. The five departments bordering El Salvador (Ocotepeque, Lempira, Intibuca, La Paz, and Valle) are projected to increase slowly between 1974 and 2000, at rates of about 2.0 per cent a year or less, with Ocotepeque growing at just under 1.0 per cent a year for the period.

**Urbanized Area Projections**

The population of each of the 13 urbanized areas in Honduras is projected to the years 1980, 1990, and 2000 by continuing the trend of its proportion of its department's population observed at the four latest censuses. The combined population of these cities is projected to more than triple from 686,000 in 1974 to 2,250,000 in the year 2000 (Table 101). The cities will increase their share of the national population from 23.7 per cent to 32.7 per cent by increasing at a rate of 4.5 per cent per annum while the non-urbanized areas grow at a rate of 2.8 per cent. Although the rate of increase is greater for the urbanized areas, the non-urbanized areas will continue to increase by greater absolute amounts throughout the rest of this century.

The projections indicate that both Tegucigalpa and San Pedro Sula will more than triple in population size by the year 2000, when they will contain 974,000 and 658,000 inhabitants, respectively (Table 102). Together they account for nearly three-fourths (72.5 per cent) of the urbanized area population and one-fourth (23.7 per cent) of the population of Honduras in the year 2000. San Pedro Sula is expected to be the most rapidly growing urbanized area in the country, averaging increases of 5.33 per cent a year during 1974–2000 (Table 103). Tegucigalpa's projected growth rate is 4.53 per cent per annum. La Ceiba will hold its rank as the third largest city by increasing at a rate of 3.85 per cent and equalling 116,000 in the year 2000. El Progreso is the fourth urbanized area projected to exceed 100,000 in population at the end of the century. It is expected to be the second fastest growing city, with a growth rate of 4.54 per cent. The average annual growth rates of Siguatepeque (4.25 per cent), Choluteca (4.16 per cent), and Juticalpa (4.00 per cent) are also projected to equal or exceed 4.0 per cent in the 1974-2000 period. On the other hand, Santa Rosa de Copan, the smallest of the 13 urbanized areas in 2000, and Tela are expected to increase at rates below that of the national population.

The major conclusions drawn from the projections of the population of Honduras and its urbanized areas are as follows: (1) the population of Honduras will continue to increase at the extremely high average rate of 3.3 per cent a year and equal nearly 6.9 million at the end of the century; (2) the combined population of the 13 urbanized areas discussed in this report will triple during 1974-2000 and comprise nearly one-third of the national population in the year 2000; and (3) Tegucigalpa is not a primate city. Although Tegucigalpa will hold 14 per cent of the population of Honduras in 2000, San Pedro Sula is projected to grow at a greater rate during the 1974-2000 interval and to be two-thirds the size of the capital in that year.

**Appendix A**

**Honduras: Population projections by sex and quinquennial age groups, 1975-2000. Recommended hypothesis**

| | year | | | | | |
|---|---|---|---|---|---|---|
| age groups | 1975 | 1980 | 1985 | 1990 | 1995 | 2000 |
| | | | males | | | |
| Total | 1,514.420 | 1,794.804 | 2,120.262 | 2,500.345 | 2,942.233 | 3,448.000 |
| 0- 4 | 294.057 | 335.048 | 383.384 | 441.419 | 505.805 | 571.977 |
| 5- 9 | 231.526 | 280.178 | 321.449 | 370.203 | 428.944 | 494.359 |
| 10-14 | 185.896 | 227.752 | 276.154 | 317.414 | 366.198 | 425.015 |
| 15-19 | 151.934 | 184.237 | 226.062 | 274.495 | 315.929 | 364.949 |
| 20-24 | 127.539 | 150.416 | 182.640 | 224.403 | 272.842 | 314.444 |
| 25-29 | 112.399 | 125.630 | 148.553 | 180.646 | 222.484 | 271.009 |
| 30-34 | 84.854 | 110.143 | 123.498 | 146.471 | 178.615 | 220.573 |
| 35-39 | 73.947 | 83.030 | 108.137 | 121.602 | 144.680 | 176.990 |
| 40-44 | 60.063 | 72.080 | 81.234 | 106.187 | 119.846 | 143.112 |
| 45-49 | 52.739 | 58.120 | 70.066 | 79.326 | 104.206 | 118.186 |
| 50-54 | 44.410 | 50.363 | 55.790 | 67.669 | 77.117 | 101.989 |
| 55-59 | 31.592 | 41.568 | 47.495 | 53.008 | 64.772 | 74.360 |
| 60-64 | 24.234 | 28.600 | 37.984 | 43.803 | 49.338 | 60.839 |
| | 18.313 | 20.857 | 24.899 | 33.447 | 39.009 | 44.429 |
| 70-74 | 10.882 | 14.551 | 16.805 | 20.341 | 27.699 | 32.741 |
| 75-79 | 6.710 | 7.620 | 10.366 | 12.176 | 14.985 | 20.742 |
| 80 + | 3.325 | 4.611 | 5.746 | 7.735 | 9.764 | 12.392 |

# Appendix A cont.

| age groups | year | | | | | |
|---|---|---|---|---|---|---|
| | 1975 | 1980 | 1985 | 1990 | 1995 | 2000 |
| | | | females | | | |
| **Total** | **1,522.790** | **1,799.924** | **2,121.215** | **2,496.269** | **2,933.010** | **3,433.346** |
| 0- 4 | 294.231 | 333.944 | 380.822 | 437.188 | 500.806 | 565.786 |
| 5- 9 | 232.704 | 281.735 | 322.163 | 369.892 | 427.229 | 492.082 |
| 10-14 | 184.981 | 228.282 | 277.137 | 317.662 | 365.531 | 423.060 |
| 15-19 | 152.311 | 182.412 | 225.602 | 274.441 | 315.168 | 363.301 |
| 20-24 | 126.680 | 150.360 | 180.526 | 223.773 | 272.808 | 313.892 |
| 25-29 | 108.698 | 124.579 | 148.297 | 178.537 | 221.882 | 271.174 |
| 30-34 | 82.642 | 106.435 | 122.396 | 146.160 | 176.485 | 219.971 |
| 35-39 | 73.298 | 80.862 | 104.512 | 120.586 | 144.465 | 174.895 |
| 40-44 | 60.580 | 71.478 | 79.147 | 102.656 | 118.856 | 142.868 |
| 45-49 | 54.551 | 58.635 | 69.452 | 77.193 | 100.488 | 116.785 |
| 50-54 | 46.076 | 52.004 | 56.148 | 66.799 | 74.562 | 97.474 |
| 55-59 | 33.238 | 42.970 | 48.767 | 52.942 | 63.323 | 71.053 |
| 60-64 | 26.270 | 30.280 | 39.427 | 45.063 | 49.262 | 59.359 |
| 65-69 | 20.445 | 23.030 | 26.790 | 35.205 | 40.659 | 45.014 |
| 70-74 | 12.893 | 16.797 | 19.146 | 22.603 | 30.234 | 35.627 |
| 75-79 | 8.461 | 9.556 | 12.692 | 14.743 | 17.731 | 24.154 |
| 80 + | 4.731 | 6.565 | 8.191 | 10.826 | 13.521 | 16.851 |
| | | | both sexes | | | |
| **Total** | **3,037.210** | **3,594.728** | **4,241.477** | **4,996.614** | **5,875.243** | **6,881.452** |
| 0- 4 | 588.288 | 668.992 | 764.206 | 878.607 | 1,006.611 | 1,137.763 |
| 5- 9 | 464.230 | 561.913 | 643.612 | 740.095 | 856.173 | 986.441 |
| 10-14 | 370.877 | 456.034 | 553.291 | 635.076 | 731.729 | 848.075 |
| 15-19 | 304.245 | 366.649 | 451.664 | 548.936 | 631.097 | 728.250 |
| 20-24 | 254.219 | 300.776 | 363.166 | 448.176 | 545.650 | 628.336 |
| 25-29 | 221.097 | 250.209 | 296.850 | 359.183 | 444.366 | 542.183 |
| 30-34 | 167.496 | 216.578 | 245.894 | 292.631 | 355.100 | 440.544 |
| 35-39 | 147.245 | 163.892 | 212.649 | 242.188 | 289.145 | 351.885 |
| 40-44 | 120.643 | 143.558 | 160.381 | 208.843 | 238.702 | 285.980 |
| 45-49 | 107.290 | 116.755 | 139.518 | 156.519 | 204.694 | 234.971 |
| 50-54 | 90.486 | 102.367 | 111.938 | 134.468 | 151.679 | 199.463 |
| 55-59 | 64.830 | 84.538 | 96.262 | 105.950 | 128.095 | 145.413 |
| 60-64 | 50.504 | 58.880 | 77.411 | 88.866 | 98.600 | 120.198 |
| 65-69 | 38.758 | 43.887 | 51.689 | 68.652 | 79.668 | 89.443 |
| 70-74 | 23.775 | 31.348 | 35.951 | 42.944 | 57.933 | 68.368 |
| 85-79 | 15.171 | 17.176 | 23.058 | 26.919 | 32.716 | 44.896 |
| 80 + | 8.056 | 11.176 | 13.937 | 18.561 | 23.285 | 29.243 |

Source: CELADE, Boletín Demográfico 7:13 (January 1974), Table 2, p. 24.

154

# NICARAGUA

Nicaragua is the largest and least densely-settled country in Central America. Its population of 2.3 million in 1975 is less than half that of Guatemala. Although it has a very long Caribbean coastline, the majority of the population is concentrated on the Pacific side of the Republic. The proportion of the population living in urban areas (48 per cent in 1971) is the highest in the region.

In the absence of reliable vital registries, which in any case cover only a limited subject area, and with continuous national level household sample survey systems still in their infancy in Latin America, a great deal of dependence must be placed on the information gathered through enumerations, normally encompassing a census of population, housing, and agriculture. During the course of an enumeration and the tabulation process accompanying it a key issue is the amount of underenumeration that has occurred. A large undercount relative to the prior census will, for example, produce a growth rate in the interval that is lower than in actual fact. This problem is always a major concern, and the normal skepticism directed in surveys of this kind to the data base almost immediately focuses on this very subject.

The amount of undercount for each of Nicaragua's enumerations is considered on the following pages. The necessary adjustments were made and figure in the projections to the year 2000. In the major tables (Tables 114 and 115) the original census data for 1950, 1963 and 1971 are reproduced unaltered. For 1980, 1990 and 2000 the projections presume complete census counts. A cautionary flag is consequently raised to note that at the point of differences between the two series, specifically in the 1971–80 interval, an artificially high growth rate is reflected, one based on the depressed census count in 1971 determined by the ISPC at a level of 4.8 per cent. The growth rate during the 1960-70 interval is also affected by differential underenumerations. Details are found on page 171.

## Growth Rate

The total population enumerated by Nicaragua's six censuses in this century is presented in Table 105. The population has more than tripled since the census of 1906. Fertility has been high and nearly constant while mortality has declined gradually to a moderate level. The result has been a steadily rising growth rate which increased the most during the 1940's and 1950's and is currently 3.3 per cent a year. The trend of the growth rate has been partially obscured by differential completeness of census enumerations. If the CELADE time series of estimates is taken as accurate, the apparent decline in the growth rate between 1906-1920 and 1920-1940 was caused by the underenumeration of 6.7 per cent in the 1940 census (see Table 105). The growth rate given by CELADE for 1920-1940 is nearly the same as that yielded by the census counts of 1906 and 1920.

The apparent decline in the growth rate from 1950–63 to 1963–71 may also be partially attributable to different levels of underenumeration in 1963 and 1971. However, the CELADE estimate of the 1971 population is, in fact, a projection from 1963 and may be somewhat high. A preliminary adjustment of the 1971 census population made by the International Statistical Programs Center (ISPC) of the U.S. Bureau

Table 105

**Enumerated and Estimated Population and Growth Rates of Nicaragua, 1906 to 1971**

| | Enumeration[a] | | CELADE Estimates[b] | | |
|---|---|---|---|---|---|
| Date of Census | Population | Ave. Annual Growth Rate (%) in Period | Population (Thousands) | Ave. Annual Growth Rate (%) in Period | Implied under-enumeration (%) |
| July 1906 | 501,849 | — | | | |
| January 1920 | 633,622 | 1.73 | 634 | — | 0.0 |
| May 1940 | 829,831 | 1.33 | 890 | 1.67 | 6.7 |
| May 1950 | 1,049,611 | 2.35 | 1,105 | 2.16 | 5.0 |
| May 1963 | 1,535,588 | 2.93 | 1,598 | 2.84 | 3.9 |
| May 20, 1971 | 1,877,952 | 2.53 | 2,020 | 2.94 | 7.0 |

[a] The population totals have been adjusted to correspond to the area within the national borders of 1963 and later.
[b] The CELADE estimates are adjusted to the census dates.

Sources: Nicaragua, Banco Central de Nicaragua-Ministerio de Economía, Industria y Comercio, *Censos Nacionales 1971, Población por Municipios*, Vol. 1, *Características Generales*, Managua, March 1975, Table A.

Centro Latinoamericano de Demografía (CELADE), *Boletín Demográfico* 9:17 (January 1976) Table 1.

of Census[1] puts the 1971 population at 1,973,000, a figure which implies that underenumeration equalled 4.8 per cent. The adjustment is based on a 10 per cent sample tabulation of the 1971 census data and differs from the census data principally in the number of persons ages 0–14. The ISPC estimate of persons 0–14 is derived using births 1956–71 adjusted for underregistration and the appropriate survival ratios. The 1963–71 intercensal growth rate estimated by ISPC (assuming a 1963 population of 1,576,000) is 2.82 per cent, virtually the same as estimated by CELADE for the 1950–63 period. The adjustment of the 1971 census population and the national projection based on it by the ISPC are employed throughout this report.

### Birth Rate

From 1920 to 1950 Collver estimated that the crude birth rate (CBR) in Nicaragua was approximately equal to 46 per thousand.[2] The registered CBR of (39.5) during the 1940–1950 period indicates that birth registration was then about 86 per cent complete (see Table 106). Compared with the CBR of 52.4 estimated by CELADE (Table 107) for the 1950's, the registered rate of 43.1 implies that registration was 82 per cent complete. The registered CBR of 45.0 for the 1960–1970 period is 91 per cent of that estimated by CELADE (49.3). For 1970–1975 the ISPC projection yields a CBR of 45.2, compared with the registered rate of 43.4.

There has been no indication of a significant decline in the crude birth rate in Nicaragua, but because the crude death rate has fallen gradually since 1940 or before (Tables 106 and 107) the population is currently increasing faster than ever, about 3.2 or 3.3 per cent a year.

Since birth registration is not complete, fertility measures must be estimated. The age-specific fertility rates for the periods 1955–60 and 1965–70 as estimated by CELADE are presented in Table 108 and graphed in Figure 30. The rates for the latter period are slightly lower than for the earlier period but the pattern is similar. The age-specific fertility rates as estimated by the ISPC for 1970 are lower and of a different distribution than the CELADE rates. ISPC places the total fertility rate at 6.76, compared with 7.10 estimated by CELADE. The rates estimated by ISPC are lower for the age groups under age 35 but higher for ages 35 and over than are the CELADE rates.

The government has sponsored a family planning program since 1967 which now includes 62 Ministry of Health clinics and seven Social Se-

---

[1] Letter from Sylvia Quick, U.S. Bureau of the Census, International Statistical Programs Center, Washington, D.C. July 3, 1975.

[2] Collver, *Birth Rates in Latin America*. p. 51.

curity clinics. In 1974 there were 25,400[1] active users of contraceptives, which represented less than six per cent of all females ages 15–44.

## Death Rate

The crude death rate (CDR) as estimated by CELADE (Table 107) has been falling steadily since 1950, declining by over a third in that period. Death registration is only about one-half complete.

## Migration Rate

According to CELADE estimates, Nicaragua has been experiencing a small amount of net emigration. Annual net emigration equalled 2.0 per thousand population during 1970–1975 and is projected to be about 1.0 per thousand for the remainder of the century, or approximately 4,000 a year.

[1]Population Reference Bureau, *World Population Growth and Response.* p. 151.

**Table 106**

**Registered Vital Rates in Nicaragua, 1940 to 1975**

| Period | Crude Birth Rate | Crude Death Rate | Rate of Natural Increase (%) |
|---|---|---|---|
| 1940–45 | 38.9 | 16.8 | 2.21 |
| 1945–50 | 40.0 | 13.1 | 2.69 |
| 1950–55 | 42.1 | 10.1 | 3.20 |
| 1955–60 | 44.0 | 9.1 | 3.49 |
| 1960–65 | 43.9 | 8.1 | 3.58 |
| 1965–70 | 46.1 | 8.0 | 3.81 |
| 1970–75 | 43.4 | 8.1 | 3.53 |

Source: Nicaragua: Banco Central de Nicaragua; Ministerio de Economía, Industria, y Comercio; and Oficina Ejecutiva de Encuestas y Censos; *Crecimiento Demográfico y Desarrollo.* Managua, 1974, p. 10.

**Table 107**

**Vital Rates in Nicaragua Estimated by CELADE, 1950 to 1975**

| Period | Crude Birth Rate | Crude Death Rate | Rate of Net International Migration | Growth Rate (per cent) |
|---|---|---|---|---|
| 1950–55 | 53.4 | 22.5 | −2.5 | 2.84 |
| 1955–60 | 51.3 | 20.1 | −3.0 | 2.82 |
| 1960–65 | 50.0 | 17.8 | −3.3 | 2.89 |
| 1965–70 | 48.6 | 15.6 | −3.6 | 2.93 |
| 1970–75 | 48.3 | 13.9 | −2.0 | 3.25 |

Source: Centro Latinoamericano de Demografía (CELADE), *Boletín Demografíco* 7:13 (January 1974) Table 3.

**Table 108**

**Estimates of Age-Specific and Total Fertility Rates in Nicaragua.**

| Age | CELADE Estimates | | ISPC Estimates, 1970 | | |
| --- | --- | --- | --- | --- | --- |
| | 1955–60 | 1965–70 | Total | Urban | Rural |
| 15–19 | .154 | .150 | .096 | .076 | .120 |
| 20–24 | .362 | .351 | .310 | .261 | .364 |
| 25–29 | .374 | .363 | .340 | .288 | .391 |
| 30–34 | .289 | .280 | .274 | .235 | .317 |
| 35–39 | .177 | .172 | .216 | .176 | .256 |
| 40–44 | .083 | .081 | .087 | 0.74 | .102 |
| 45–49 | .025 | .024 | .028 | .021 | 0.35 |
| **Total Fertility Rate** | **7.32** | **7.10** | **6.76** | **5.65** | **7.93** |

Sources: Centro Latinoamericano de Demografía (CELADE), *Boletín Demografíco* 9:17 (January 1976) p. 31.

U.S. Bureau of the Census, International Statistical Programs Center, Washington, D.C., 1975.

**Figure 30**
**Age-specific fertility rates, Nicaragua; 1955–60, 1965–70.**

Age-specific
fertility rate

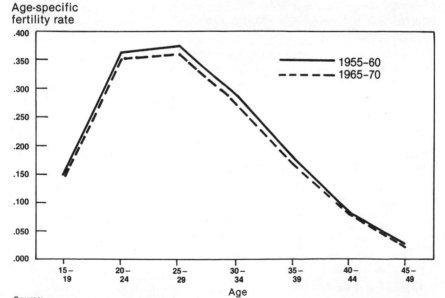

Age

Source:
Centro Latinoamericano de Demografia (CELADE), *Boletin*
Demografico 9:17 (January, 1976) p. 31.

159

## Age Distribution

Fertility and mortality dynamics combined to increase the percentage of the population under age 15 from 47.8 to 49.5 between 1960 and 1970 (Table 109). Fertility remained about constant or may have risen during the period (Table 106) while mortality declined somewhat. A decrease in mortality may raise the proportion of a population in younger age groups through its impact on infant and child mortality. The dependency ratio of Nicaragua's very young population increased from 103.7 in 1960 to 111.2 in 1970.

Age distribution patterns corresponding to the population projections for Nicaragua are presented in Table 110. Nicaragua fits well into the general pattern for the region, whereby a very large 40-50 per cent of each country's population is consistently found in the age bracket 0-14. This compares with 24 per cent projected for the United States in 1980 and 28 per cent for Argentina. The burden this places on social and economic systems throughout Central America is enormous, whether viewed at the family level as basic necessities for health care, proper nutrition, and training, or at the community and public institution level where, if available, large capital outlays are required for health and education, among other systems. A decline from 46 to 39 per cent of the total population in this age group is projected in Nicaragua in the 1970-2000 interval. This again is similar to declines projected in the other countries of the region. Between 1970-2000 and in absolute terms the largest single net increase per decade in Nicaragua for the group 0-14 should occur between 1980-90. The respective net gains in population for this age group are 274,000 (1970-80), 378,000 (1980-90), and 293,000 (1990-2000).

The proportion of those in their productive years, conventionally defined as the population ages 15-64, should increase in Nicaragua from 47 (1970) to 58 (2000) per cent of the total. Absolute net gains for this age group during each decade are 465,000 (1970-80), 596,000 (1980-90),

**Table 109**

**Percentage of Population in Broad Age Groups, and Dependency Ratios for Nicaragua, by Residence; 1960 and 1970.**

| Age | 1960 | | | 1970 | | |
|---|---|---|---|---|---|---|
| | Total | Urban | Rural | Total | Urban | Rural |
| All Ages | 100.0% | 100.0% | 100.0% | 100.0% | 100.0% | 100.0% |
| 0-14 | 47.8 | 45.5 | 49.4 | 49.5 | 47.5 | 51.3 |
| 15-64 | 49.1 | 50.6 | 48.1 | 47.3 | 48.7 | 46.1 |
| 65 | 3.1 | 3.9 | 2.5 | 3.1 | 3.7 | 2.6 |
| Dependency Ratio[a] | 103.7 | 97.6 | 107.9 | 111.2 | 105.1 | 116.9 |

[a] The dependency ratio is $(P(0-14) + P(65+))/P(15-64) \times 100$, where P(a) is the population age "a".

Source: U.S. Bureau of the Census, International Statistical Programs Center, computer printout for urban/rural projection series dated September 13, 1974 (recommended series).

160

and a very substantial 800,000 individuals between 1990–2000. A more detailed breakdown of the projected population by age groups is found in Appendix A of this chapter.

## Urban-Rural Fertility Differentials

Although the fertility of urban women is only 71 per cent of that of rural women, fertility in both areas of Nicaragua is high. The total fertility rate for urban women is 5.65 and for rural women is 7.93 (Table 108).

The rural population exhibits a slightly younger age distribution than the urban because of higher rural fertility and rural-to-urban migration (Table 109). Among the rural population, 51.3 per cent are under age 15, compared with 47.5 per cent of the urban population. The rural dependency ratio is 117; the urban ratio is 105. The dependency ratios for both the urban and rural populations increased between 1960 and 1970.

Only a modest number of males migrates from rural to urban areas, and many of these return to rural areas (Figure 31). The percentages of males 0–4 living in urban areas is 43.5. This rises to 46 per cent for ages 10–14 and 15–19, but falls to 44 per cent at ages 20–24 and to about 42 per cent at ages 25–29. Migration of females from rural to urban areas is more substantial and more lasting. Fifty-four per cent of females 15–19 live in urban areas. The percentage in urban areas drops to 50 for ages 25–29 and 35–39 but then rises steadily with age.

## Economically Active Population and Labor Force Participation, by Age and Sex.

The population of Nicaragua increased 22 per cent in the 1963–71 census interval, but during the same period the economically active group increased by just 6.4 per cent. The latter figure is inordinately low, and cannot be explained by such factors as larger numbers of children (ages 10–14) retained in the school system, fewer females participating in the labor force, or greater numbers retiring from the labor force at earlier ages. While there is the possibility that changes in census definitions may have served to moderately lower the economically active total

**Table 110**

**Projected Population in Broad Age Groups 1980–2000**

| Age Group | 1980 | 1990 | 2000 | 1980 | 1990 | 2000 |
|---|---|---|---|---|---|---|
| Total | 2,669,517 | 3,671,606 | 4,811,925 | 100.0 | 100.0 | 100.0 |
| 0–14 | 1,226,345 | 1,603,669 | 1,897,045 | 45.9 | 43.7 | 39.4 |
| 15–64 | 1,374,217 | 1,969,628 | 2,769,662 | 51.5 | 53.6 | 57.6 |
| 65+ | 68,953 | 98,310 | 145,217 | 2.6 | 2.7 | 3.0 |

Source: See source note, Table 109.

**Figure 31**
**Urban residence ratios by age and sex, Nicaragua, 1970.**

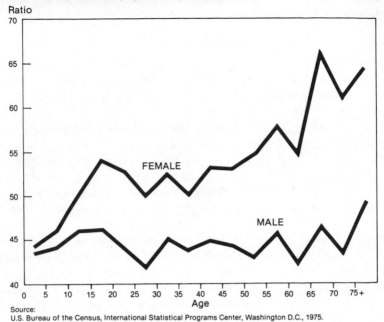

Ratio

Age

Source:
U.S. Bureau of the Census, International Statistical Programs Center, Washington D.C., 1975.

in 1971, it appears that the economically active proportion simply did not keep pace with the general rise in population. Only limited information on this theme is available for study from census documents—particularly for 1971—but the data do seem internally consistent, and there appear to be no major changes in industrial classification schemes that bias the 1963–71 comparison.

A summary of trends by major industrial classification appears in Table 111. The feature of prime interest is the sharp drop in the population engaged in agricultural activities. Accordingly, those in this group declined by approximately 46,000 in just an eight-year period. This represents a decline of 19 per cent. Should further study of the data using more refined statistics firmly support these initial findings, this would represent as sharp a drop in this category as found anywhere in Latin America during the 1960's.

Further information, unfortunately, is not available to study this development by age group. The data do permit an examination of the degree of decline among agriculturalists by department between 1963 and 1971 (Table 112).

The decline is general throughout the Republic. Overall, agriculturalists dropped as a percentage of all economically active Nicaraguans from 60 to 47 per cent. Only in the Department of Zelaya is there a substantial increase. This is a region of recent colonization, and the census documents show a net gain of more than 10,000 agriculturalists in the eight-year period.

The agricultural decline seems nonetheless consistent with the trends of high urban and low rural population growth. Depending on the urban and rural definition used (urban by census definition vs. those in cities and towns of 10,000 and more) the urban population increased in a range of 43 to 48 per cent in the interval, and the rural population in a range from 8 to 12 per cent.

A second feature of Table 111 is the rapid rise among those classified in services, increasing from 60,078 to 99,907 in the interval- an overall gain of 66 per cent. Among females the increase was 39 per cent, but among the economically active male population there is a very high increase of 123 per cent. Thus it seems that among males the urbanization surge combined with a vast increase among those in services accounts at least partially for the reduced agricultural labor force.

Figure 32 provides a profile on the percentage of each age group that is economically active. The information is from the census of 1963. Comparable data for 1971 are not available. The profile is quite similar to the pattern found for other countries of the region e.g., the highest labor force participation rates for males are in the rural areas and the lowest rates for females are similarly found there.

## Urban Population Growth

The urban population referred to in previous sections of this chapter is

Table 111

**Economically Active Population by Industrial Classification, by Sex and Urban and Rural, 1950, 1963, and 1971.**

| Industrial Classification[a] | 1971 | | | 1963 | | | 1950 | | |
|---|---|---|---|---|---|---|---|---|---|
| | Total | Male | Female | Total | Male | Female | Total | Male | Female |
| | **505,445** | **395,005** | **110,440** | **474,960** | **379,305** | **95,665** | **329,976** | **283,799** | **46,177** |
| Agriculture | 237,327 | 228,455 | 8,872 | 283,106 | 268,770 | 14,336 | 223,426 | 218,257 | 5,169 |
| Mining & Quarrying | 2,958 | 2,834 | 124 | 4,013 | 3,876 | 137 | 3,178 | 3,162 | 16 |
| Manufacturing | 62,473 | 44,459 | 18,014 | 55,631 | 38,108 | 17,523 | 37,706 | 26,920 | 10,786 |
| Utilities | 3,017 | 2,841 | 176 | 1,264 | 1,228 | 36 | 615 | 604 | 11 |
| Construction | 20,252 | 19,975 | 277 | 15,852 | 15,821 | 31 | 8,684 | 8,600 | 84 |
| Commerce | 47,376 | 24,972 | 22,404 | 39,499 | 17,664 | 21,835 | 20,071 | 12,466 | 7,605 |
| Transportation & Storage | 17,318 | 16,603 | 715 | 12,009 | 11,716 | 293 | 6,127 | 5,993 | 134 |
| Financial | 5,893 | 4,744 | 1,149 | 2,522 | 2,157 | 365 | 266 | 224 | 42 |
| Services | 99,907 | 43,474 | 56,433 | 60,078 | 19,471 | 40,607 | 29,903 | 7,573 | 22,330 |
| Not Specified | 8,924 | 6,648 | 2,276 | 986 | 494 | 492 | | | |

[a] The 1950 and 1963 figures are adjusted to conform to the 1968 International Standard Industrial Classification (ISIC).

Source: 1950 Census Report, Table 47. 1963 Census Report, Tables 15 and 42. 1971 Census Report, Table 6.

163

## Table 112

### Economically Active Population and Population in Agriculture by Industrial Classification, for Departments, Urban and Rural, 1963 and 1971

| Department | 1963 Economically Active Population Total | Urban | Rural | 1963 In Agriculture Total | Urban | Rural | 1971 Economically Active Population Total | Urban | Rural | 1971 In Agriculture Total | Urban | Rural | Total Percentage of Economically Active in Agriculture 1963 | 1971 |
|---|---|---|---|---|---|---|---|---|---|---|---|---|---|---|
| National Totals | 474,960 | 189,442 | 285,518 | 283,106 | 31,103 | 252,003 | 505,445 | 244,702 | 260,743 | 237,327 | 27,651 | 209,676 | 60 | 47 |
| Boaco | 22,020 | 2,860 | 19,160 | 17,224 | 626 | 16,598 | 18,580 | 4,032 | 14,548 | 13,349 | 971 | 12,378 | 78 | 72 |
| Carazo | 18,561 | 7,907 | 10,654 | 11,012 | 1,852 | 9,160 | 17,782 | 8,482 | 9,300 | 8,016 | 1,227 | 6,789 | 59 | 45 |
| Chinandega | 42,316 | 17,740 | 24,576 | 27,006 | 4,705 | 22,301 | 40,983 | 19,041 | 21,942 | 19,196 | 2,885 | 16,311 | 64 | 47 |
| Chontales | 22,403 | 3,849 | 18,554 | 17,817 | 849 | 16,968 | 17,749 | 4,657 | 18,092 | 12,423 | 986 | 11,437 | 80 | 70 |
| Estelí | 20,288 | 5,743 | 14,545 | 14,970 | 1,589 | 13,381 | 19,663 | 7,568 | 12,095 | 11,734 | 1,453 | 10,281 | 74 | 60 |
| Granada | 19,112 | 10,737 | 8,375 | 9,085 | 1,698 | 7,387 | 18,140 | 12,474 | 5,666 | 5,470 | 1,279 | 4,191 | 48 | 30 |
| Jinotega | 24,032 | 3,437 | 20,595 | 18,666 | 649 | 18,017 | 24,631 | 4,293 | 20,338 | 19,678 | 1,174 | 18,504 | 78 | 80 |
| León | 45,977 | 19,423 | 26,554 | 29,000 | 4,980 | 24,020 | 43,567 | 21,493 | 22,074 | 21,408 | 3,971 | 17,437 | 63 | 49 |
| Madriz | 15,636 | 2,750 | 12,886 | 12,615 | 989 | 11,626 | 14,085 | 2,833 | 11,252 | 10,867 | 902 | 9,965 | 81 | 77 |
| Managua | 100,718 | 76,602 | 24,116 | 21,139 | 2,674 | 18,465 | 139,750 | 114,884 | 24,866 | 16,024 | 2,991 | 13,033 | 21 | 11 |
| Masaya | 23,595 | 11,939 | 11,656 | 13,139 | 3,318 | 9,821 | 23,373 | 13,789 | 9,584 | 9,586 | 2,641 | 6,945 | 56 | 41 |
| Matagalpa | 54,063 | 8,660 | 45,403 | 44,240 | 2,090 | 42,150 | 45,537 | 10,875 | 34,662 | 32,839 | 2,002 | 30,837 | 82 | 72 |
| Nueva Segovia | 14,112 | 2,983 | 11,129 | 11,861 | 1,326 | 10,535 | 18,908 | 4,753 | 14,155 | 13,581 | 1,634 | 11,947 | 84 | 72 |
| Río San Juan | 5,310 | 895 | 4,415 | 4,222 | 239 | 3,983 | 6,348 | 1,829 | 4,519 | 5,018 | 945 | 4,073 | 80 | 79 |
| Rivas | 18,446 | 5,501 | 12,945 | 12,598 | 1,878 | 10,720 | 17,952 | 6,462 | 11,490 | 10,368 | 1,904 | 8,464 | 68 | 58 |
| Zelaya | 28,371 | 8,416 | 19,955 | 18,512 | 1,641 | 16,871 | 38,397 | 7,237 | 31,160 | 27,770 | 686 | 27,084 | 65 | 72 |

Sources: For 1963, Nicaragua, Dirección General de Estadística y Censos, *Censos Nacionales 1963. Población*, Vol. III, Managua, July, 1967, Table 15. For 1971, Nicaragua, Banco Central de Nicaragua, Ministerio de Economía, Industria, y Comercio, *Censos Nacionales, 1971. Población por Municipios. Vol. I. Características Generales*, Mangua, March 1975, Tables 5 and 6.

**Figure 32**
**Economically active population, urban and rural,
by sex, Nicaragua, 1963.**

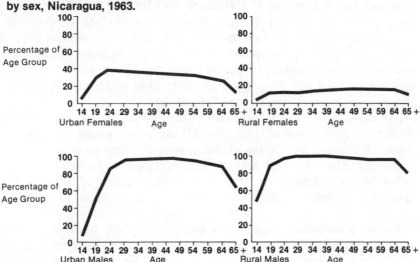

Source:
Nicaragua, Direccion General de Estadistica y Censos,
*Censos Nacionales 1963,* Vol. 4, Table 30.

that defined by the *Dirección General de Estadística y Censos*. In 1950 this definition included only the population in department and *municipios cabeceras*. In 1963 the definition of urban was expanded to include localities which contained at least 1,000 inhabitants; which had certain characteristics such as a street plan or electricity or in which the predominant activity was non-agricultural such as mining or sugar-milling.[1] The change in definition had a negligible effect on the urban proportion of the population, which increased from 35.2 per cent in 1950 to only 40.9 per cent in 1963. Volume 1 of the 1971 census report gives no definition of "urban,"[2] but gives the urban population as 47.7 per cent of the total.

A definition of "urbanized area" used for the projections here includes only cities of 10,000 or more inhabitants in 1971. The urbanized area populations are as delimited by the census. The urbanized area of Managua in 1971 includes the city proper plus the peripheral *barrios* of

---

[1] Nicaragua, Dirección General de Estadística y Censos, *Censos Nacionales 1963, Población,* Vol. 1, Managua, December 1964, p. 16.

[2] Nicaragua, Banco Central de Nicaragua-Ministerio de Economía, Industria, y Comercio, *Censos Nacionales 1971. Población por Municipios,* Vol. 2, Caracteristicas Generales, Managua, March 1975.

165

Sabana Grande, Bella Cruz, Open No. 3, San Isidro de La Cruz Verde, Cofradia, and Ticuantepe.[3] Following the earthquake which devastated Managua in 1972, killing 16,000 people and leveling 53,000 dwellings, the population of the city dropped to as low as 200,000. However, reports indicate that most of the survivors returned to the general area of the capital. These reports include a special census of Managua and surrounding towns conducted approximately two years after the earthquake, which counted the population as far away as Tipitapa, Granada, Masaya, Jinotepe, Diriamba, and San Marcos.

For the purpose of the projections, and based on the available information it is assumed that the Managua earthquake caused no permanent loss of population or decrease in the long-term growth rate of the city. The urbanized area of Leon is defined to include the population of the nearby town of Poneloya. The suburb of Ingenio San Antonio is included in the urbanized area of Chichigalpa in 1963 and after.

Fourteen urbanized areas in Nicaragua contained populations of a least 10,000 in 1971. Their total population was 661,600, or 35.2 per cent of the national population (Table 113). This percentage is an increase over 23.6 per cent in 1950 and 29.1 per cent in 1963. Table 114 presents the population of Nicaragua's urbanized areas as counted by the three most recent censuses. Managua is rapidly increasing its primacy among the urbanized areas. In 1950 it was 3.6 times as large as the second largest city, Leon, and 1.6 times the size of Leon, Granada, and Masaya combined. By 1970, both of these ratios had about doubled to 7.0 and 3.2, respectively. The capital city contained 20 per cent of the national population and 58 per cent of the urbanized area population in 1971.

---

[3] Ibid., p. 26.

**Table 113**

**Enumerated and Projected Population of Nicaragua, Fourteen Urbanized Areas, and Remaining Population, 1950 to 2000.**

| | | Fourteen Urbanized Areas | | Remaining Population | |
|---|---|---|---|---|---|
| Year | Nicaragua | Population in Thousands | Per Cent of Total | Population in Thousands | Per Cent of Total |
| 1950 | 1,049.6 | 247.2 | 23.6 | 802.4 | 76.4 |
| 1963 | 1,535.6 | 446.8 | 29.1 | 1,088.7 | 70.9 |
| 1971 | 1,878.0 | 661.6 | 35.2 | 1,216.4 | 64.8 |
| 1980 | 2,669.5 | 1,061.2 | 39.8 | 1,608.3 | 60.2 |
| 1990 | 3,671.6 | 1,627.4 | 44.3 | 2,044.2 | 55.7 |
| 2000 | 4,811.9 | 2,324.2 | 48.3 | 2,487.7 | 51.7 |

Source: Table 114.

Managua is Nicaragua's fastest-growing city; it increased at an annual rate of 6.2 per cent between 1963 and 1971 (Table 115). Leon, which is the only other urbanized area with more than 50,000 inhabitants grew at 2.5 per cent a year, or just under the national rate, during the latest intercensal period. The four cities in the 20–50,000 population range all increased at rates above the national average: Matagalpa at 4.0 per cent, Chinandega at 3.6 per cent, Masaya at 3.4 per cent, and Granada at 2.7 per cent. The urbanized area of Diriamba decreased from 10,500 to 10,200 during the 1963–1971 interval. Each of the other seven urbanized areas of 10–20,000 grew more rapidly than the total population, with Esteli (5.5 per cent) and Bluefields (4.9 per cent) registering the highest rates.

The growth of the population of Nicaragua, of the 14 urbanized areas, of non-urbanized areas, and of Managua are graphed in Figure 33. The 1963–71 intercensal period was the first in which the population of the urbanized areas increased by a greater absolute amount than did the non-urbanized area population.

## Population Projections

A ratio-trend methodology[1] is employed to project the total population of urbanized areas in Nicaragua to the years 1980, 1990, and 2000 by allocating the previously projected national population first to departments then to urbanized areas.

## National Projection

The projection of the population of Nicaragua to the year 2000 by the International Statistical Programs Center of the U.S. Bureau of the Census appears in Table 116. It is based on the population enumerated on April 20, 1971, and adjusted for underenumeration and age misreporting. It assumes that fertility will decline 41 per cent and that life expectancy will increase 18 per cent between 1970 and the year 2000. The total fertility rate in the projection falls from 6.8 in 1970 to 4.0 in 2000. Expectation of life at birth for males increases from 54.7 to 64.9 years and for females from 58.4 to 68.5 years between 1970 and 2000. Net international migration is assumed to be negligible for the purposes of the projection. The annual rate of population growth is expected to decline by 21 per cent, from 3.30 per cent in 1970–1975 to 2.61 in 1995–2000.

Nicaragua's population in the year 2000 is projected to be 4.8 million, or 2.5 times as large as in 1970. The population projected for the year 2000 has a significantly older age structure due to the assumed de-

---

[1]Pickard, *Dimensions to Metropolitanism.* pp. 53–56.

**Table 114**

**Enumerated and Projected Population of Departments and Urbanized Areas of Nicaragua, 1950 to 2000**

| Department and Urbanized Area | Enumerated Population in Thousands | | | Projected Population in Thousands (midyear) | | |
|---|---|---|---|---|---|---|
| | May 1950[a] | May 1963 | Apr. 20 1971 | 1980 | 1990 | 2000 |
| National Total | 1,049.6 | 1,535.6 | 1,878.0 | 2,669.5 | 3,671.6 | 4,811.9 |
| Boaco | 50.0 | 71.6 | 69.2 | 86.5 | 101.5 | 113.2 |
| Carazo | 52.1 | 65.9 | 71.1 | 89.0 | 105.7 | 119.3 |
| Diriamba | 7.6 | 10.5 | 10.2 | 12.5 | 14.5 | 15.9 |
| Jinotepe | 7.1 | 9.1 | 12.5 | 17.2 | 22.6 | 28.0 |
| Remainder | 37.5 | 46.3 | 48.5 | 59.3 | 68.6 | 75.3 |
| Chinandega | 81.8 | 128.6 | 155.3 | 223.9 | 310.1 | 407.7 |
| Chinandega | 13.1 | 22.4 | 29.9 | 46.3 | 68.8 | 96.3 |
| Chichigalpa[b] | 4.3 | 11.2 | 14.6 | 21.7 | 31.1 | 42.3 |
| Corinto | 4.8 | 9.2 | 13.4 | 22.0 | 34.6 | 50.7 |
| Remainder | 59.6 | 85.9 | 97.4 | 134.0 | 175.6 | 218.3 |
| Chontales | 50.5 | 75.6 | 68.8 | 85.3 | 98.8 | 108.7 |
| Estelí | 43.7 | 69.3 | 79.2 | 111.5 | 149.9 | 191.5 |
| Estelí | 3.6 | 12.7 | 19.8 | 33.4 | 32.7 | 76.6 |
| Remainder | 38.2 | 56.5 | 59.4 | 78.1 | 97.2 | 114.9 |
| Granada | 48.7 | 65.6 | 71.1 | 91.4 | 111.7 | 129.6 |
| Granada | 21.0 | 28.5 | 35.4 | 48.2 | 62.5 | 76.6 |
| Remainder | 27.7 | 37.1 | 35.7 | 43.2 | 49.2 | 53.1 |
| Jinotega | 48.3 | 76.9 | 90.6 | 129.8 | 178.2 | 232.3 |
| Jinotega | 4.0 | 7.7 | 10.2 | 16.3 | 25.0 | 35.8 |
| Remainder | 44.3 | 69.2 | 80.4 | 113.5 | 153.2 | 196.5 |
| León | 123.6 | 150.1 | 166.8 | 208.3 | 247.8 | 280.0 |
| León | 30.5 | 45.0 | 54.8 | 75.3 | 98.0 | 119.8 |
| Remainder | 93.1 | 105.0 | 112.0 | 133.0 | 149.8 | 160.2 |
| Madriz | 33.2 | 50.2 | 53.4 | 71.5 | 90.7 | 109.4 |
| Managua | 161.5 | 318.8 | 485.8 | 797.8 | 1,244.8 | 1,800.3 |
| Mangua | 109.4 | 234.6 | 384.9 | 661.9 | 1,075.2 | 1,604.1 |
| Remainder | 52.2 | 84.2 | 100.9 | 135.9 | 169.6 | 196.2 |
| Masaya | 72.4 | 76.6 | 92.2 | 113.5 | 134.4 | 151.1 |
| Masaya | 16.7 | 23.4 | 30.8 | 42.5 | 55.8 | 68.4 |
| Remainder | 55.7 | 53.2 | 61.4 | 71.0 | 78.6 | 82.6 |
| Matagalpa | 135.4 | 171.5 | 168.1 | 200.9 | 225.9 | 241.2 |
| Matagalpa | 10.3 | 15.0 | 20.7 | 28.8 | 37.8 | 46.0 |
| Remainder | 125.1 | 156.4 | 147.5 | 172.1 | 188.1 | 195.3 |
| Nueva Segovia | 26.0 | 45.9 | 65.8 | 104.9 | 160.7 | 230.8 |
| Río San Juan | 9.1 | 15.7 | 20.8 | 32.2 | 47.9 | 67.1 |
| Rivas | 45.3 | 64.4 | 74.1 | 100.4 | 129.9 | 159.8 |
| Rivas | 4.8 | 7.7 | 10.0 | 14.8 | 21.0 | 28.1 |
| Remainder | 40.5 | 56.6 | 64.1 | 85.5 | 108.9 | 131.7 |
| Zelaya | 67.7 | 89.0 | 145.5 | 222.6 | 333.5 | 470.0 |
| Bluefields | 8.0 | 9.8 | 14.4 | 20.3 | 27.8 | 35.7 |
| Remainder | 59.7 | 79.2 | 131.1 | 202.3 | 305.8 | 434.3 |

[a] The 1950 census figures for the Republic and for the departments of Jinotega, Nueva Segovia, and Zelaya are adjusted to correspond to the area of these departments in 1963, conforming to the new northern border resulting from litigation with Honduras.
[b] The "suburb" of Ingenio San Antonio is included in the urbanized area in 1963 and 1971, but not in 1950.

Sources: 1950 and 1963: Nicaragua, Dirección General de Estadística y Censos, *Censos Nacionales 1963. Población,* vol. 1, Managua, December 1964, p. xi.

1971: Nicaragua, Banco central de Nicaragua-Ministerio de Economía, Industria y Comercio, *Censos Nacionales 1971. Población por Municipios, vol. I, Características Generales,* Mangua, March 1975, Tables A and 1.

# Table 115

## Observed and Projected Population Growth Rates of Departments and Urbanized Areas in Nicaragua, 1950 to 2000

| Department and Urbanized Area | Average Annual Growth Rate (%) of Enumerated Population | | Average Annual Growth Rate (%) of Projected Population | | |
|---|---|---|---|---|---|
| | 1950–1963 | 1963–1971 | 1971–1980 | 1980–1990 | 1990–2000 |
| **National Total** | **2.93** | **2.58** | **3.82** | **3.19** | **2.70** |
| **Boaco** | **2.76** | **−0.43** | **2.42** | **1.60** | **1.09** |
| **Carazo** | **1.80** | **0.96** | **2.43** | **1.72** | **1.21** |
| Diriamba | 2.53 | −0.42 | 2.28 | 1.47 | 0.95 |
| Jinotepa | 1.93 | 3.93 | 3.48 | 2.77 | 2.13 |
| Remainder | 1.62 | 0.59 | 2.18 | 1.46 | 0.94 |
| **Chinandega** | **3.48** | **2.36** | **3.98** | **3.26** | **2.74** |
| Chinandega | 4.10 | 3.63 | 4.74 | 3.96 | 3.37 |
| Chichigalpa | 7.35 | 3.36 | 4.31 | 3.61 | 3.06 |
| Corinto | 5.04 | 4.72 | 5.41 | 4.53 | 3.83 |
| Remainder | 2.81 | 1.58 | 3.47 | 2.71 | 2.18 |
| **Chontales** | **3.10** | **−1.18** | **2.34** | **1.47** | **0.95** |
| **Estelí** | **3.53** | **1.68** | **3.72** | **2.96** | **2.45** |
| Estelí | 6.38 | 5.53 | 5.67 | 4.58 | 3.74 |
| Remainder | 3.02 | 0.62 | 2.98 | 2.19 | 1.67 |
| **Granada** | **2.29** | **1.00** | **2.73** | **2.00** | **1.49** |
| Granada | 2.34 | 2.73 | 3.35 | 2.61 | 2.02 |
| Remainder | 2.26 | −0.50 | 2.09 | 1.28 | 0.77 |
| **Jinotega** | **3.58** | **2.06** | **3.91** | **3.17** | **2.65** |
| Jinotega | 5.02 | 3.58 | 5.09 | 4.23 | 3.60 |
| Remainder | 3.43 | 1.88 | 3.75 | 3.00 | 2.49 |
| **León** | **1.49** | **1.33** | **2.41** | **1.74** | **1.22** |
| León | 2.99 | 2.47 | 3.45 | 2.63 | 2.00 |
| Remainder | 0.93 | 0.81 | 1.87 | 1.19 | 0.68 |
| **Madriz** | **3.19** | **0.77** | **3.17** | **2.38** | **1.87** |
| **Managua** | **5.23** | **5.29** | **5.39** | **4.45** | **3.69** |
| Managua | 5.87 | 6.21 | 5.89 | 4.85 | 4.00 |
| Remainder | 3.69 | 2.27 | 3.24 | 2.21 | 1.46 |
| **Masaya** | **0.43** | **2.32** | **2.27** | **1.68** | **1.17** |
| Masaya | 2.58 | 3.45 | 3.51 | 2.71 | 2.04 |
| Remainder | −0.36 | 1.79 | 1.59 | 1.02 | 0.50 |
| **Matagalpa** | **1.82** | **−0.25** | **1.94** | **1.17** | **0.66** |
| Matagalpa | 2.89 | 4.01 | 3.61 | 2.71 | 1.95 |
| Remainder | 1.72 | −0.74 | 1.68 | 0.89 | 0.37 |
| **Nueva Segovia** | **4.38** | **4.52** | **5.07** | **4.27** | **3.62** |
| **Río San Juan** | **4.19** | **3.57** | **4.74** | **3.97** | **3.37** |
| **Rivas** | **2.70** | **1.77** | **3.29** | **2.58** | **2.07** |
| Rivas | 3.67 | 3.25 | 4.28 | 3.50 | 2.89 |
| Remainder | 2.58 | 1.56 | 3.13 | 2.41 | 1.90 |
| **Zelaya** | **2.10** | **6.17** | **4.62** | **4.04** | **3.43** |
| Bluefields | 1.51 | 4.89 | 3.74 | 3.13 | 2.51 |
| Remainder | 2.17 | 6.32 | 4.72 | 4.13 | 3.51 |

Source: Table 114.

169

**Figure 33**
**Enumerated and projected population of Nicaragua, fourteen urbanized areas, non-urbanized areas, and Managua, 1950 to 2000.**

Population
in thousands

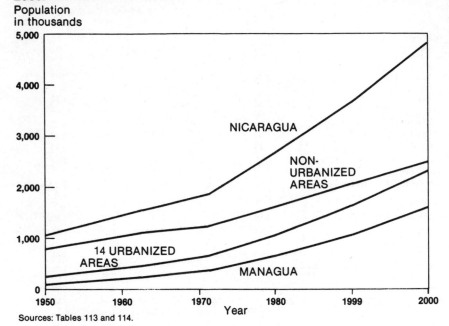

Sources: Tables 113 and 114.

**Table 116**

**Projected Population, Crude Birth Rate, Crude Death Rate, and Rate of Increase; Nicaragua; 1970 to 2000**

| Period | Population at Beginning of Period (in Thousands) | Crude Birth Rate | Crude Death Rate | Average Annual Rate of Increase (%) |
|---|---|---|---|---|
| 1970–1975 | 1,921.2 | 45.2 | 12.2 | 3.30 |
| 1975–1980 | 2,260.8 | 44.3 | 11.0 | 3.33 |
| 1980–1985 | 2,669.5 | 42.7 | 9.9 | 3.28 |
| 1985–1990 | 3,145.2 | 39.9 | 8.8 | 3.11 |
| 1990–1995 | 3,671.6 | 36.3 | 7.8 | 2.85 |
| 1995–2000 | 4,228.5 | 33.0 | 6.9 | 2.61 |
| 2000 | 4,811.9 | | | |

Source: U.S. Bureau of the Census, International Statistical Programs Center, Washington, D.C., 1975.

170

creases in fertility and mortality. Of the projected population, 39.4 per cent is ages 0-14, 57.6 per cent is 15-64, and 3.0 per cent is 65 and over (compare with Table 109). The dependency ratio in the year 2000 would equal 73.6, compared with 111.2 in 1970.

**Department Projections**

The population of each department is projected to mid-year 1980, 1990, and 2000 by continuing the trend of the ratio of the department's population to the national population observed in 1950, 1963, and 1971. Data from the 1940 census could also be incorporated in the projection; but since it is estimated that the census of 1940 undercounted the population by 6.7 per cent (Table 105), it is felt that such data would add little accuracy to the projection. Table 114 presents the results of the projections. The Department of Managua is projected to reach 1.2 million by 1990 and 1.8 million by 2000 when it will be 3.7 times its size of 1971. It will grow from 25.9 per cent to 37.4 per cent of the national population between 1971 and 2000. In 1971 there was a second tier of departments all between 145,000 and 169,000 in population: Matagalpa, Leon, Chinandega, and Zelaya. By the year 2000, Zelaya is projected to be the largest of these with a population of 470,000. Chinandega's projected population for the year 2000 is 408,000, Leon's is 280,000 and Matagalpa's is 241,000.

The coastal departments of Nicaragua have been gaining population at the expense of the inland departments. The proportion of the national population in the Pacific Region increased from 55.8 per cent in 1950 to 59.5 in 1971, and is projected to equal 63.3 per cent at the end of the century (see Table 117). The Atlantic Region's two departments' share of the national population equalled 7.3 per cent in 1950 and 8.9 in 1971, and is expected to be 11.2 per cent in the year 2000. The North-Central Region's percentage has declined from 36.9 in 1950 to 31.7 in 1971, and is projected to decrease further to 25.5 by 2000.

Average annual rates of growth of the projected population of Nicaragua's departments are shown in Table 115 by decade for the 1971–2000 period. Because the population totals for 1971 presented in Table 114 are from the census of that year and are not adjusted for underenumeration (which was greater than in 1963), and the totals for 1980 are projected from the adjusted 1971 census, the growth rates in Table 115 for 1963–71 understate the true ones and those given for 1971–80 overstate the actual rates. According to the analysis by the U.S. Bureau of the Census employed in this report, the 1960–70 average annual growth rate of Nicaragua was 2.82 per cent (compared with 2.53 per cent for 1963-1971 based on unadjusted census results) and the projected 1970-1980 growth rate is 3.32 per cent (rather than 3.82 per cent as shown in Table 115).

The Department of Managua is not only Nicaragua's largest but also the fastest-growing (Table 117). Managua's population is projected to increase at an average annual rate of 4.49 per cent between 1971 and the year 2000. Nueva Segovia (4.30 per cent), Zelaya (4.02 per cent), and Rio San Juan (4.01 per cent) are also expected to grow at annual rates of over four per cent for the 1971-2000 period. The projected average growth rate for the remainder of the century is 3.31 per cent for Chinandega and 3.22 per cent for Jinotega. All other departments are expected in increase at less than the national average of 3.22 per cent a year.

## Urbanized Area Projections

The population of each of Nicaragua's 14 urbanized areas is projected to the years 1980, 1990, and 2000 by continuing the trend of the proportion of the department's population observed at the three latest censuses. To prevent past growth from annexation from exerting an undue influence on the projection, the urbanized area of Chichigalpa is treated as though it included the suburb of Ingenio San Antonio in 1950. The 1950 population of Ingenio San Antonio is estimated from its 1963 total by assuming that it increased at the same rate as that of Chichigalpa proper during the 1950-1963 intercensal period. The projected population of the urbanized areas is presented in Table 114. Table 113 indicates that the combined population of the 14 urbanized areas is projected to increase to 3.5 times its 1971 size by reaching one million in 1980 and 2.3 million by 2000, when these cities will contain nearly half (48.3 per cent) of Nicaragua's population. The urbanized areas collectively are projected to grow at an average annual rate of 4.3 per cent between 1971 and 2000. The projected population of the

Table 117

Percentage of the Population of Nicaragua in Regions[a] as Enumerated in 1950 1963, and 1971; and as Projected to 1980, 1990, and 2000

| Year | Nicaragua | Pacific Region | North–Central Region | Atlantic Region |
|------|-----------|----------------|----------------------|-----------------|
| 1950 | 100.0% | 55.8 | 36.9 | 7.3 |
| 1963 | 100.0% | 56.7 | 36.5 | 6.8 |
| 1971 | 100.0% | 59.5 | 31.7 | 8.9 |
| 1980 | 100.0% | 60.8 | 29.6 | 9.5 |
| 1990 | 100.0% | 62.2 | 27.4 | 10.4 |
| 2000 | 100.0% | 63.3 | 25.5 | 11.2 |

[a] The departmental composition of the regions is as follows: Pacific: Carazo, Chinandega, Granada, León, Managua, Masaya, and Rivas.

North–Central: Boaco, Chontales, Estelí, Jinotega, Madriz, Matagalpa, and Nueva Segovia.

Atlantic: Rio San Juan and Zelaya.

Source: Table 114.

urbanized and non-urbanized areas (or all remaining population) is graphed in Figure 33. The Managua urbanized area alone is expected to increase by a larger number than the combined non-urbanized areas during the 1990–2000 decade.

The projections show the population of the urbanized area of Managua quadrupling by the end of the century, reaching one million in 1990 and 1.6 million in 2000. One-third of Nicaragua's population and over two-thirds of the urbanized area population will then reside in the capital. Managua's projected average growth rate of 4.9 per cent a year during the 1971–2000 interval is the greatest of any of the urbanized areas. In the year 2000 Managua's population is expected to be 13.4 times that of Leon and 5.5 times the population of Leon, Chinandega, and Esteli combined.

Leon, the only other urbanized area expected to surpass 100,000 in population in the year 2000, is nevertheless projected to increase at rates below the national average (Table 115). Chinandega's average annual rate of increase of 4.0 per cent would make it the third largest urbanized area (93,300) in the year 2000, compared with its fifth in rank in 1971. Esteli and Granada are projected to have equal populations (76,000) in the year 2000, but Esteli's growth rate (4.6 per cent) for the 1971–2000 period is much higher than Granada's (2.6 per cent). The two urbanized areas of Corinto and Masaya, whose population in the year 2000 will range at about 50–75,000, are expected to increase at average rates of 4.6 and 2.7 per cent, respectively. Of the urbanized areas that will not attain populations of 50,000 by the year 2000, Chichigalpa, Jinotega, and Rivas are projected to grow at rates above the national average of 3.2 per cent a year; while Jinotepe, Matagalpa, Bluefields, and Diriamba are expected to increase at rates below this average.

The projections of Nicaragua's population yield four principal conclusions: (1) the national population will reach 4.8 million by the year 2000, 2.6 times its 1971 size; (2) the 14 urbanized areas considered in this chapter will attain a combined size of 2.3 million, 48 per cent of the national population in the year 2000; (3) although urbanization is expected to increase steadily, half of the 14 urbanized areas are projected to grow at average rates below the national growth rate of 3.2 per cent a year for the 1971–2000 period; and (4) the Managua urbanized area will increase its primacy among cities and comprise one-third of Nicaragua's population at the end of the century.

## Appendix A

## Nicaragua: Population projections by sex and quinquennial age groups, 1970–2000

| Age | 1970 Total | Male | Female | Age | 1990 Total | Male | Female |
|-----|-----|------|--------|-----|-----|------|--------|
|  | 1,921,228 | 945,871 | 975,357 | Total | 3,671,606 | 1,836,578 | 1,835,029 |
| 0–4 | 373,180 | 189,227 | 183,953 | 0–4 | 606,715 | 310,021 | 296,694 |
| 5–9 | 309,595 | 156,671 | 152,924 | 5–9 | 535,497 | 273,279 | 262,217 |
| 10–14 | 268,759 | 136,002 | 132,757 | 10–14 | 461,457 | 235,213 | 226,244 |
| 15–19 | 207,631 | 102,466 | 105,165 | 15–19 | 386,213 | 196,597 | 189,616 |
| 20–24 | 157,164 | 75,447 | 81,717 | 20–24 | 349,264 | 176,579 | 172,685 |
| 25–29 | 125,699 | 59,484 | 66,215 | 25–29 | 297,593 | 150,132 | 147,462 |
| 30–34 | 99,711 | 45,801 | 53,910 | 30–34 | 256,708 | 129,381 | 127,327 |
| 35–39 | 85,203 | 41,405 | 43,798 | 35–39 | 196,374 | 96,353 | 100,021 |
| 40–44 | 67,524 | 31,481 | 36,043 | 40–44 | 147,160 | 70,100 | 77,059 |
| 45–49 | 58,337 | 28,932 | 29,405 | 45–49 | 116,136 | 54,331 | 61,805 |
| 50–54 | 44,820 | 21,614 | 23,206 | 50–54 | 90,220 | 40,670 | 49,550 |
| 55–59 | 35,725 | 17,184 | 18,541 | 55–59 | 74,299 | 35,088 | 39,211 |
| 60–64 | 27,474 | 13,034 | 14,440 | 60–64 | 55,661 | 24,807 | 30,853 |
| 65–69 | 21,047 | 9,875 | 11,172 | 65–69 | 43,471 | 20,304 | 23,167 |
| 70–74 | 15,403 | 7,117 | 8,286 | 70–74 | 28,240 | 12,555 | 15,685 |
| 75+ | 23,956 | 10,131 | 13,825 | 75+ | 26,599 | 11,168 | 15,431 |

| Age | 1980 Total | Male | Female | Age | 2000 Total | Male | Female |
|-----|-----|------|--------|-----|-----|------|--------|
|  | 2,669,517 | 1,326,609 | 1,342,908 | Total | 4,811,925 | 2,417,346 | 2,394,578 |
| 0–4 | 479,694 | 244,793 | 234,901 | 0–4 | 675,717 | 345,716 | 330,001 |
| 5–9 | 391,679 | 199,560 | 192,120 | 5–9 | 631,105 | 322,542 | 308,563 |
| 10–14 | 354,972 | 179,728 | 175,244 | 10–14 | 590,223 | 301,311 | 288,912 |
| 15–19 | 304,030 | 153,717 | 150,313 | 15–19 | 530,207 | 270,327 | 259,879 |
| 20–24 | 263,218 | 132,989 | 130,229 | 20–24 | 456,171 | 232,209 | 223,962 |
| 25–29 | 202,027 | 99,434 | 102,593 | 25–29 | 380,333 | 193,258 | 187,075 |
| 30–34 | 152,247 | 72,864 | 79,384 | 30–34 | 342,904 | 173,007 | 169,897 |
| 35–39 | 121,295 | 57,191 | 64,104 | 35–39 | 291,276 | 146,566 | 144,711 |
| 40–44 | 95,655 | 43,696 | 51,959 | 40–44 | 250,008 | 125,533 | 124,475 |
| 45–49 | 80,868 | 38,958 | 41,910 | 45–49 | 189,643 | 92,460 | 97,183 |
| 50–54 | 63,060 | 28,973 | 34,087 | 50–54 | 140,101 | 65,995 | 74,106 |
| 55–59 | 52,937 | 25,706 | 27,231 | 55–59 | 108,045 | 49,614 | 58,431 |
| 60–64 | 38,880 | 18,182 | 20,698 | 60–64 | 80,974 | 35,456 | 45,519 |
| 65–69 | 28,675 | 13,247 | 15,428 | 65–69 | 62,539 | 28,429 | 34,110 |
| 70–74 | 19,234 | 8,673 | 10,561 | 70–74 | 41,951 | 17,758 | 24,193 |
| 75+ | 21,044 | 8,898 | 12,146 | 75+ | 40,727 | 17,166 | 23,561 |

Source: U.S. Bureau of the Census, International Statistical Programs Center, computer printout. n. d.

# PANAMA

The quality and accessibility of demographic data for Panama, so frequently a major problem for many countries, posed no difficulty in the preparation of this chapter. This is largely due to the excellent organization and functioning of the Panamanian Department of Statistics and Census, a dependency of the General Accounting Office of the Republic.

Panama has conducted seven population censuses, the results of which are shown in Table 118. Collver[1] has concluded that the enumeration of the total population has been accurate in all of the censuses. The highly divergent growth rates for 1911-20 and 1920-30 resulted from the effects of international migration. "A large number of workers were brought to the Canal Zone from the West Indies (after 1903). Upon completion of the Canal Zone in 1913 many of these workers were transferred to the Republic of Panama, whence most of them eventually returned to their homes or emigrated to other areas."[2] Hence, net immigration was sizeable between 1911 and 1920, and net emigration was great between 1920 and 1930. Net international migration after 1930 was negligible according to Collver. The 2.87 per cent average annual growth rate between 1930 and 1940 appears exaggerated, however, and casts some doubt on these censuses, especially the former.

---

[1]Collver, *Birth Rates in Latin America.* p. 152.
[2]Ibid.

## Growth Rate

Panama's population has grown at a sustained high rate since 1930; the average annual rate from 1930 to 1970 equalled 2.8 per cent. The population has quadrupled this century and has doubled since 1945.

A high and nearly constant crude birth rate has combined with a low and gradually declining crude death rate to produce the rapid growth of Panama's population during the last 40 years. The crude rates based on the vital registration system appear in Table 119. The differences between the rates of increase derived in Table 119 and those shown in Table 118 reflect some error in either the vital registration system or in the decennial censuses, or both, and perhaps a small amount of net emigration as well.

The extent of census underenumeration in Panama is not great. In a thorough study of the population of Panama, Medica estimates the census undercount only for the 0–4 age group.[1] For the 1970 census it is estimated that males 0–4 were underenumerated by 5.1 per cent, and females 0–4 by 3.9 per cent. The respective estimates for the 1960 census (non-indigenous population) were 6.0 per cent and 4.2 per cent. These undercounts amount to only 0.7 per cent of the total 1970 population and 0.85 per cent of the 1960 population. The true extent of underenumeration is no doubt greater than these percentages indicate but is not a major obstacle to the use of census data for demographic analysis. The difference in completeness of enumeration between 1960 and 1970 is not sufficient to have any effect on the computation of the average annual intercensal growth rate.

---

[1] Vilma N. Medica. "Estimación de Indicadores Demográficos de la Republica de Panamá para el Período 1950–1970 y Proyecciones de Poblacíon por Sexo y Grupos de Edades, Años 1960 al 2000," *Estadística Panameña,* Suplemento, año 33, Panamá, Dirección de Estadístics y Censo, 1973.

**Table 118**

**Enumerated Population and Intercensal Growth Rates of Panama, 1911 to 1970.**

| Year | Enumerated population | Average annual rate of increase (%) during intercensal period |
|------|-----------------------|----------------------------------------------------------------|
| 1911 | 336,742 | |
| 1920 | 446,098 | 3.12 |
| 1930 | 467,459 | 0.47 |
| 1940 | 622,576 | 2.87 |
| 1950 | 805,285 | 2.57 |
| 1960 | 1,075,541 | 2.89 |
| 1970 | 1,428,082 | 3.01 |

Source: Panamá, Dirección de Estadística y Censo, *Censos Nacionales de 1970, Resultados Generales.* Table 1.

## Birth Rate

The registration of births is close to complete. Medica estimates that only 2.0 per cent of the births which occurred in 1960 through 1964 were not reported and that 3.9 per cent of the births 1951-55 went unregistered. The recent crude birth rates presented in Table 119 are quite accurate. If Medica's findings are accepted, the slight increase in the recorded crude birth rate after 1955 is probably due primarily to an improvement in the coverage of the vital registration system.

The crude birth rate (CBR) in Panama appears to have begun a modest decline in 1964. There is no reason to suspect that it is due to a decline in the completeness of birth registration. Table 120 shows the registered CBR for single years from 1960 to 1971. The decline is not simply an artifact of a changing age distribution since the proportion of the total population made up of females ages 15-44 dropped from

**Table 119**

**Reported Crude Birth Rate, Crude Death Rate, and Rate of Natural Increase for Panama, 1930 to 1970.**

| Period | Crude birth rate | Crude death rate | Rate of natural increase (%) |
|--------|------|------|------|
| 1930–34 | 36.5 | 12.9 | 2.36 |
| 1935–39 | 36.4 | 12.9 | 2.35 |
| 1940–44 | 37.5 | 8.8 | 2.87 |
| 1945–49 | 36.1 | 10.9 | 2.52 |
| 1950–54 | 37.5 | 8.8 | 2.87 |
| 1955–59 | 39.8 | 9.1 | 3.07 |
| 1960–64 | 40.2 | 7.8 | 3.24 |
| 1965–70 | 38.5 | 7.1 | 3.14 |

Sources: The rates for 1930 through 1959 are from U.S., Bureau of the Census, *Population of Panama, Estimated and Projections: 1961 to 2001.* Demographic Reports for Foreign Countries, Series P-96, No. 2, U.S. Government Printing Office, Washington, D.C.

The rates for 1960 through 1970 are from Panamá, Dirección de Estadística y Censo, *La Población de Panamá,* 1973, pp. 16, 31.

**Table 120**

**Registered Crude Birth Rate of Panama, Single Years 1960 to 1971**

| Year | CBR | Year | CBR |
|------|------|------|------|
| 1960 | 39.9 | 1966 | 39.9 |
| 1961 | 40.4 | 1967 | 38.8 |
| 1962 | 41.1 | 1968 | 38.9 |
| 1963 | 40.2 | 1969 | 38.0 |
| 1964 | 39.6 | 1970 | 37.1 |
| 1965 | 39.2 | 1971 | 37.2 |

Sources: For 1960-1970, Panamá, Dirección de Estadística y Censo, *La Población de Panamá,* 1973, p. 16.

For 1971, *Population Index* 40:3 (July 1974) 597.

20.7 per cent in 1960 only to 20.6 per cent in 1970. The decline in fertility is also reflected by the gross reproduction rate which fell from 2.66 in 1960 to 2.48 in 1970.[1] Thus, the level of fertility and the population growth rate appear to have reached a peak in the 1960-64 period and to have declined slightly since then.

## Death Rate

Death registration is not as complete as birth registration. Medica estimated that deaths were underregistered by 12.5 per cent for both the 1950-1960 and 1960-1970 decades.

The 1960-1970 reported vital rates adjusted for the percentage of underregistration estimated by Medica are as follows:

| Year | CBR | CDR | RNI (%) |
|---|---|---|---|
| 1960–64 | 41.0 | 8.8 | 3.22 |
| 1965–70 | 39.3 | 8.0 | 3.13 |

The rate of natural increase is barely changed by this adjustment since the birth rate and death rate are adjusted by nearly the same absolute amount.

## Net Migration Rate

Collver estimated that net international migration was +37,000 during 1910-19 and -37,000 during 1920-29.[2] The former figure yields an average annual net migration rate of +9.55 per thousand for the 1911-20 intercensal period when applied to the mid-period population. If this rate is subtracted from the growth rate of 3.12 per cent (Table 118) the implied rate of natural increase is 2.16 per cent, which is the same as estimated by Collver for 1910-19 (2.15 per cent).

The average annual net migration rate for the 1920-30 intercensal period was -8.10 per thousand. This rate, in conjunction with the growth rate of 0.47 per cent, implies a rate of natural increase of 1.28 per cent. Since Collver estimates the rate of natural increase for 1920-29 as 2.25 per cent, the lower rate computed above is further evidence of a certain of underenumeration in the 1930 census.

Panama experienced a net loss of 6,111 males and 9,726 females in the 10-year period from January 1, 1960 to January 1, 1970 according to estimates by Medica. These totals represent an average annual net migration rate of -0.13 per cent. If 0.13 percentage points are sub-

---

[1] Panama, Dirección de Estadística y Censo, *La Población de Panama,* 1973, p. 21.
[2] Collver, *Birth Rates in Latin America.* p. 155.

tracted from the adjusted rates of natural increase based on vital registration calculated in the previous paragraph, the resultant growth rates are nearly identical to the rate of increases of 3.01 per cent implied by the unadjusted 1960 and 1970 census totals. The close correspondence between growth rates calculated by the two different methods is an indication of the general reliability of census totals and of registration statistics when adjusted by the suggested amounts.

## Age Distribution

The relatively high level of fertility and the low and declining level of mortality over the past four decades or more has resulted in a young age structure: 43 per cent of the population is below age 15 (see Table 121). For every 100 persons aged 15–64 there are 89 who are either young or older than this conventional definition of working age. The age distribution remained essentially unchanged between 1960 and 1970.

Supporting the national population projection series detailed later in this chapter is a contemplated modest fall in the crude birth rate to the year 2000, one descending slightly faster than the continuing decline in the death rate (Table 119). This, combined with a longer life expectancy pattern for the population in general, will produce shifts in the age structure, and will in turn affect the dependency ratio.

According to CELADE projections to the year 2000 (Table 122), those in the age group 0–14 will continue to decline as a proportion of the total population. They represented 43.5 per cent of the total in 1960, and should represent 37.5 per cent in 2000. In the category 65 and older, the share increases from 3.5 per cent (1960) to 5.0 per cent (2000). Among those of working ages 15–64, the projections show an

Table 121

**Percentage of Population in Broad Age Groups, and Dependency Ratios for Panama, 1960 and 1970**

| Age | 1970 | 1960 | | |
|---|---|---|---|---|
| | | Total | Urban | Rural |
| all ages | 100.0% | 100.0% | 100.0% | 100.0% |
| 0–14 | 43.4 | 43.5 | 38.2 | 47.1 |
| 15–64 | 52.8 | 53.0 | 57.5 | 49.8 |
| 65+ | 3.7 | 3.5 | 4.3 | 3.1 |
| Dependency ratio[a] | 89.2 | 88.6 | 73.9 | 100.9 |

[a] The dependency ratio is $(P(0-14) + P(65+))/P(15-64) \times 100$, where P(a) is the population age "a".

Sources: For 1970, Panamá, Dirección de Estadística y Censo, *Censos Nacionales de 1970, Resultados Generales,* (calculated from Table 6).

For 1960, Panamá, Dirección de Estadística y Censos, *Censos Nacionales de 1960, Compendio General de Población,* (calculated from Table 12).

increase from 53 to 58 per cent in the same period. The CELADE data in 5 year age intervals (1975-2000) and by 5 year age groups are shown in Appendix A of this chapter.

The decrease in the dependency ratio for Panama is only moderate in comparison to Costa Rica, for example, which has experienced a sharp drop in the birth rate. In Costa Rica the dependency ratio reached 104 in 1963, dipped sharply to 91 by 1973, and by 1980 an index number of 75 is projected. With shifts in the age structure continuing, the ratio should stand at around 63 by the year 2000, a number substantially lower than in Panama.

## Urban-Rural Fertility Differentials

The urban-rural demographic differentials cited here are based on 1960 data because similar data on this point for 1970 are not yet available. It is observed from Table 123 that the crude birth rate in urban areas (37.5) is substantially below that in rural areas (44.4). The CBR is also lower in Panama City and in the city of Colon than for the urban population as a whole. The CBR camouflages much of the actual rural-

Table 122

**Population in Broad Age Groups, and Dependency Ratios for Panama, 1980-2000 as Projected by CELADE.**

| Age Group | Population | | | Percentage Distribution | | |
|---|---|---|---|---|---|---|
| | 1980 | 1990 | 2000 | 1980 | 1990 | 2000 |
| Total | 1,926,709 | 2,524,593 | 3,217,565 | 100.0 | 100.0 | 100.0 |
| 0-14 | 797,578 | 1,005,012 | 1,198,429 | 41.4 | 39.8 | 37.2 |
| 15-64 | 1,049,751 | 1,406,553 | 1,868,016 | 54.5 | 55.7 | 58.1 |
| 65+ | 79,380 | 113,028 | 151,120 | 4.1 | 4.5 | 5.0 |
| Dependency Ratios | 84 | 79 | 72 | | | |

Source: Centro Latinoamericano de Demografía (CELADE); *Boletín Demográfico*, 7:13 (January, 1974). Note that these projections (year 2000) differ slightly from those of Medica (Table 128).

Table 123

**Crude Birth Rate (CBR) and Gross Reproduction Rate (GRR) of Various Areas of Panama, 1960 [a]**

| Area | CBR | Index (rural 100) | GRR | Index (rural 100) |
|---|---|---|---|---|
| Panama | 39.9 | 90 | 2.7 | 79 |
| Rural | 44.4 | 100 | 3.4 | 100 |
| Urban | 37.5 | 84 | 2.2 | 65 |
| Panama City | 35.4 | 80 | 2.0 | 59 |
| Colon (city) | 32.7 | 74 | 2.2 | 65 |

[a] Rates are unadjusted for underregistration.

Source: Panamá, Dirección de Estadística y Censo, *La Población de Panamá*, 1973, p. 24.

180

urban fertility differential because it does not control for the fact that the urban population comprises a greater proportion of women of child-bearing age than the rural population (see Figure 35). As a measure of fertility, the gross reproduction rate (GRR) has the effect of controlling for the age distribution of a population; thus, it more accurately reflects the difference between fertility in rural and urban places. Urban fertility is seen to be only about 65 per cent as great as rural fertility and the fertility of women in Panama City in 1960 was only 59 per cent as great as that of rural women.

A significantly smaller percentage of the urban population than of the rural population is under age 15 (Table 121). The combination of lower urban fertility and the concentration of rural-urban migrants between the ages of 15 and 30 produces an urban population which is older than the rural population. Consequently, the urban dependency ratio (74) is much lower than the rural (101).

The much greater propensity for females than for males to migrate to urban areas is demonstrated in Figures 34 and 35. Figure 34 shows the urban residence ratios (URR) by sex and 5-year age group, based on the 1960 census of Panama. The URR is the percentage of each sex-age group which lives in an urban area. Males and females below age 10 were about equally urbanized in 1960, but females ages 10–14 and especially 15–19 were decidedly more urban than their male cohorts. Above age 20 the greater propensity for females to live in urban areas is maintained at a roughly constant level.

The sex ratios by age group and area of residence presented in Figure 35 confirm that a greater proportion of females than of males lives in urban areas. This phenomenon is typical of Latin American countries. The sex ratios in Figure 35 are defined as the number of males in each age-residence group per 100 females in that group. In a closed population with a Western-style mortality pattern, the sex ratios at ages above approximately 20 would be expected to be below 100. The fact that Panama's sex ratios above age 20 are greater than 100 and increases between ages 20 and 54 is explained by international migration which is differentially selective by sex. Of the 44,240 foreign-born persons counted in the 1960 census, 25,809 were males. Medica estimated that males and females emigrated from Panama in equal numbers between 1960 and 1970, but because more males immigrated the net rate of emigration for females was 50 per cent greater than that for males.[1]

**Occupational Structures, Labor Force Participation, by Age and Sex**

The dependency ratio is only an arithmetic expression of the relation-

---

[1] Medica, *Estimación de Indicadores.* p. 43.

**Figure 34**
**Urban residence ratios by age and sex, Panama, 1960**

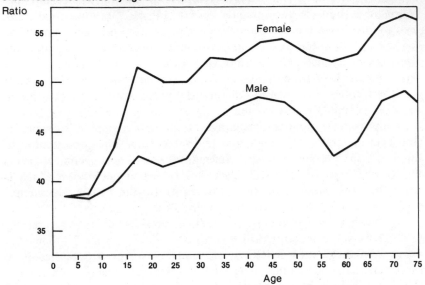

**Figure 35**
**Sex ratios by age group for the total, urban and rural**
**Population of Panama, 1960.**

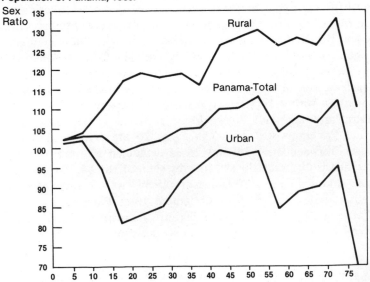

ship between those in various age groups, and does little to differentiate between those who are actually working and the population remaining. This topic deserves scrutiny since the "absorption" of the rapidly increasing population in economic activities by age, sex, and urban or rural place of residence is of central interest. A very recent publication from Panama makes this examination possible.[1]

In 1960, some 299,386 persons comprised the labor force—or 42.9 per cent of the non-indigenous population 10 and older. The labor force by 1970 increased to 419,781, or 44.9 per cent of the population. Taking those under 10 into account, this represents 29.5 per cent in 1960, and in 1970, 31.0 per cent of the Panamanian non-indigenous population. Modifying the dependency ratio accordingly produces index numbers of 239 (1960) and 222 in 1970. Thus, at each interval there were about two dependents for each person working. Aside from children under 10, the single largest category outside the labor force consists of "amas de casa," essentially housewives, numbering 174,285 women in 1960, and 214,656 in 1970.

Labor force growth trends by sex in the 1950–70 period are shown in Table 124. Females joining the work force have not only kept pace but have significantly gained on the overall increase in the number of females 10 and older. This is seen in the jump from a 17.4 per cent to a 22.0 per cent participation rate (1960–70). In proportional terms, participation among males has slightly declined from 72.7 per cent in 1950 to 66.9 per cent by 1970. The key reason for this decline seems to be that greater number of boys are retained in the school system than in the past.

The highest percent of labor force expansion between 1950–70 occurred in the service sector as noted in Figure 36 and Table 125. This is consistent with existing patterns for other Latin American countries.

**Table 124**

**Economically Active Population of Panama, by sex, 1950–1970[a]**

| | (A) Population 10 and Older | | | (B) Population Economically Active | | | (B) as Percentage of (A) | | |
|---|---|---|---|---|---|---|---|---|---|
| | 1950 | 1960 | 1970 | 1950 | 1960 | 1970 | 1950 | 1960 | 1970 |
| Male | 269,583 | 356,487 | 476,211 | 195,974 | 239,951 | 318,791 | 72.7% | 67.3% | 66.9% |
| Female | 257,594 | 342,137 | 459,242 | 45,130 | 59,435 | 100,990 | 17.5% | 17.4% | 22.0% |

[a] Excluding the indigenous population.

Source: For 1950 and 1960, Panama Census and Statistics Institute, *Compendio General de Población, Censos Nacionales de 1960,* Table 34, Panama, 1965. For 1970; *Compendio General de Población,* Volume III, Table 8 and 30, Panama, n.d.

[1] Panama, Dirección de Estadística y Censo, *Censos Nacionales de 1970, Compendio General de Población, Volumen III, 1975.*

The tertiary, or service sector, in 1970 employed about the same number as did agriculture—the primary sector—but in the 1960-70 interval those in services increased by 71 per cent and agriculture by just 10 per cent. Quite evidently, among the three, the service sector will dominate by 1980.

Figures 37 and 38 illustrate by age groups, and by urban and rural sectors the radical differences between male and female participation in the labor force. For comparative purposes information for Costa Rica is also shown (1973). The pattern for males (Figure 37), either urban or rural, is rather similar for both countries. A large number of urban males below age 24 are withheld from the labor market while attending school; on the rural side, the slope rises sharper and earlier. Regardless of age group among males, there are only slight variations in proportions in the category "unemployed or looking for employment for the

**Table 125**

**Panama, Economically Active Population by Activity and Economic Sector: 1950-1970[1]**

| Economic Sector and Activity | (Population 10 and Older) | | | Percentage Distribution | | |
|---|---|---|---|---|---|---|
| | 1950 | 1960 | 1970 | 1950 | 1960 | 1970 |
| Total | 277,262 | 346,540 | 471,250 | 100.0 | 100.0 | 100.0 |
| Primary Sector | 146,246 | 171,577 | 187,947 | 52.7 | 49.5 | 39.9 |
| Agriculture, hunting, forestry and fishing | 146,246 | 171,577 | 187,947 | | | |
| Secondary Sector | 33,701 | 42,576 | 71,669 | 12.2 | 12.3 | 15.2 |
| Mine and quarry exploitation | 445 | 450 | 650 | | | |
| Manufacturing industries | 21,927[a] | 26,079[a] | 38,847 | | | |
| Electricity, gas, and water | 1,427 | 1,683 | 4,226 | | | |
| Construction | 9,902 | 14,364 | 27,946 | | | |
| Tertiary Sector | 72,736 | 108,656 | 186,260 | 26.2 | 31.4 | 39.5 |
| Wholesale and retail business and restaurants and hotels: | 22,018[b] | 30,749[b] | 57,751 | | | |
| Transportation, storage and communications | 7,885 | 10,004 | 16,934 | | | |
| Financial establishments, insurance, real estate and business services | c | c | 9,652 | | | |
| Communal, social and personal services | 42,833[d] | 67,903[d] | 101,923 | | | |
| Panama Canal Zone | 22,427 | 18,848 | 21,805 | 8.1 | 5.4 | 4.6 |
| Activities not specified | 2,152 | 4,883 | 3,569 | 0.8 | 1.4 | 0.8 |

[1] Excludes new workers.

[a] Includes "repair shops" which according to the 1970 classification belong in the service branch.
[b] Excludes "restaurants and hotels" which were considered part of the service branch.
[c] Belongs to the commerce branch.
[d] Excludes "repair shops" and includes "restaurants and hotels."

Source: Panamá, Dirección de Estadística y Censo, *Censos Nacionales de 1970, Compendio General de Población, Volumen III,* p. 176.

**Figure 36**
**Panama, economically active population according
to economic sector, census of 1950 to 1970.**

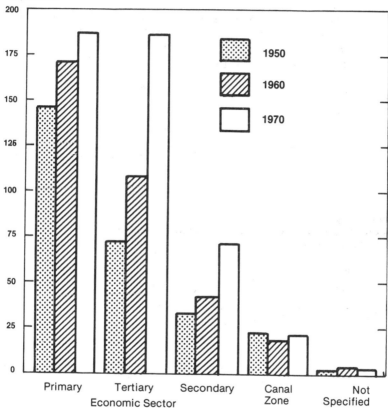

Thousands
of persons

Primary Sector- Agriculture, hunting, forestry, and fishing.

Secondary Sector- Mine and quarry exploitation; manufacturing industries; electricity, gas, and water, construction.

Tertiary Sector- Wholesale and retail business; restaurants and hotels; transportation, storage, and communications; financial establishments, insurance, real estate; personal, business, and other services.

Source: Panama, Direccion de Estadistica y Censo, *Censos Nacionales de 1970, Compendio General de Poblacion, Volumen III*, p. 175.

## Figure 37
## Economically active males, urban and rural, in Panama (1970) and Costa Rica (1973), by age.

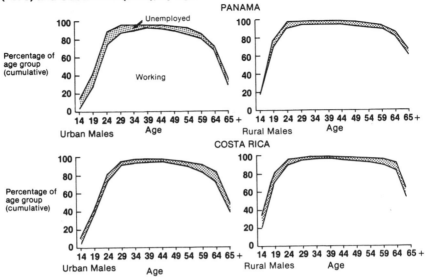

PANAMA

Percentage of age group (cumulative)

Unemployed

Working

Urban Males — Age

Rural Males — Age

COSTA RICA

Percentage of age group (cumulative)

Urban Males — Age

Rural Males — Age

## Figure 38
## Economically active females, urban and rural, in Panama (1970) and Costa Rica (1973), by age.

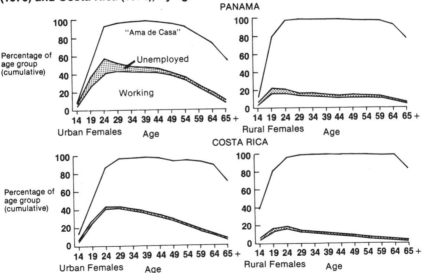

PANAMA

Percentage of age group (cumulative)

"Ama de Casa"

Unemployed

Working

Urban Females — Age

Rural Females — Age

COSTA RICA

Percentage of age group (cumulative)

Urban Females — Age

Rural Females — Age

Sources: Costa Rica, Direccion General de Estadística y Censos, Censos Nacionales de 1970: Población, Volumes 1 and 2, San Jose, 1974–75.
Panama, Dirección de Estadística y Censo, Compendio General de Población, Vol. III, 1975.

first time." And the downturn in the figure after roughly age 59 reflects retirement from the labor force. This is less pronounced in the rural sector, since few options to remaining employed are available there.

The proportion of economically active females (Figure 38) is sharply lower than for males. Rural, rather than urban females are also clearly at a greater disadvantage since few employment opportunities exist in the tradition-bound rural occupational structure.

A higher proportion of Panamanian than Costa Rican females are noted as unemployed or looking for work for the first time. Census reports from Panama for the entire 1950–70 period give a rate of 14–17 per cent in this regard. Among males the rate has wavered between 8–9 per cent for the three census years.

To account for the majority of the remaining Panamanian and Costa Rican female population, those in the "ama de casa" category are also shown in Figure 38.

## Population Projections

The total population of cities and urbanized areas in Panama is projected to the years 1980, 1990, and 2000 by allocating the projected national totals first to provinces then to the cities using the ratio-trend methodology as elaborated by Jerome P. Pickard.[1] Since this method progresses from a population projection for the country as a whole, to regional projections, to urban projections, it is termed a "step-down" system.

## National Projection

Province and urban area totals are derived from the national population projection prepared by Vilma N. Medica for the *Dirección de Estadística y Censo.*[2] Medica prepared four series of projections which differ in their hypotheses of future fertility levels. Hypothesis I is that the 1970 age-specific fertility rates remain constant until the year 2000. This assumption yields a total population of 3.7 million in 2000. The other hypotheses assume various degrees of fertility decline and produce populations of 3.5, 3.2, and 2.9 million by the end of the century. The series 3 projection (Table 126) has been accepted as the most feasible by the *Centro Latinoamericano de Demografía* (CELADE)[3] and is employed in this chapter.

Medica adjusted the 1970 census population upward by 1.6 per cent before using it as the base for the projections. This adjustment of the enumerated population has not been carried out here because there is

---

[1] Pickard, *Dimensions to Metropolitanism,* pp. 53-56.
[2] Medica, *Estimación de Indicadores.* p. 43.
[3] CELADE, *Boletín Demográfico 7:13* (January 1974).

no information concerning differential completeness of enumeration among provinces or between urban and rural areas. At any rate, the degree of adjustment is well within the margin of error to be anticipated for the population projections.

The population of Panama as projected to the year 2000 by Medica is shown in Table 126 along with the projected rates of the components of population change. When Table 126 is compared with Table 119 it is seen that the assumed decline of the crude birth rate is a reasonable continuation of the incipient decline observed during the 1960's. The crude birth rate minimizes the extent of an actual decline in fertility. As the number of births declines (or increases more slowly) the total population is affected in the same direction but to a lesser degree. Thus, a change in the number of births affects both the numerator and denominator in the calculation of the crude birth rate. The total fertility rate is simply the sum of single-year age-specific fertility rates, hence the denominator is not affected by a change in fertility. For this reason the total fertility rate (TFR) may be considered a less biased measure of fertility. From Table 127 it is observed that the crude birth rate is projected to decline by 19 per cent between 1970–75 and 1995–2000, but the corresponding total fertility rate would fall by 25 per cent during the same interval. Since changes in the net reproduction rate (NRR) reflect not only changes in the level of fertility but also (in this case) improving survival rates, the projected decline of the NRR (21 per cent) is less than that for the TFR.

It is difficult to project the future trend of fertility accurately particularly when it appears to be in a stage of incipient decline. The results of

Table 126

**Projected Population, Crude Birth Rate, Crude Death Rate, Net Migration Rate, and Rate of Increase for Panama, 1970 to 2000.**

| Period | Population at beginning of period (in thousands) (1) | Crude birth rate (2) | Crude death rate (3) | Net migration rate (4) | Average annual rate of increase (%) (5) |
|---|---|---|---|---|---|
| 1970–75 | 1,458 | 36.2 | 7.2 | −1.0 | 2.80 |
| 1975–80 | 1,678 | 35.5 | 6.6 | −0.9 | 2.80 |
| 1980–85 | 1,930 | 34.6 | 6.2 | −0.7 | 2.77 |
| 1985–90 | 2,217 | 33.1 | 5.8 | −0.7 | 2.66 |
| 1990–95 | 2,533 | 31.1 | 5.5 | −0.5 | 2.51 |
| 1995–2000 | 2,871 | 29.2 | 5.2 | −0.5 | 2.35 |
| 2000 | 3,230 | | | | |

In the projection the net number of migrants is held constant. The net migration rate here is calculated as a residual: (4) = (5) − (2) + (3).

Source: Vilma N. Médica, "Estimación de Indicadores Demográficos de la República de Panamá para el Período 1950–70 y Proyecciones de Población por Sexo y Grupos de Edades, Años 1960 al 2000," *Estadística Panameña*, Suplemento, año 33, Panamá, Dirección de Estadística y Censo, 1973, hypothesis III.

the national population projection, and consequently of the projections for provinces and urbanized areas, will be inaccurate at least to the extent that actual fertility trends differ from those projected by Medica. Fertility rates in Panama over the next several years will bear close watching since a declining trend is apparent and since the accuracy of these projections obviously depends heavily upon the fertility decline assumed.

It must be noted that the rate of increase of the population is not projected to decline by as great a proportion of the 1970–75 level as is the fertility level. The decline in fertility can be expected to be partially offset by a drop in the crude death rate. Barring exceptional circumstances, death rates operate within a narrower range than birth rates and their projection is less problematical. The crude death rate in Panama is low not only because the average life expectancy is 65 years (for 1965–70) but because of the youthfulness of the population. The combination of a decline in both fertility and mortality will age the population somewhat. From the distribution by age group shown in Table 121, the population as projected to the end of the century by Medica would be 37.3 per cent in the ages 0–14, 58.0 per cent ages 15–64, and 4.7 per cent ages 65 and over. The dependency ratio would be 72 in the year 2000. The projected broad age distribution for 2000 is quite similar to the age distribution of the urban population in 1960. (See Appendix A to this chapter).

Medica assumes a constant net international out-migration of 3,250 males and 5,000 females during each five-year period of the projection.

## Provincial Projections

The provincial populations are not projected by the component method, as is the national total. Instead, the trend of each province's proportion of the national population is projected to 1980, 1990, and 2000. The

Table 127

**Projected Crude Birth Rate, Total Fertility Rate, and Net Reproduction Rate for Panama, 1970 to 2000.**

| Period | Crude birth rate | Index (1970–75 =100) | Total fertility rate | Index (1970–75 =100) | Net reproduction rate | Index (1970–75 =100) |
|--------|------|------|------|------|------|------|
| 1970–75 | 36.2 | 100 | 5.06 | 100 | 2.22 | 100 |
| 1975–80 | 35.5 | 98 | 4.80 | 95 | 2.14 | 96 |
| 1980–85 | 34.6 | 96 | 4.55 | 90 | 2.05 | 92 |
| 1985–90 | 33.1 | 91 | 4.29 | 85 | 1.95 | 88 |
| 1990–95 | 31.1 | 86 | 4.04 | 80 | 1.85 | 83 |
| 1995–2000 | 29.2 | 81 | 3.78 | 75 | 1.75 | 79 |

Source: Vilma N. Médica, "Estimación de Indicadores Demográficos de la República de Panamá para el Período 1950-1970 y Proyecciones de Población por Sexo y Grupos de Edades, Años 1960 al 2000," *Estadística Panameña,* Suplemento, año 33, Panamá, Dirección de Estadística y Censo, 1973, p. 87.

projected trend is dependent upon the observed intercensal trends, with greater weight assigned to the trends of more recent periods. The projected provincial proportions of the national population are then converted to absolute population figures.

Table 128 presents the population of each province as projected to mid-year 1980, 1990, and 2000. No change in the ranking of the six largest provinces is projected. The Province of Panama is projected to increase its dominance in terms of size by surpassing one million before 1990 and by reaching nearly 1.7 million by the year 2000. The proportion of the national total residing in the Province of Panama is projected to increase from 40 per cent in 1970 to 52 per cent in the year

**Table 128**

**Enumerated and Projected Population of Provinces and Urbanized Areas in Panama, 1950 to 2000**

| Province and Urbanized Area | Enumerated Population in Thousands | | | | | Projected Population in Thousands (midyear) | | |
|---|---|---|---|---|---|---|---|---|
| | 1930 | 1940 | Dec. 10 1950 | Dec. 11 1960 | May 10 1970 | 1980 | 1990 | 2000 |
| **National Total** | **467.5** | **622.6** | **805.3** | **1,075.5** | **1,428.1** | **1,930.8** | **2,532.8** | **3,230.2** |
| **Bocas del Toro** | **15.9** | **16.5** | **22.4** | **32.6** | **43.5** | **60.6** | **79.1** | **103.9** |
| **Coclé** | **48.2** | **55.7** | **73.1** | **93.2** | **118.0** | **151.4** | **188.5** | **230.0** |
| Aguadulce | 3.7 | 4.4 | 6.3 | 8.4 | 11.4 | 15.4 | 20.0 | 25.6 |
| Penonomé | 3.2 | 2.4 | 3.5 | 4.3 | 5.1 | 6.1 | 7.0 | 8.2 |
| Remainder | 41.1 | 48.9 | 63.3 | 80.5 | 101.6 | 129.9 | 161.5 | 196.1 |
| **Colón** | **57.2** | **78.1** | **90.1** | **105.4** | **134.3** | **167.7** | **203.9** | **238.0** |
| Colón | 36.9 | 52.3 | 67.0 | 79.5 | 103.0 | 130.8 | 163.1 | 194.0 |
| Remainder | 20.2 | 25.9 | 23.2 | 25.9 | 31.3 | 36.9 | 40.8 | 44.0 |
| **Chiriquí** | **76.9** | **111.2** | **138.1** | **188.4** | **236.2** | **307.8** | **396.6** | **488.9** |
| David | 5.0 | 9.2 | 14.8 | 22.9 | 40.8 | 61.8 | 89.0 | 121.5 |
| Puerto Armuelles | 0.7 | 3.3 | 5.7 | 10.7 | 12.0 | 16.0 | 23.2 | 30.3 |
| La Concepción | 1.8 | 2.2 | 3.1 | 6.5 | 9.2 | 14.3 | 20.4 | 28.5 |
| Remainder | 69.4 | 96.5 | 114.5 | 148.2 | 174.1 | 215.7 | 236.9 | 308.6 |
| **Darién** | **13.4** | **14.9** | **14.7** | **19.7** | **22.7** | **27.7** | **31.6** | **35.7** |
| **Herrera** | **31.0** | **38.1** | **50.1** | **61.7** | **72.5** | **87.3** | **105.5** | **122.1** |
| Chitré | 5.3 | 6.2 | 9.8 | 12.3 | 19.0 | 24.7 | 31.7 | 39.2 |
| Remainder | 25.7 | 32.0 | 40.3 | 49.4 | 53.6 | 62.6 | 73.7 | 82.9 |
| Chitré-Los Santos (Urbanized Area)[a] | 7.1 | 8.1 | 12.4 | 15.4 | 22.9 | 29.5 | 37.4 | 45.7 |
| **Los Santos** | **41.2** | **49.6** | **61.4** | **70.6** | **72.4** | **77.2** | **85.3** | **88.8** |
| Los Santos | 1.8 | 2.0 | 2.6 | 3.2 | 3.9 | 4.8 | 5.7 | 6.4 |
| Remainder | 39.4 | 47.7 | 58.8 | 67.4 | 68.4 | 72.5 | 79.7 | 82.3 |
| **Panamá** | **114.1** | **173.3** | **248.3** | **372.4** | **576.6** | **870.2** | **1,228.7** | **1,679.5** |
| Panama City | 92.9 | 148.4 | 216.6 | 331.8 | 519.6 | 794.3 | 1,135.9 | 1,567.6 |
| Remainder | 21.2 | 25.0 | 31.8 | 40.6 | 57.0 | 75.9 | 92.8 | 111.9 |
| **Veraguas** | **69.5** | **85.0** | **107.0** | **131.7** | **151.8** | **180.2** | **213.7** | **243.4** |
| Santiago | 2.2 | 4.3 | 5.9 | 8.7 | 14.6 | 21.7 | 29.5 | 38.2 |
| Remainder | 67.3 | 80.7 | 101.1 | 122.9 | 137.3 | 158.5 | 184.3 | 205.1 |

Some province totals do not agree with the sum of the component populations because all numbers in the table are independently rounded.

[a] The Chitré and Los Santos urbanized areas were projected within their respective provinces and the results were summed to obtain the population of the Chitré-Los Santos urbanized area.

2000. Chiriqui, the second largest province, is projected to pass the 300,000 mark by 1980, to reach 400,000 in 1990, and 489,000 in 2000. The provinces of Cocle, Colon, and Veraguas are all expected to contain between 230,000 and 243,000 inhabitants by the year 2000.

Panama, already the largest province, is projected to be the fastest-growing with an average annual growth rate of well above 3 per cent for the remainder of this century (Table 129). Bocas del Toro, while beginning with a small base population, is projected to maintain the second highest growth rate between 1970 and 2000 and still to be increasing at 2.7 per cent year at the end of the century. The growth of Panama is expected to dominate in such a way the increase of the national population that all other provinces, except Bocas del Toro, are projected to

**Table 129**

**Observed and Projected Population Growth Rates of Provinces and Urbanized Areas in Panama, 1930 to 2000**

| Province and Urbanized Area | Average annual growth rate (%) based on enumerated population | | | | Average annual growth rates (%) based on projected population | | |
|---|---|---|---|---|---|---|---|
| | 1930–1940 | 1940–1950 | 1950–1960 | 1960–1970 | 1970–1980 | 1980–1990 | 1990–2000 |
| National Total | 2.87 | 2.57 | 2.89 | 3.01 | 2.97 | 2.72 | 2.43 |
| Bocas del Toro | 0.42 | 3.04 | 3.76 | 3.07 | 3.26 | 2.66 | 2.73 |
| Coclé | 1.44 | 2.71 | 2.42 | 2.51 | 2.46 | 2.20 | 1.99 |
| Aguadulce | 1.32 | 3.53 | 2.84 | 3.19 | 3.00 | 2.63 | 2.48 |
| Penonomé | −2.82 | 3.74 | 1.94 | 1.83 | 1.85 | 1.40 | 1.60 |
| Remainder | 1.72 | 2.58 | 2.41 | 2.47 | 2.42 | 2.18 | 1.94 |
| Colón | 3.12 | 1.43 | 1.57 | 2.57 | 2.19 | 1.95 | 1.55 |
| Colón | 3.47 | 2.48 | 1.72 | 2.75 | 2.35 | 2.21 | 1.74 |
| Remainder | 2.46 | −1.09 | 1.10 | 2.00 | 1.64 | 1.00 | 0.74 |
| Chiriquí | 3.69 | 2.17 | 3.10 | 2.40 | 2.61 | 2.53 | 2.09 |
| David | 6.04 | 4.76 | 4.34 | 6.13 | 4.04 | 3.64 | 3.11 |
| Puerto Armuelles | 15.23 | 5.44 | 6.25 | 1.22 | 2.84 | 3.72 | 2.66 |
| La Concepción | 1.95 | 3.48 | 7.57 | 3.69 | 4.31 | 3.56 | 3.32 |
| Remainder | 3.30 | 1.71 | 2.58 | 1.71 | 2.11 | 2.02 | 1.56 |
| Darién | 1.09 | −0.18 | 2.96 | 1.49 | 1.96 | 1.32 | 1.24 |
| Herrera | 2.06 | 2.73 | 2.08 | 1.72 | 1.83 | 1.89 | 1.47 |
| Chitré | 1.48 | 4.61 | 2.27 | 4.64 | 2.60 | 2.50 | 2.13 |
| Remainder | 2.17 | 2.33 | 2.03 | 0.86 | 1.54 | 1.63 | 1.17 |
| Chitré-Los Santos (Urbanized Area) | 1.28 | 4.22 | 2.20 | 4.20 | 2.48 | 2.37 | 2.01 |
| Los Santos | 1.86 | 2.13 | 1.39 | 0.27 | 0.64 | 0.99 | 0.40 |
| Los Santos | 0.67 | 2.89 | 1.94 | 2.32 | 1.91 | 1.68 | 1.31 |
| Remainder | 1.91 | 2.10 | 1.36 | 0.16 | 0.56 | 0.95 | 0.33 |
| Panamá | 4.18 | 3.60 | 4.05 | 4.64 | 4.06 | 3.45 | 3.13 |
| Panama City | 4.68 | 3.78 | 4.27 | 4.76 | 4.18 | 3.58 | 3.22 |
| Remainder | 1.62 | 2.41 | 2.45 | 3.61 | 2.82 | 2.01 | 1.87 |
| Veraguas | 2.01 | 2.30 | 2.08 | 1.51 | 1.69 | 1.71 | 1.30 |
| Santiago | 6.53 | 3.25 | 3.96 | 5.44 | 3.89 | 3.08 | 2.61 |
| Remainder | 1.82 | 2.25 | 1.95 | 1.17 | 1.42 | 1.51 | 1.07 |

Source: Table 128.

experience growth rates below the national average, as they did during the 1960's.

## Urbanized Area Projections

The methodology employed in projecting the population of urbanized areas in Table 129 is the same as that used for projecting provincial populations. In this step the trend of the ratio of an urbanized area's population to the appropriate provincial population is projected. Thus, the projected population of a city area is determined as a proportion of the previously projected population of the province in which the area is located.

This projection procedure acts in two distinct ways to produce conservative projections of the future population of the cities. First, past intercensal changes in the ratios are averaged so that a large change in the most recent period is not the sole determinant of projected changes. Second, the projection procedure imposes on the ratios an asymptote of 100 per cent which may be approached only gradually.

## Urban Population Growth

Heretofore the definition of "urban" employed in this chapter has been that established by the *Dirección de Estadística y Censo*. Accordingly, thirty-three localities were designed as urban in 1970. Each had at least 1,500 inhabitants and, in addition, was largely served by electricity, a public water and sewerage system, and paved streets. The total population of these localities was 679,418 in 1970, or 47.6 per cent of the national total.

More basic to the purpose here is to project the population of the larger urbanized or metropolitan areas of Panama. Accordingly, a definition of "urbanized area" is established which includes the city and its respective suburbs or, alternatively, twin cities. Only cities of 5,000 or more inhabitants are defined as urbanized areas.[1] The delineation of the components of specific urbanized areas is that given by Boyce[2] and shown in Table 130.

Although only nine cities are defined as urbanized areas, their total population is larger than the urban population as defined for the 1970 census because the inclusion of the population of entire districts into Panama City and Colon more than offsets the exclusion of those urban areas as defined by the census of less than 5,000 population in 1970. The total population of the nine 1970 urbanized areas is 738,680, which is 51.7 per cent of the national total. These areas, when treated as a

---

[1] For consistency with the other countries, only cities with 10,000 and more inhabitants are considered in the regional section of this report.

[2] Information provided by Charles Boyce, UNDP Project PAN/72/008.

unit, are labeled "1970 urbanized areas" to indicate that some of the cities did not meet the present definition of urbanized in earlier periods and that other cities will qualify as urbanized in later censuses but are not considered in this study.

The population of Panama's nine cities as enumerated in the last three censuses was shown earlier in Table 128. Three cities had over 25,000 inhabitants in 1970: Panama City, 520,000; Colon, 103,000; and David, 41,000. In no province has urbanization progressed so far as to cause the remaining—or rural—population to decline. However, the rural population of Los Santos increased by only 1,000 between 1960 and 1970. There also appears to have been net out-migration from the town of Los Santos during the period, since it grew at a rate less than the national rate of natural increase (see Table 129 for growth rates of provinces and urbanized areas). The fastest-growing urbanized areas in

**Table 130**

**Components and Size of Urbanized Areas of Panama, 1970**

| Urbanized Area Component | 1970 Population |
|---|---|
| **Panama City (Panama)** [a] | **519,643** |
| Panamá D | 386,527 |
| San Miguelito D | 68,400 |
| La Chorrera D | 45,269 |
| Arraiján D | 19,347 |
| **Colón (Colón)** | **103,029** |
| Colón D | 95,421 |
| Chagres D | 6,063 |
| Portobelo D | 1,545 |
| **Davíd (Chiriquí)** | **40,819** |
| Davíd U | 35,677 |
| San José U | 5,142 |
| **Chitré-Los Santos** | **22,914** |
| Chitré (Herrera) U | 12,379 |
| Los Santos (Los Santos) U | 3,939 |
| Mongrillo (Herrera) U | 3,832 |
| La Arena (Herrera) U | 2,764 |
| **Santiago (Veraguas) U** | **14,595** |
| **Puerto Armuellas (Chiriquí) U** | **12,015** |
| **Aguadulce (Coclé)** | **11,354** |
| Aguadulce U | 7,980 |
| Pocrí U | 3,374 |
| **La Concepción (Chiriquí) U** | **9,245** |
| **Penonomé (Coclé) U** | **5,066** |

[a] Province names are in parentheses.

D Includes the total population of the district.

U Includes only the urban area as defined for the 1970 census.

Source: Boyce, UNDP project PAN/72/008.

Panama are David, which increased at an annual rate of 6.1 per cent between 1960 and 1970; Santiago, 5.4 per cent and Panama City, 4.8 per cent. The second largest city, Colon, increased more slowly than the national population.

An impression of the rapid and sustained growth of population in Panama over the past 40 years is given in Figure 39. The population of urbanized areas recently surpassed that of the remaining rural numbers. The true rate of increase of the urbanized population is actually under-represented by Figure 40 because of the use of a cohort of urbanized areas which excludes growth due to the reclassification of towns from rural to urban status.

Primacy is the dominance in size of the largest city in a country over other cities of the country. Various indexes of primacy are presented in Table 131 for selected Latin American countries. Although Panama City is five times larger than Colon and three times the size of Colon, David, and Chitre-Los Santos added together, the ratio of the population of the Panama City metropolitan area to that of other cities in the country is not unusual for Latin America. However, Panama City has as large a share (36 per cent) of the population of Panama as Buenos Aires has of the population of Argentina.

The nine urbanized areas of more than 5,000 population in 1970 contained a total of 739,000 inhabitants. Between 1960 and 1970 the population of this group of cities increased at a rate of 4.4 per cent per year, compared with 1.7 per cent for the remaining population of Panama (Table 132). By the year 2000 the population of this group of cities is projected to increase by a multiple of 2.8, to over two million. This figure would be 64 per cent of the national population. The projected growth rates of the urbanized and non-urban areas are, respectively, 3.0 per cent and 1.5 per cent annually for the 1990–2000 decade.

**Table 131**

**Indexes of Primacy for Seven Latin American Countries, 1970.**

| Country (Largest Metropolitan area) | $I_1$ | $I_2$ | $I_3$ |
|---|---|---|---|
| Panama (Panama City) | 5 | 3.1 | 36 |
| Argentina (Buenos Aires) | 10 | 4.0 | 36 |
| Brazil (São Paulo) | 1.1 | 0.8 | 8 |
| Chile (Santiago) | 6 | 2.7 | 32 |
| Mexico (Mexico City) | 6 | 2.4 | 18 |
| Peru (Lima-Callao) | 11 | 4.5 | 24 |
| Venezuela (Caracas) | 3 | 1.4 | 20 |

$I_1 = P_1/P_2$, where $P_1$ is the population of the largest metropolitan area, and $P_2$ is the population of the second largest metropolitan area.

$I_2 = P_1/P_2 + P_3 + P_4$.

$I_3 = (P_1/\text{national population}) \times 100$.

Source: "Urban Population Growth Trends in Latin America", *op. cit.*

**Figure 39**
**Increases in the population of Panama, 1970 urbanized areas, rural sector, Panama City, Colon, and David, 1930–2000 (3,230 in year 2000)**

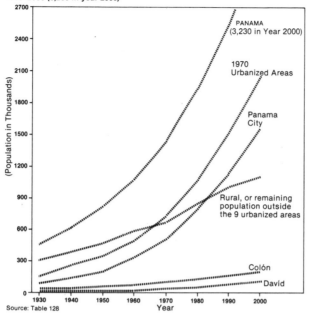

Source: Table 128

The only change in rank projected for the urbanized areas involves Aguadulce and La Concepcion. The former was the seventh ranking city in 1970 and its population exceeded that of La Concepcion by about 2,000 inhabitants. By 1990, however, La Concepcion is expected to have edged into the seventh rank and its population may be about 3,000 larger than Aguadulce's in the year 2000.

**Table 132**

**Urbanized and Rural Areas, 1930 to 2000.**

| Year | Population in thousands | | | | |
|------|---------|-------------------------------|----------------------|----------------|----------------------|
| | Panama | 1970 Urbanized areas[a] | Per cent of total | Rural areas | Per cent of total |
| 1930 | 467.5 | 153.8 | 32.9 | 313.7 | 67.1 |
| 1940 | 622.6 | 254.6 | 37.7 | 388.0 | 62.3 |
| 1950 | 805.3 | 335.3 | 41.6 | 470.0 | 58.4 |
| 1960 | 1,075.5 | 488.3 | 45.4 | 587.2 | 54.6 |
| 1970 | 1,428.1 | 738.6 | 51.7 | 689.5 | 48.3 |
| 1980 | 1,930.0 | 1,089.8 | 56.5 | 840.2 | 43.5 |
| 1990 | 2,532.8 | 1,525.5 | 60.2 | 1,007.3 | 39.8 |
| 2000 | 3,230.2 | 2,059.7 | 63.8 | 1,170.5 | 36.2 |

[a] Urbanized areas as of 1970 are defined in Table 130.

Source: Table 128.

According to the projection, the population of the Panama City metropolitan area will triple between 1970 and 2000, when it will be nearly 1.6 million and will represent about half of the national population (48.5 per cent) and three fourths of the total population of the nine urban areas (76 per cent). It is expected that the growth rate of Panama City will remain high, and equal 3.2 per cent a year during the final decade of this century. Colon's population is projected to reach 194,000 by 2000, but its growth rate will remain below the national rate. David's rapid rate of increase (3.1 per cent during 1990–2000) will triple its population to 122,000 by the end of the century. The fastest projected rate of growth is that for La Concepcion, which is expected to be 4.3 per cent for 1970-80, 3.6 per cent for 1980-90, and 3.3 per cent for 1990-2000. Among the "remainder," or rural portions of provincial populations, that of Bocas del Toro (the entire province) is projected to grow the fastest while that of Los Santos has the lowest projected growth rate.

The primacy of Panama City will increase substantially by 2000 according to the projections. Panama City is expected to be eight times larger than Colon; 4.3 times larger than Colon, David, and Chitre-Los Santos as a group; and to comprise 49 per cent of the national population in the year 2000.

Three main conclusions emerge from the population projections for Panama: (1) the total population will continue to grow rapidly and to exceed three million by the end of this century; (2) the urban population will increase more rapidly and comprise 64 per cent of the total in the year 2000; and (3) an increasing share of the national and urban populations will be located in Panama City, which by the year 2000 will contain nearly half the country's population.

**Appendix A**

**Panama: Population projections by sex and quinquennial age groups, 1975-2000. Recommended hypothesis.**

| age groups | year | | | | | |
|---|---|---|---|---|---|---|
| | 1975 | 1980 | 1985 | 1990 | 1995 | 2000 |
| | males | | | | | |
| Total | 857.216 | 984.789 | 1,129.697 | 1,289.247 | 1,460.522 | 1,642.054 |
| 0- 4 | 135.860 | 154.186 | 173.986 | 191.624 | 206.629 | 220.132 |
| 5- 9 | 120.748 | 132.686 | 151.007 | 170.815 | 188.521 | 203.638 |
| 10–14 | 108.991 | 119.537 | 131.487 | 149.799 | 169.602 | 187.322 |
| 15–19 | 91.267 | 107.863 | 118.422 | 130.386 | 148.685 | 168.482 |
| 20–24 | 75.547 | 90.171 | 106.711 | 117.286 | 129.264 | 147.545 |
| 25–29 | 62.711 | 74.491 | 89.045 | 105.521 | 116.111 | 128.101 |
| 30–34 | 52.101 | 61.788 | 73.506 | 87.991 | 104.400 | 115.001 |
| 35–39 | 42.146 | 51.238 | 60.866 | 72.519 | 86.929 | 103.271 |
| 40–44 | 36.644 | 41.316 | 50.327 | 59.887 | 71.467 | 85.793 |
| 45–49 | 30.823 | 35.735 | 40.379 | 49.292 | 58.771 | 70.261 |
| 50–54 | 27.115 | 29.824 | 34.671 | 39.275 | 48.060 | 57.430 |

196

## Appendix A cont.

| age groups | year | | | | | |
|---|---|---|---|---|---|---|
| | 1975 | 1980 | 1985 | 1990 | 1995 | 2000 |
| 55–59 | 23.448 | 25.914 | 28.597 | 33.350 | 37.893 | 46.500 |
| 60–64 | 18.935 | 21.870 | 24.278 | 26.909 | 31.513 | 35.950 |
| 65–69 | 13.163 | 16.934 | 19.675 | 21.971 | 24.493 | 28.846 |
| 70–74 | 8.510 | 10.863 | 14.077 | 16.479 | 18.541 | 20.826 |
| 75–79 | 5.458 | 6.063 | 7.794 | 10.177 | 12.008 | 13.623 |
| 80 + | 3.749 | 4.310 | 4.869 | 5.966 | 7.635 | 9.333 |

### females

| | 1975 | 1980 | 1985 | 1990 | 1995 | 2000 |
|---|---|---|---|---|---|---|
| Total | 819.099 | 941.920 | 1,081.532 | 1,235.346 | 1,400.505 | 1,575.511 |
| 0– 4 | 130.749 | 148.336 | 167.307 | 184.181 | 198.505 | 211.369 |
| 5– 9 | 116.506 | 128.030 | 145.638 | 164.645 | 181.598 | 196.039 |
| 10–14 | 104.554 | 114.803 | 126.343 | 143.948 | 162.957 | 179.929 |
| 15–19 | 86.378 | 102.821 | 113.085 | 124.640 | 142.240 | 161.250 |
| 20–24 | 70.847 | 85.096 | 101.488 | 111.770 | 123.343 | 140.932 |
| 25–29 | 59.215 | 69.850 | 84.037 | 100.372 | 110.669 | 122.256 |
| 30–34 | 48.765 | 58.236 | 68.826 | 82.950 | 99.225 | 109.532 |
| 35–39 | 39.813 | 47.841 | 57.256 | 67.796 | 81.852 | 98.061 |
| 40–44 | 34.940 | 38.938 | 46.902 | 56.253 | 66.733 | 80.710 |
| 45–49 | 29.080 | 34.053 | 30.033 | 45.919 | 55.188 | 65.593 |
| 50–54 | 25.372 | 28.163 | 33.064 | 37.015 | 44.793 | 53.951 |
| 55–59 | 21.555 | 24.295 | 27.045 | 31.840 | 35.741 | 43.363 |
| 60–64 | 17.730 | 20.248 | 22.902 | 25.582 | 30.220 | 34.034 |
| 65–69 | 12.874 | 16.194 | 18.566 | 21.082 | 23.643 | 28.042 |
| 70–74 | 8.687 | 11.233 | 14.184 | 16.329 | 18.622 | 20.977 |
| 75–79 | 6.350 | 7.032 | 9.117 | 11.548 | 13.339 | 15.271 |
| 80 + | 5.684 | 6.751 | 7.739 | 9.476 | 11.837 | 14.202 |

### both sexes

| | 1975 | 1980 | 1985 | 1990 | 1995 | 2000 |
|---|---|---|---|---|---|---|
| Total | 1,676.315 | 1,926.709 | 2,211.229 | 2,524.593 | 2,861.027 | 3,217.565 |
| 0– 4 | 266.609 | 302.522 | 341.293 | 375.805 | 405.134 | 431.501 |
| 5– 9 | 237.254 | 260.716 | 296.645 | 335.460 | 370.119 | 399.677 |
| 10–14 | 213.545 | 234.340 | 257.830 | 293.747 | 332.559 | 367.251 |
| 15–19 | 177.645 | 210.684 | 231.507 | 255.026 | 290.925 | 329.732 |
| 20–24 | 146.394 | 175.267 | 208.199 | 229.056 | 252.607 | 288.477 |
| 25–29 | 121.926 | 144.341 | 173.082 | 205.893 | 226.780 | 250.357 |
| 30–34 | 100.866 | 120.024 | 142.332 | 170.941 | 203.625 | 224.533 |
| 35–39 | 81.959 | 99.079 | 118.122 | 140.315 | 168.781 | 201.332 |
| 40–44 | 71.584 | 80.254 | 97.229 | 116.140 | 138.200 | 166.503 |
| 45–49 | 59.903 | 69.788 | 78.412 | 95.211 | 113.959 | 135.854 |
| 50–54 | 52.487 | 57.987 | 67.735 | 76.290 | 92.853 | 111.381 |
| 55–59 | 45.003 | 50.209 | 55.642 | 65.190 | 73.634 | 89.863 |
| 60–64 | 36.665 | 42.118 | 47.180 | 52.491 | 61.733 | 69.984 |
| 65–69 | 26.037 | 33.128 | 38.241 | 43.053 | 48.136 | 56.888 |
| 70–74 | 17.197 | 22.096 | 28.261 | 32.808 | 37.163 | 41.803 |
| 75–79 | 11.808 | 13.095 | 16.911 | 21.725 | 25.347 | 28.894 |
| 80 + | 9.433 | 11.061 | 12.608 | 15.442 | 19.472 | 23.535 |

Source: CELADE, Boletín Demográfico 7:13 (January 1974), Table 2, p. 26.

# APPENDICES

## Appendix 1
## List of Tables

**Appendix 2**
**List of Charts**

205

## Appendix 3

## Methodology for Projection of Total Population of Urbanized Areas

Essentially the same methodology is used for each of the countries in this study, although its application varies slightly depending on the number of past censuses from which observed population totals may be usefully employed.

An adaptation of Pickard's ratio-trend methodology is used to project the population totals of urbanized areas.[1] The projection methodology allocates the projected population of a country in 1980, 1990, and 2000 first to the departments (or provinces), then to the specified urbanized areas. The allocation is based on the observed trend of each department's proportion of the national population and of each urbanized area's proportion of its department's population.

### National Projections

Projections of the national populations to the years 1980, 1990, and 2000 which were previously prepared by other sources are employed here. The projections for Costa Rica, El Salvador, and Honduras were made by CELADE. The Guatemala and Nicaragua projections are from the International Statistical Programs Center of the U.S. Bureau of the Census, and the Panama projection was prepared by Vilma Medica. Full citations and descriptions of the results of the projections appear in the individual country chapters of this publication.

### Department Projections

The projected national population is distributed among a country's departments (or provinces) using the ratio-trend method. The observed trend of the ratio of each department's population to the national population is projected to 1980, 1990, and 2000. The observed percentages are calculated from the three, four, or five most recent censuses. All intercensal periods should be of equal length in order for the method of weighting the intercensal change in a department's observed proportion of the total population to be accurate. For this reason, national, departmental, and urbanized area population totals are adjusted to midyear 1950, 1960, and 1970 (also 1930 and 1940 where available) using intercensal growth rates.

The projection methodology for each department is diagramed in Figure 1 and outlined below:

---

[1] Jerome P. Pickard, *Dimensions to Metropolitanism,* Urban Land Institute Research Monograph 14A, Washington, D.C., 1966, pp. 53–56.

a. Each department's percentage (P) of the national population is calculated for 1950, 1960, and 1970. Five previous censuses are taken into account for Panama, and four for Honduras, so this step is also carried out for 1930 for Panama and for 1940 for both countries.

b. The ratio of the department's percentage of the national population at the end of each of the two (or three or four) previous decades to the percentage at the beginning of the decade is calculated ($R_3$ and $R_4$). $R_3$ (relating the 1950 to the 1940 percentage) is calculated for Panama and Honduras, and $R_4$ (for 1940 and 1930) is computed for Panama. These ratios describe the relative change in a department's proportion of the national population during a decade.

c. The ratio $R_5$ is calculated as a weighted average of $R_4$ and $R_3$ by the formula given in Figure 1 for the departments of all six countries.

**Figure 1. Schema of Methodology for Projecting Departmental Population.**

| Year | Department population | | Percentage of national population | Ratio |
|------|----------------------|---|----------------------------------|-------|
| 1950 | $POP_{50}$ | $\longrightarrow$ | $P_{50}$ | $R_3$ |
| 1960 | $POP_{60}$ | $\longrightarrow$ | $P_{60}$ | |
| | | | | $R_4$ |
| 1970 | $POP_{70}$ | $\longrightarrow$ | $P_{70}$ | |
| **enumerated** | | | | |
| - - - - - - - - - - - - - - - - - - - - - - - - - - - - - - - - - - - - - - - - - - - - | | | | |
| **projected** | | | | |
| | | | | $R_5$ |
| 1980 | $POP_{80}$ | $\longleftarrow$ | $P_{80}$ | |
| 1990 | $POP_{90}$ | $\longleftarrow$ | $P_{90}$ | |
| 2000 | $POP_{00}$ | $\longleftarrow$ | $P_{00}$ | |

$$R_3 = P_{60}/P_{50} \qquad R_4 = P_{70}/P_{60} \qquad R_5 = \frac{2(R_4) + R_3}{3}$$

$$P_{80} = P_{70} \times R_5 \qquad P_{90} = P_{80} \times R_5 \qquad P_{00} = P_{90} \times R_5$$

$POP_a = P_a \times$ projected national population, for $a = 80, 90, 00$.

In addition, the ratios $R_6$ and $R_7$ corresponding to the decades 1980–1990 and 1990–2000, respectively, are projected for Honduras and Panama by the following formulas:

*Honduras*

$$R_6 = \frac{6(R_4) + 4(R_3) + 3(R_2)}{13}$$

$$R_7 = \frac{12(R_6) + 6(R_5) + 4(R_4) + 3(R_3) + 2.4(R_2)}{27.4}$$

*Panama*

$$R_6 = \frac{6(R_4) + 4(R_3) + 3(R_2) + 2(R_1)}{15}$$

$$R_7 = \frac{6(R_5) + 4(R_4) + 3(R_3) + 2(R_2)}{15}$$

These formulas assign to the relative changes (R) weights which are inversely proportional to the length of time between the midpoint of the observed decade and the midpoint of the decade for which the population is being projected.

d. The 1970 percentage ($P_{70}$) is multipled by $R_5$ to obtain the department's percentage of the national population in 1980 ($P_{80}$). For Costa Rica, El Salvador, Guatemala, and Nicaragua $P_{80}$ is multiplied by $R_5$ to obtain $P_{90}$, which is multiplied by $R_5$ to yield $P_{00}$. In the calculations for Honduras and Panama $P_{80}$ is multiplied by $R_6$ to obtain $P_{90}$, which is multiplied by $R_7$ to give $P_{00}$.

e. The percentages for all the departments of a country are adjusted to sum to 100.0 in 1980, 1990, and 2000. The adjusted percentages are then applied to the previously projected national population for the corresponding year to derive the projected population of each department.

This projection methodology acts in two distinct ways to produce conservation projections of the future population of departments. First, the relative change in a department's proportion of the national population for an observed intercensal period (R) is averaged with the relative change for other intercensal periods. Thus, the greatest relative change is always averaged with a smaller change before being used to project a department's percentage (P).

Second, if a department's percentage (P) of the total population increased between 1950 and 1970, it is subtracted from 100 before entering the calculations. This step allows the methodology to project only decreasing percentages at the intermediate stage. As an example, consider the simplified case of only two observed percentages, $P_1 = 50\%$ and $P_2 = 60\%$. If these are not subtracted from 100%, $R_1 = 60/50 =$

1.20. To project the percentage one interval the projection ratio ($R_2$) is also 1.20. Thus $P_3 = 60\%$ x $1.20 = 72\%$. The department's percentage is projected to increase by 12 percentage points by this method.

If the percentages are first subtracted from 100, $P_1' = 50\%$ and $P_2' = 40\%$. Then $R_1$ is .80, as is $R_2$. $P_3' = 40\%$ x .80 $= 32\%$. The percentages projected in this manner (in step "d" of the methodology) are then resubtracted from 100 before entering step "e". When $P_3'$ is subtracted from 100%, a $P_3$ of 68% is yielded. By this method, the department's percentage of the total population is projected to increase by just 8 percentage points. This procedure has the effect of imposing on each department's percentages an asymtote of 100 per cent which can be approached only gradually.

## Urbanized Area Projections

The population of each urbanized area of 10,000 or more inhabitants (5,000 for Panama) in the 1970 census round is projected to 1980, 1990, and 2000. At this step the percentages calculated are of the population of each urbanized area to the population of its department. Aside from this difference, this step of the projection methodology is identical to the first, as illustrated by the above projection schema.

In order to force the sum of the projected urbanized areas to the projected departmental populations, as required by step "e" above, all of the department's population which is not located in an urbanized area being projected is lumped into one category and treated exactly the same as the urbanized areas throughout the projections. This category is labeled "remainder" in the tables containing projection results.

Since the population of the urbanized area of La Lima in Honduras is not given in the 1940 and 1950 census reports, it is estimated by assuming that La Lima increased at the same rate as the department of Cortes during 1940-1950 and 1950-1960 (Table 103).

Since the component areas of urbanized areas in Panama in 1970 have not remained fixed since 1930, a few minor adjustments to the observed population of urbanized areas are made. San Miguelito in the province of Panama was established as a district only in the 1970 census. For 1960 the population of the administrative division corresponding to the district as defined in 1970 is included in the population of Panama City. The area is not considered a component of Panama City prior to 1960.

San Jose (a component of David) and La Arena (a component of Chitre) were not defined as urban areas for census purposes previous to the census of 1970. To prevent the effect of these reclassifications on the observed 1960-1970 growth rates of David and Chitre from unduly influencing the projected growth rates, San Jose and La Arena are treated as though they had existed as urban areas prior to 1970. The

210

populations of San Jose and La Arena are assumed to have grown at the same rates since 1930 as the populations of David and Chitre, respectively. Clearly this assumption is unlikely to reflect the actual situation, but it eliminates the effect of aereal reclassification on the observed growth rates. Tables 128 and 129 are based on population reported by the national censuses and do not show these adjustments.

Since the urbanized area of Chitre-Los Santos is located in both the provinces of Herrera and Los Santos, the proportion in each province is projected as an urbanized area of that province. The portions are then summed to obtain the population of the Chitre-Los Santos urbanized area.

## Appendix 4

**Table 1. Costa Rica, Population of Provinces and Urbanized Areas, with data adjusted to mid-year 1960 and 1970**

| Province and urbanized area | Population (in Thousands) | | | |
|---|---|---|---|---|
| | 1950 | 1960 | 1970 | 1980 |
| **National Total** | **800.9** | **1,185.3** | **1,677.1** | **2,285.7** |
| **Alajuela** | **148.8** | **214.0** | **296.1** | **390.5** |
| Alajuela | 13.9 | 18.1 | 28.5 | 40.7 |
| Remainder | 134.9 | 195.9 | 267.6 | 349.8 |
| **Cartago** | **100.7** | **140.7** | **187.3** | **239.3** |
| Cartago | 12.9 | 16.7 | 27.9 | 40.9 |
| Turrialba | 5.4 | 7.7 | 10.9 | 14.6 |
| Remainder | 82.3 | 116.3 | 148.5 | 183.8 |
| **Guanacaste** | **88.2** | **126.8** | **166.1** | **210.8** |
| Liberia | 3.4 | 5.3 | 9.0 | 13.6 |
| Remainder | 84.8 | 121.5 | 157.1 | 197.2 |
| **Heredia** | **51.8** | **75.9** | **115.8** | **165.6** |
| Heredia | 12.0 | 17.3 | 23.6 | 31.1 |
| Remainder | 39.8 | 58.6 | 92.2 | 134.5 |
| **Limón** | **41.4** | **60.7** | **97.5** | **143.9** |
| Puerto Limón | 11.3 | 17.1 | 25.9 | 36.9 |
| Remainder | 30.1 | 43.6 | 71.6 | 107.0 |
| **Puntarenas** | **88.2** | **136.8** | **196.4** | **272.6** |
| Puntarenas | 13.3 | 17.9 | 24.0 | 30.3 |
| Remainder | 74.9 | 118.9 | 172.4 | 242.3 |
| **San José** | **281.8** | **429.2** | **620.4** | **863.1** |
| San José | 146.1 | 224.7 | 347.7 | 507.8 |
| Remainder | 135.7 | 204.5 | 272.7 | 355.3 |

212

# Appendix 4 (continued)

## Table 2. El Salvador, Population of Departments and Urbanized Areas, with data adjusted to mid-year 1960 and 1970

| Department and urbanized area | Population (in thousands) | | | |
|---|---|---|---|---|
| | 1950 | 1960 | 1970 | 1980 |
| **National Total** | **1,855.9** | **2,446.1** | **3,392.4** | **4,812.7** |
| **Ahuachapán** | **94.6** | **124.7** | **172.0** | **241.9** |
| Ahuachapán | 10.3 | 12.9 | 16.0 | 20.3 |
| Remainder | 84.4 | 111.8 | 156.0 | 221.7 |
| **Cabañas** | **77.6** | **92.7** | **124.5** | **165.9** |
| **Cuscatlán** | **90.1** | **110.9** | **146.1** | **195.9** |
| Cojutepeque | 10.0 | 11.3 | 18.5 | 28.0 |
| Remainder | 80.1 | 99.6 | 127.6 | 167.9 |
| **Chalatenango** | **105.9** | **127.8** | **166.5** | **218.0** |
| **La Libertad** | **144.0** | **197.3** | **270.2** | **385.4** |
| Antiguo Cuscatlán | | | | |
| Nueva San Salvador(a) | 19.7 | 27.5 | 39.7 | 58.2 |
| Quezaltepeque | 6.4 | 9.0 | 12.2 | 17.1 |
| Remainder | 117.9 | 160.8 | 218.3 | 310.1 |
| **La Paz** | **96.8** | **127.6** | **176.6** | **249.4** |
| Zacatacoluca | 9.2 | 11.9 | 16.1 | 22.2 |
| Remainder | 87.7 | 115.7 | 160.5 | 227.2 |
| **La Unión** | **109.7** | **144.6** | **209.0** | **305.3** |
| La Unión | 7.9 | 11.0 | 16.2 | 24.6 |
| Remainder | 101.8 | 133.6 | 192.8 | 280.7 |
| **Morazán** | **96.7** | **116.7** | **153.1** | **200.4** |
| **San Miguel** | **171.2** | **225.6** | **310.3** | **434.5** |
| San Miguel | 26.7 | 38.4 | 58.3 | 89.9 |
| Remainder | 144.5 | 187.2 | 252.0 | 344.6 |
| **San Salvador** | **296.5** | **443.0** | **688.3** | **1,081.7** |
| San Salvador(b) | 193.6 | 300.7 | 490.1 | 799.6 |
| Remainder | 102.8 | 142.3 | 198.2 | 282.1 |
| San Salvador Metropolitan Area(c) | 213.4 | 328.2 | 534.5 | 857.8 |
| **San Vicente** | **87.6** | **109.9** | **149.9** | **205.9** |
| San Vicente | 11.0 | 15.1 | 18.1 | 23.3 |
| Remainder | 76.6 | 94.8 | 131.0 | 182.6 |
| **Santa Ana** | **202.5** | **254.1** | **323.7** | **421.2** |
| Chalchuapa | 9.9 | 13.1 | 18.0 | 25.4 |
| Santa Ana | 51.7 | 70.8 | 95.0 | 131.1 |
| Remainder | 140.9 | 170.2 | 210.7 | 264.7 |
| **Sonsonate** | **120.3** | **161.7** | **223.5** | **317.6** |
| Ajacutla | 2.0 | 3.4 | 8.8 | 17.6 |
| Sonsonate | 17.9 | 22.9 | 32.0 | 44.7 |
| Remainder | 100.4 | 135.4 | 182.7 | 255.2 |
| **Usulután** | **162.3** | **201.7** | **279.8** | **389.8** |
| Usulután | 9.5 | 12.2 | 18.7 | 28.0 |
| Remainder | 152.9 | 189.5 | 261.1 | 361.8 |

(a) The combined urban population of Antiguo Cuscatlán and Nueva San Salvador are included in the San Salvador Metropolitan Area.

(b) The total urban population of the municipios of San Salvador, Mejicano, Soyapongo, Delgado, Cuscatancingo, Ayutuxtepeque, Ilopango, and San Marcos.

(c) The San Salvador Metropolitan Area is comprised of population in the Department of both San Salvador (note b) and La Libertad (note a).

## Appendix 4 (continued)

### Table 3. Guatemala, Population of Departments and Urbanized Areas, with data adjusted to mid-year 1960 and 1970

| Department and Urbanized Area | Population (in Thousands) | | | |
|---|---|---|---|---|
| | 1950 | 1960 | 1970 | 1980 |
| **National Total** | **3,005.7** | **3,961.5** | **5,218.7** | **6,939.8** |
| **Alta Verapaz** | **204.4** | **249.2** | **290.0** | **343.2** |
| Cobán | 7.7 | 8.8 | 11.6 | 14.6 |
| Remainder | 196.7 | 240.4 | 278.4 | 328.6 |
| **Baja Verapaz** | **71.4** | **90.5** | **110.6** | **137.0** |
| **Chimaltenango** | **130.8** | **156.3** | **196.2** | **242.4** |
| Chimaltenango | 6.0 | 7.8 | 12.0 | 17.4 |
| Remainder | 124.9 | 148.5 | 184.2 | 255.0 |
| **Chiquimula** | **121.5** | **145.2** | **166.7** | **193.5** |
| Chiquimula | 8.6 | 12.0 | 15.2 | 21.6 |
| Remainder | 113.0 | 133.2 | 151.5 | 171.9 |
| **El Progreso** | **51.6** | **62.9** | **75.7** | **91.5** |
| **Escuintla** | **133.3** | **233.4** | **309.9** | **448.2** |
| Escuintla | 9.5 | 17.8 | 33.4 | 59.3 |
| Sta. Lucia Cotzumalguapa | 3.7 | 6.6 | 12.3 | 21.9 |
| Tiquisate | 4.5 | 7.4 | 10.9 | 16.3 |
| San José | 2.7 | 4.6 | 8.7 | 15.6 |
| Remainder | 112.9 | 187.0 | 244.6 | 335.2 |
| **Guatemala** | **472.7** | **706.7** | **1,081.7** | **1,611.6** |
| Guatemala City | 336.6 | 527.8 | 898.4 | 1,430.0 |
| Remainder | 136.1 | 178.9 | 183.3 | 181.6 |
| **Huehuetenango** | **215.5** | **270.5** | **362.8** | **481.2** |
| Huehuetenango | 6.0 | 8.3 | 11.6 | 16.2 |
| Remainder | 209.5 | 262.2 | 351.2 | 465.1 |
| **Izabal** | **59.3** | **97.5** | **160.3** | **254.0** |
| Puerto Barrios | 15.1 | 19.0 | 21.3 | 37.3 |
| Remainder | 44.2 | 78.5 | 139.0 | 216.8 |
| **Jalapa** | **81.0** | **95.9** | **119.2** | **146.9** |
| Jalapa | 6.4 | 8.5 | 12.9 | 18.5 |
| Remainder | 74.6 | 87.4 | 106.3 | 128.4 |
| **Jutiapa** | **149.6** | **184.2** | **234.2** | **294.5** |
| Jutiapa | 5.0 | 6.3 | 9.4 | 13.3 |
| Remainder | 144.6 | 177.9 | 224.8 | 281.2 |
| **Petén** | **17.1** | **23.9** | **50.1** | **88.5** |
| **Quetzaltenango** | **198.4** | **254.0** | **318.1** | **403.4** |
| Quetzaltenango | 26.9 | 36.5 | 47.1 | 61.5 |
| Coatepéque | 6.1 | 10.2 | 15.6 | 23.5 |
| Remainder | 165.4 | 207.3 | 255.4 | 318.4 |
| **Quiché** | **188.4** | **236.4** | **302.1** | **387.3** |
| **Retalhuleu** | **72.0** | **104.5** | **137.3** | **186.4** |
| Retalhuleu | 8.9 | 12.2 | 18.7 | 28.1 |
| Remainder | 63.1 | 92.3 | 118.6 | 158.3 |
| **Sacatepéquez** | **64.8** | **78.2** | **99.6** | **125.7** |
| Antigua Guatemala | 10.4 | 12.2 | 16.8 | 22.4 |
| Remainder | 54.3 | 66.0 | 82.8 | 103.4 |
| **San Marcos** | **250.5** | **317.6** | **395.8** | **499.4** |
| San Pedro Sacatepéquez & San Marcos | 10.5 | 12.9 | 16.7 | 21.3 |
| Remainder | 240.0 | 304.7 | 379.1 | 478.0 |

# Appendix 4 (continued)

## Table 3. cont.

| Department and Urbanized Area | Population (in Thousands) | | | |
|---|---|---|---|---|
| | 1950 | 1960 | 1970 | 1980 |
| **Santa Rosa** | **118.3** | **148.5** | **182.3** | **224.6** |
| **Sololá** | **89.3** | **104.7** | **128.9** | **156.6** |
| Santiago Atitlán | 7.0 | 8.2 | 11.1 | 14.4 |
| Remainder | 82.3 | 96.5 | 117.8 | 142.2 |
| **Suchitepéquez** | **134.0** | **173.3** | **217.9** | **276.2** |
| Mazatenango | 10.7 | 15.5 | 23.2 | 33.8 |
| Remainder | 123.3 | 157.8 | 194.7 | 242.5 |
| **Totonicapán** | **107.0** | **134.3** | **169.5** | **213.7** |
| **Zacapa** | **74.9** | **92.2** | **110.7** | **134.0** |
| Zacapa | 8.0 | 9.7 | 12.6 | 16.1 |
| Remainder | 66.9 | 82.5 | 98.1 | 118.0 |

## Appendix 4 (continued)

### Table 4. Honduras, Population of Departments and Urbanized Areas, with data adjusted to mid-year 1960 and 1970

| Department and Urbanized Areas | Population (in Thousands) | | | |
|---|---|---|---|---|
| | 1950 | 1960 | 1970 | 1980 |
| **National Total** | **1,368.6** | **1,839.4** | **2,523.7** | **3,594.7** |
| **Atlántida** | **63.6** | **89.7** | **135.7** | **208.4** |
| La Ceiba | 16.6 | 23.9 | 35.8 | 54.1 |
| Tela | 12.6 | 13.5 | 18.4 | 23.7 |
| Remainder | 34.3 | 52.3 | 81.5 | 130.5 |
| **Choluteca** | **107.3** | **144.2** | **189.6** | **256.6** |
| Choluteca | 7.1 | 11.0 | 20.8 | 35.8 |
| Remainder | 100.2 | 133.2 | 168.8 | 220.8 |
| **Colón** | **35.5** | **41.2** | **67.2** | **109.5** |
| **Comayagua** | **68.2** | **93.4** | **129.1** | **184.9** |
| Comayagua | 5.2 | 8.1 | 12.3 | 19.4 |
| Siguatepeque | 4.6 | 5.8 | 10.2 | 16.7 |
| Remainder | 58.4 | 79.5 | 106.6 | 148.8 |
| **Copán** | **95.9** | **122.8** | **152.2** | **195.5** |
| Santa Rosa de Copán | 6.4 | 7.8 | 11.2 | 15.9 |
| Remainder | 89.5 | 115.0 | 141.0 | 179.6 |
| **Cortés** | **125.7** | **191.4** | **324.0** | **538.9** |
| La Lima(a) | 6.2 | 9.4 | 14.0 | 19.8 |
| Puerto Cortés | 12.2 | 16.6 | 24.0 | 34.1 |
| San Pedro Sula | 21.1 | 51.8 | 116.1 | 238.9 |
| Remainder | 86.2 | 113.6 | 169.9 | 246.1 |
| **El Paraíso** | **82.6** | **104.7** | **136.9** | **184.0** |
| Danlí | 4.2 | 6.1 | 9.9 | 15.9 |
| Remainder | 78.4 | 98.6 | 127.0 | 168.1 |
| **Francisco Morazán** | **190.4** | **273.8** | **415.5** | **637.0** |
| Tegucigalpa | 72.4 | 126.0 | 228.5 | 405.6 |
| Remainder | 118.0 | 147.8 | 187.0 | 231.4 |
| **Gracias a Dios(b)** | **—** | **—** | **18.1** | **30.6** |
| **Intibucá** | **59.4** | **71.7** | **83.6** | **101.7** |
| **Islas de la Bahía** | **8.1** | **9.0** | **12.5** | **16.8** |
| **La Paz** | **51.2** | **60.0** | **68.1** | **79.7** |
| **Lempira** | **90.9** | **109.7** | **129.8** | **159.0** |
| **Ocotepeque** | **45.7** | **52.0** | **54.9** | **60.6** |
| **Olancho** | **83.9** | **108.5** | **145.7** | **201.4** |
| Juticalpa | 3.2 | 6.6 | 9.6 | 15.4 |
| Remainder | 80.7 | 101.9 | 136.1 | 186.1 |
| **Santa Bárbara** | **96.4** | **141.3** | **183.5** | **253.9** |
| **Valle** | **65.3** | **79.6** | **93.4** | **113.5** |
| **Yoro** | **98.7** | **127.6** | **182.6** | **262.8** |
| El Progreso | 9.2 | 13.4 | 23.7 | 40.3 |
| Remainder | 89.5 | 114.2 | 158.9 | 222.5 |

(a) The population of the city of La Lima is not given in the census reports for 1950. The figure shown here is an approximation derived by assuming that La Lima grew at the same rate as the Department of Cortés during 1950–1961.

(b) Gracias a Dios formerly comprised part of the Department of Colón and was not established as a separate department until after the 1950 census.

# Appendix 4 (continued)

## Table 5. Nicaragua, Population of Departments and Urbanized Areas, with data adjusted to mid-year 1960 and 1970

| Department and Urbanized Areas | Population (in Thousands) | | | |
|---|---|---|---|---|
| | 1950(a) | 1960 | 1970 | 1980 |
| **National Total** | **1,049.6** | **1,397.0** | **1,825.8** | **2,669.5** |
| **Boaco** | **50.0** | **65.9** | **67.3** | **86.5** |
| **Carazo** | **52.1** | **62.3** | **70.6** | **89.0** |
| Diriamba | 7.6 | 9.7 | 9.9 | 12.5 |
| Jinotepe | 7.1 | 8.6 | 11.9 | 17.2 |
| Remainder | 37.5 | 44.0 | 48.8 | 59.3 |
| **Chinandega** | **81.8** | **115.4** | **151.9** | **223.9** |
| Chinandega | 13.1 | 19.6 | 28.7 | 46.3 |
| Chichigalpa (b) | 4.3 | 8.8 | 14.2 | 21.7 |
| Corinto | 4.8 | 7.8 | 12.7 | 22.0 |
| Remainder | 59.6 | 79.2 | 96.3 | 134.0 |
| **Chontales** | **50.5** | **68.5** | **66.9** | **85.3** |
| **Estelí** | **43.7** | **61.7** | **78.0** | **111.5** |
| Estelí | 5.6 | 10.4 | 18.5 | 33.4 |
| Remainder | 38.2 | 51.3 | 59.5 | 78.1 |
| **Granada** | **48.7** | **61.1** | **70.3** | **91.4** |
| Granada | 21.0 | 26.4 | 34.3 | 48.2 |
| Remainder | 27.7 | 34.7 | 36.0 | 43.2 |
| **Jinotega** | **48.3** | **68.8** | **89.0** | **129.8** |
| Jinotega | 4.0 | 6.5 | 9.9 | 16.3 |
| Remainder | 44.3 | 62.3 | 79.1 | 113.5 |
| **León** | **123.6** | **143.5** | **163.6** | **208.3** |
| León | 30.5 | 41.0 | 53.5 | 75.3 |
| Remainder | 93.1 | 102.5 | 110.1 | 133.0 |
| **Madriz** | **33.2** | **45.5** | **53.1** | **71.5** |
| **Managua** | **161.5** | **268.1** | **457.5** | **797.8** |
| Managua | 109.4 | 194.1 | 357.5 | 661.9 |
| Remainder | 52.2 | 74.0 | 100.0 | 135.9 |
| **Masaya** | **72.4** | **75.4** | **89.9** | **113.5** |
| Masaya | 16.7 | 21.6 | 29.8 | 42.5 |
| Remainder | 55.7 | 53.8 | 60.1 | 71.0 |
| **Matagalpa** | **135.4** | **161.8** | **163.4** | **200.9** |
| Matagalpa | 10.3 | 13.7 | 19.7 | 28.8 |
| Remainder | 125.1 | 148.1 | 143.7 | 172.1 |
| **Nueva Segovia** | **26.0** | **40.0** | **62.5** | **104.9** |
| **Río San Juan** | **9.1** | **13.7** | **20.1** | **32.2** |
| **Rivas** | **45.3** | **59.1** | **73.0** | **100.4** |
| Rivas | 4.8 | 6.9 | 9.7 | 14.8 |
| Remainder | 40.5 | 52.2 | 63.3 | 85.5 |
| **Zelaya** | **67.7** | **83.3** | **135.6** | **222.6** |
| Bluefields | 8.0 | 9.3 | 13.7 | 20.3 |
| Remainder | 59.7 | 74.0 | 121.9 | 202.3 |

(a) The 1950 census figures for the Republic and for the departments of Jinotega, Nueva Segovia, and Zelaya are adjusted to correspond to the area of these departments in 1963, conforming to the new northern border resulting from litigation with Honduras.

(b) The "suburb" of Ingenio San Antonio is included in the urbanized area in 1963 and 1971, but not in 1950.

# List of References

## General

Centro Latinoamericano de Demografía and University of Chicago Community and Family Study Center. *Fertility and Family Planning in Metropolitan Latin America*. Chicago: University of Chicago, 1972.

Fox, Robert W. *Urban Population Growth Trends in Latin America*. Washington, D.C.: Inter-American Development Bank, 1975.

Inter-American Development Bank. "Evaluating Social Change in Latin America: The Statistical Foundations." *Economic and Social Progress Report in Latin America*. Washington, D.C.: Inter-American Development Bank, 1975.

Nortman, Dorothy and Ellen Hofstatter. "Population and Family Planning Programs: A Factbook." *Reports on Population/Family Planning*. No. 2, 7th ed. New York: The Population Council, October, 1975.

Pickard, Jerome P. *Dimensions to Metropolitanism*. Research Monograph 14-A. Washington, D.C.: Urban Land Institute, 1966.

Population Reference Bureau. *World Population Growth and Response, 1965–1975: A Decade of Global Action*. Washington, D.C.: Population Reference Bureau, 1976.

Ravenholt, R. T. and Chao, J. "Availability of Family Planning Services, the Key to Rapid Fertility Reduction." *Family Planning Perspectives*. 6:4. New York: Planned Parenthood Federation of America, 1974.

United Nations. *Demographic Yearbook 1972*. New York: United Nations, 1972.

U. S. Bureau of the Census. *World Population: 1973, Recent Demographic Estimates for the Countries and Regions of the World*. Washington, D.C.: International Statistical Programs Center, 1973.

U.S. Bureau of the Census. *Projections of the Population of the United States, 1975–2050*. Report P 25, No. 601. October, 1975.

## Regional

Centro Latinoamericano de Demografía. "América Latina. Evaluación de la Situación Demográfica en el Quinquenio 1970–1975. Comparación de las Estimaciones Previas con las que Resultan de Datos Recientes." Santiago, Chile: Centro Latinoamericano de Demografía. November, 1976.

_____ "América Latina: Indice de Crecimiento de la Población en el Período 1950–2000. Por Países." *Boletín Demográfico*, VII, No. 13. Santiago, Chile: Centro Latinoamericano de Demografía, January 1974.

_____"America Latina: Población Menor de 80 Años, Total y Económicamente Activa, Según Sexo Y Grupos de Edad 1975." *Boletín Demográfico*. VII, No. 16, Santiago, Chile: Centro Latinoamericano de Demográfica, July 1975.

_____ *América Latina, Situación Demográfica alrededor de 1973 y Perspectivas para el Año 2000*. San José, Costa Rica: Centro Latinoamericano de Demografía, January 1975.

Collver, Andrew O. *Birth Rates in Latin America: New Estimates of Historical Trends and Fluctuations*. California: Institute of International Studies, University of California, 1965.

Pons, Gabriel. *Ecología Humana en Centroamérica.* San Salvador, El Salvador: Secretaría General de la Organización de Estados Centroaméricanos, August, 1970.

Rath, Ferdinand. "América Central: Tendencias Pasadas y Perspectivas de su Población." Serie AS. No. 1. San José, Costa Rica: Centro Latinoamericano de Demografía, 1970.


## Costa Rica

Alberts, Joop. Costa Rica: *Tablas Abreviadas de Mortalidad por Provincias, 1962–1964.* Serie AS. No. 9. San José, Costa Rica: Centro Lationamericano de Demografía, 1970.

Bogan, Mark W. "Costa Rica, Population Projections, San José Metropolitan Area and Costa Rica by Sex and Single Years." University of Costa Rica, 1976.

_____ "Population Projections: Totals by Age and Sex, Costa Rica 1975-2050." Instituto de Estudios de Población, University of Costa Rica, 1976.

Chackiel, Juan. *La Fecundidad y la Mortalidad en Costa Rica 1963–1973.* Serie A, No. 1023. San José, Costa Rica: Centro Latinoamericano de Demografía, September 1976.

Dirección General de Estadística y Censos. *Censo Agropecuario 1963.* San José, Costa Rica: Dirección General de Estadística y Censos. November, 1965.

_____ *Censo de Población de Costa Rica (22 de mayo de 1950).* 2nd ed. 1975. San José, Costa Rica: Dirección General de Estadística y Censos, 1953.

_____ *Censo de Población 1963.* San José, Costa Rica: Dirección General de Estadística y Censos, April 1966.

_____ *Censos Nacionales de 1973, Población.* Volumes 1 and 2. Costa Rica: Dirección General de Estadística y Censos, December 1974, April 1975.

_____ *Evaluación del Censo de 1973 y Proyección de la Población por Sexo y Grupos de Edades.* San José, Costa Rica: Dirección General de Estadística y Censos, June 1976.

_____ *Población de la República de Costa Rica por Provincias, Cantones y Distritos.* San José, Costa Rica: Dirección General de Estadística y Censos, 1975.

_____ "Tablas Abreviadas de Vida, Costa Rica - 1963." *Revista de Estudios y Estadísticas.* No. 6 Serie 4. San José, Costa Rica: Dirección General de Estadística y Censos, March 1967.

_____ *1963 Censo de Vivienda.* San José, Costa Rica: Dirección General de Estadística y Censos, October 1966.

Dirección de Urbanismo. *Delimitación de la Región Metropolitana de San José.* San José, Costa Rica: Dirección de Urbanismo, September 1969.

Gómez, Miguel B. *Proyecciones de la Población de Costa Rica por Sexo y Grupos de Edades.* Costa Rica: University of Costa Rica, Research Unit, 1971.

Gómez, Miguel B. and Bermudez, Vera V. *Costa Rica: Country Profiles.* New York: The Population Council, 1974.

Gómez, Miguel B. and Reynolds, Jack. "Numerator Analysis of Fertility Change in Costa Rica: A Methodological Examination." *Studies in Family Planning.* 4:12. New York: The Population Council, December 1973, pp. 317-326.

219

Huguet, Jerrold. "The Costa Rican Labor Force: Age Patterns by Industry in 1950, 1963, and 1973." University of Pennsylvania, January 1976.

Huyck, Earl E. "Fecundidad y Planificación Familiar: El Caso de Costa Rica." *Quinto Seminario Nacional de Demografía, Informe San José.* Costa Rica: Dirección General de Estadística y Censos, September 1970.

Jiménez, Ricardo J. "Proyección de la Población de Costa Rica por Sexo y Grupos de Edad, 1965-1990." *Revista de Estudios y Estadísticas.* Serie 5 No. 8. Costa Rica: Dirección General de Estadística y Censos, October 1967. p. 37.

Macció, Guillermo. "Costa Rica: Proyecciones de Población por Sexo y Grupos de Edad, 1950-1978." Serie C. No. 95. Santiago, Chile: Centro Latinoamericano de Demografía, 1967.

Nunley, Robert E. *The Distribution of Population in Costa Rica.* Publication 743. Washington, D.C.: National Academy of Science and National Research Council, 1960.

Thiel, Bernardo A. "Monografía de la Población de la República de Costa Rica en el Siglo XX." *Revista de Estudios y Estadísticas.* No. 8. Serie 5. Costa Rica: Dirección General de Estadística y Censos, October 1967.

United Nations, Population Division. "An Analytic Study of the Urban and Rural Population of Costa Rica." Working paper No. 22. November 1967.

Zumbado, Fernando. "La Evolución de la Distribución de la Población en Costa Rica." San José, Costa Rica, Oficina de Planificación y Política Económica. n. d.


*El Salvador*

Alens, Alex A. *La Población de El Salvador por Sexo y Edad en un Período 1950-2000, Principales Indicadores Demográficos.* San Salvador, El Salvador: Consejo Nacional de Planificación y Coordinación Económica y Dirección General de Estadística y Censos, February 1976.

Blutstein, Howard I., et al., *Area Handbook for El Salvador.* DA PAM 550-150. Washington, D.C.: U. S. Government Printing Office, 1971. pp. 53-54.

Dirección General de Estadística y Censos. "Adjuste de la Población Censal de 1971, por Sexo, Según Grupos de Edades Quinquenales." (Estudio Preliminar) El Salvador: Dirección General de Estadística y Censos, January 1974.

_____ *Censos Nacionales de 1971, III de Vivienda IV de Población.* (Cifras preliminares obtenidas por muestreo). El Salvador: Dirección General de Estadística y Censos, June 1972.

_____ "Comentarios acerca del Volumen y Comportamiento de la Población Urbana del Area Metropolitana de El Salvador, para los Años 1950, 1961, 1971, y 30 de agosto de 1974." El Salvador: Dirección General de Estadística y Censos, 1974. (Mimeographed)

_____ "La Estructura de Edad Según Sexo de Población de El Salvador y su Distribución en las Areas Urbana y Rural, (Un Estudio Demográfico Comperativo con Base en los Censos de 1961 y 1971), Trabajo Preliminar." El Salvador: Dirección General de Estadística y Censos, December 1973.

_____*Primer Censo Agropecuario, Octubre, Noviembre y Diciembre de 1950.* San Salvador, El Salvador: Dirección General de Estadística y Censos, 1954.

220

_____ *Segundo Censo Agropecuario, 1961.* San Salvador, El Salvador: Dirección General de Estadística y Censos, December 1967.

_____ *Segundo Censo de Población, Junio 13 de 1950.* San Salvador, El Salvador: Dirección General de Estadística y Censos, 1954.

_____ *Tercer Censo Nacional de Población 1961.* San Salvador, El Salvador: Dirección General de Estadística y Censos, June 1965.

_____ *Cuarto Censo Nacional de Población 1971.* Vol. 1 San Salvador, El Salvador: Dirección General de Estadística y Censos, December 1974.

_____ *Segundo Censo de Vivienda, 1961.* San Salvador, El Salvador: Dirección General de Estadística y Censos, March 1968.

McGreevey, William P. "Population Dynamics and Policies: El Salvador." Washington, D.C.: Interdisciplinary Communications Program, Smithsonian Institution, May 1974. p. 15.

Rodriguez, Carlos A. and Castañeda Rugamas, Ricardo. *El Salvador, Perfil Demográfico.* San Salvador, El Salvador: Asociación Demográfica Salvadoreña, September 1971.

Struyk, Albert J. "Adjuste de la Población Censal de 1971, por Sexo, según Grupos de Edades Quinquenales (Estudio Preliminar)." San Salvador, El Salvador: Dirección General de Estadística y Censos, January 1974, pp. 29-31.

*Guatemala*

Arias, Jorge B. "Demografía Guatemalteca 1960-1978 - Una Bibliografía Anotada." Guatemala, 1977. (Mimeographed)

_____ *La Población de Guatemala.* Guatemala: Instituto Centroamericano de Investigación y Tecnología Industrial y Universidad del Valle, 1976.

Banco Nacional de La Vivienda. "Población." Guatemala: Banco Nacional de la Vivienda, n. d. (Mimeographed)

Camisa, Zulma C. *Guatemala: Proyecciones de la Población Total 1965-2000.* Serie AS No. 3. Costa Rica: Centro Latinoamericano de Demografía, 1970.

_____ *Las Estadísticas Demográficas y la Mortalidad en Guatemala hacia 1950 y 1964.* No. 2, Serie AS. San José, Costa Rica: Centro Latinoamericano de Demografía, 1969.

Centro Urbano Intergrado. *Analisís de los Factores Condicionantes para el Desarrollo de un Centro Urbano Integrado al Area Metropolitana de la Ciudad de Guatemala.* Informe Final, Primera Parte. Guatemala: Banco Nacional de la Vivienda, 1975.

Dirección General de Estadística y Censos. *VII Censo de Población, 1964.* Vol. I. Guatemala: Dirección General de Estadística y Censos, 1971.

_____ *VIII Censo de Población.* Serie III, Vol. 1 Guatemala: Dirección General de Estadística y Censos, 1975. Tables 21 and 49.

_____ *VIII Censo de Población, 26 de Marzo 1973.* (Cifras Definitivas) Vol. 1, Serie III. Guatemala: Dirección General de Estadística y Censos, August 1975.

_____ *VIII Censo de Población y III de Habitación, 26 de Marzo de 1973, Población.* (Cifras Preliminares) Vol. 1, Series I. Guatemala: Dirección General de Estadística y Censos, 1973.

_____VIII *Censo de Población y III de Habitación, Resultados de Tabulación por Muestreo, población; Total Indígena.* Tomo II, Serie II. Guatemala: Dirección General de Estadística y Censos, 1974.

_____ *III Censo de Vivienda, 26 de Marzo de 1973.* (edición especial referente a los departamentos afectados, terremoto Febrero 1976). Guatemala: Dirección General de Estadística y Censos, February 1976.

_____ *Evaluación del Censo de 1973 y Estimación de los Indices Vitales.* (Documento de trabajo para uso interno). Guatemala: Dirección General de Estadística y Censos, May 1976.

Fahsen, Federico, Sherman, Andrew J., and Goubaud, Ricardo. "Urbanización y Desarrollo Económico en Guatemala. Vol. 1. Guatemala, 1972.

International Statistics Program Center (ISPC). "Population of Guatemala 1973-2000 by 5-year Age Groups and Sex." Computer Printouts.

_____ Analysis of the 1973 Guatemalan population census, 1975.

Sherman, Andrew. "Proyección de la Población de Guatemala por Municipios Clasificada en Urbana y Rural para los Años 1975-1980". Guatemala, February, 1977.

*Honduras*

Arretx, Carmen. "Proyecciones de la Población de Honduras por Sexo y Grupos de Edad, 1961-1981." (edición provisional), Serie A. No. 70 Mimeo. Santiago, Chile, CELADE. June, 1967.

Dirección General de Estadística y Censos. *Anuario Estadístico 1963.* Tegucigalpa, Honduras. July, 1964, p. 25.

_____ *Datos Preliminares del Censo Nacional de Población, Abril 1961, Obtenidos por Medio de Muestra.* Tegucigalpa, Honduras. May, 1962.

_____ *Censo Nacional de Honduras, Características Generales y Educativas de la Población, Abril 1961.* Honduras, December, 1964. p. 20-27.

_____ *Censo Nacional de Población, Resumen por Departmento y Municipio.* Vol. I. Tegucigalpa, Honduras. November, 1976.

_____ *Censo Nacional de Población y Vivienda. Marzo 1974, Cifras Preliminares.* Introducción. Honduras. January, 1975.

_____ *Censo de Población y Vivienda, 1974, Resultado Muestra.* Cuadro 1, Honduras, July, 1975.

_____ *Segundo Censo Nacional de Vivienda de Honduras, Abril 1961.* (Reedition). Tegucigalpa, Honduras, May, 1967.

Dirección General de Estadística y Censos de Honduras y Centro Latinoamericano de Demografía (CELADE). *Encuesta Demográfica Nacional de Honduras (EDENH).* Santiago, Chile. Vol. I: Macció, Guillermo A., *Informe General,* Jan. 1975; Vol. II: Somoza, Jorge L. and Packer, Abel, *Resultados y Elaboración de Datos,* April, 1975; Vol.III: Camisa, Zulma C., *Fecundidad y Nupcialidad,* May, 1975; Vol.IV: Ortega, Antonio and Rincón, Manuel, *Mortalidad,* August, 1975; Vol.V: Arévalo, Jorge, *Migraciones,* October 1975; Vol.VI: Bocaz, Albino, *Descripción de la Muestra,* October, 1975.

Ortega, Antonio y Rincón, Manuel. *Mortalidad*. Encuesta Demográfica Nacional de Honduras, Parte 4. Series A, No. 129. Costa Rica. Dirección General de Estadística y Censos y Centro Latinoamericano de Demografía. August, 1975, p. 13.

## Nicaragua

Banco Central de Nicaragua and Ministerio de Economía, Industria y Comercio. *Anuario Estadístico 1972*. Nicaragua. March, 1974. Table 1, p. 11.

Banco Central de Nicaragua. *Censos Nacionales 1971. Población por Municipios*. Vol. IV. *Características Generales*. Ministerio de Economía, Industria y Comercio. Nacaragua. Marzo, 1975.

Banco Central de Nicaragua and Ministerio de Economía, Industria y Comercio. *Compendio Estadístico, 1965-1974*. Managua, Nicaragua. February, 1976.

Banco Central de Nicaragua; Ministerio de Economía, Industria y Comercio; and Oficina Ejecutiva de Encuestas y Censos. *Crecimiento Demográfico y Desarrollo*. Managua, Nicaragua, 1974. p. 10.

Consejo Nacional de Economía, Oficina de Planificación. *Estadísticas del Desarrollo Social de Nicaragua 1960-1967 y Proyecciones, 1968-1972*. Managua, February, 1968.

_____ *Censos Nacionales 1963, Población*. Vol.I. Nicaragua, December 1964. p. 16.

Dirección de Estadística y Censos. *Censos Nacionales 1963, Población*. Vol. III, Managua, Nicaragua. July 1967, Table 15.

_____ *Nicaragua, Boletín de Estadística, Demografía al 31 de diciembre de 1967*. Serie IV, Año I, No. I., Managua. Ministerio de Economía, Industria y Comercio y Banco Central de Nicaragua. July, 1968.

_____Población (Resultados de Tabulación por Muestreo). Boletín No. 3, Nicaragua, May, 1964.

_____ *Población y Viviendas por Municipios y Comarcas - Resumen*. Nicaragua. May 1964.

_____ *Resumen Estadístico, 1950-1960*. Segunda Edición. Managua, June 1961.

International Statistical Programs Center. "Computer printout for urban/rural projection series." September 13, 1974.

_____ *"Population of Nicaragua 1970-2000 by Age Groups and Sex."* Computer Printouts.

Macció Guillermo. *Nicaragua: Proyecciones de Población por Sexo y Grupos de Edad, 1950-1978."* (Provisional edition) Serie A. No. 71. Mimeo. Santiago, Chile, CELADE. June, 1967.

Perez-Palacio, Guillermo. "Conceptos Generales y Objetivos del Sistema Metropolitano de Managua para el Plan de Acción Inmediata (PAI)." Managua, Nicaragua. Ministry of Planning, August, 1974.

## Panamá

Information provided by Charles Boyce. UNDP Project. PAN/72/008.

Dirección de Estadística y Censo. *Censos Nacionales de 1960, Lugares Poblados de la República*. Vol. I, Panamá. September 1966.

_____ *Censos Nacionales de 1970, Compendio General de Población.* Vol. III, Panamá, 1975.

_____ *Censos Nacionales de 1970, Resultados Generales.* Panamá. September, 1971.

_____ "Proyecciones de la Población Total de la República de Panamá, por Sexo y Grupos de Edad: Años 1960 a 2000" *Estadística Panameña* Año XXXIII Suplemento. Panamá, 1974.

Médica, Vilma N. "Estimación de Indicadores Demográficos de la República de Panamá para el Período 1950-1970 y Proyecciones de Población por Sexo y Grupos de Edades, 1960-2000." *Estadística Panameña.* Año 33. Dirección de Estadística y Censo. 1973.

_____*La Población de Panamá.* Dirección de Estadística y Censo, 1973. Oficina de Estudios de Población.

Oficina de Estudios de Población, Ministerio de Salud. *Atlas de Salud de Panamá, 1975.* Panamá, 1975.

Panamá Census and Statistics Institute. *Compendio General de Población, Censos Nacionales de 1960.* Table 34, Panamá, 1965.

*Population Index.* 40:3, July, 1974.

U.S. Bureau of the Census. *Population of Panama, Estimated and Projections: 1961 to 2001.* Demographic Reports for Foreign Countries, Series P-96, No. 2. U.S. Government Printing Office, Washington, D.C.

372 4
49